Richard Hooker
and the
Via Media

Philip B. Secor

To Norman Glover Best wishes Philip Secor

Bloomington, IN Milton Keynes, UK

authorHOUSE®

AuthorHouse™
1663 Liberty Drive, Suite 200
Bloomington, IN 47403
www.authorhouse.com
Phone: 1-800-839-8640

AuthorHouse™ UK Ltd.
500 Avebury Boulevard
Central Milton Keynes, MK9 2BE
www.authorhouse.co.uk
Phone: 08001974150

First published by AuthorHouse 8/17/2006

ISBN: 1-4259-4766-2 (sc)

Library of Congress Control Number: 1425947662

Printed in the United States of America
Bloomington, Indiana

This book is printed on acid-free paper.

Table of Contents

List of Illustrations

Sources:
Front cover, #'s 3, 6, 9, 13 by courtesy of the National Portrait Gallery, London; #2, Royal Albert Memorial Museum, Exeter; #5, Bridgeman Art Gallery, London/New York; #11, H. Henry Meeter Center for Calvin Studies, Calvin College and Seminary, Grand Rapids, Michigan; all others by the author.

Preface

For centuries after his death in 1600, Richard Hooker had been one of the brightest luminaries of western culture. But then he was gradually forgotten through a kind of benign neglect. In 1999 I wrote the first full biography of Hooker, published in England by Burns & Oates and in Canada by the Anglican Book Centre, under the title *Richard Hooker Prophet of Anglicanism*. Subsequent editions and printings followed on into the early years of the twenty-first-century. This book is an abridged and edited version of that work and is intended for a more general reading audience.

Richard Hooker is one of the most important founders of our so-called modern era, now almost over. Along with the martyred Archbishop Thomas Cranmer, who wrote the *Book of Common Prayer*, he is the founding intellect and spirit of Anglicanism, an ecumenical cultural strain that has textured the religion, politics, literature, and social fabric of every corner of the earth touched by English language and culture for more than four centuries.

His great contribution was to provide the foundation for the so called *via media*, or "middle way," between the medieval religious, intellectual and social synthesis that defined a world based on corporate well-being, often ruled by the Roman Catholic Church, and the modern world with its emphasis on individualism in the political religious and social realms—a world in which Protestantism was the religious norm in much of the western world. This broad middle way provided for the retention of much that was of value in earlier centuries and its assimilation into modern perspectives and institutions.

Hooker's great opus, *Of the Laws of Ecclesiastical Polity*, is without equal in the literature explaining and extolling the theory and practice of the many churches around the globe that have developed from the emergent Anglicanism of the sixteenth-century. His theory of law is one of the most eloquent and influential ever conceived. His political and religious ideas are among the most important bridges between medieval and modern thought.

In the broadest sense, Hooker's genius was to make sense out of much of the clamor of a tumultuous formative age in which he too was an important actor. He translated many of the confusing and destructive conflicts of his time into a useful legacy for future generations, a legacy of order, reason, toleration, compromise--a pragmatic and tolerant *via media* between the tempting dogmatisms of his day. Both in his writings and in his life, he provides an example of how to live intelligently and morally in times of massive social and intellectual disorder. As such, he represents a useful guide for those of us who try to find our way through the wreckage and promise of our own day.

Hooker's life and personality exemplify a little known Elizabethan archetype--the thoughtful, tolerant, intellectual counterpoint to the more exuberant characters from that incredible era: Raleigh, Drake, Shakespeare, Spenser, Marlowe, Burghley, and, of course, the colorful, enigmatic Virgin Queen who presided over it all.

For all his importance, Hooker is virtually unknown today except to a handful of scholars who still perfunctorily cite him to justify their opinions on a wide range of topics ranging from theology, English literature, classical rhetoric, law and government, to ethics, aesthetics, prayer, liturgy, and even personal morality. With notable exceptions, few of these scholars have read the corpus of Hooker's works or know anything of the man behind the quotations they pluck from his writings and carefully plant in their footnotes. And as for more popular literature, Hooker has almost disappeared.

There is, of course, always the wonderful exception. After years of searching, usually in vain, for references to Hooker in our popular culture, I was jolted a few years ago by a surprisingly accurate and unselfconscious citation in, of all places, a mystery novel by Margaret Truman Daniels, daughter of former U. S. President Harry Truman. In one of her popular potboilers, entitled *Murder at the Washington Cathedral*, the dean of the cathedral explains the idiosyncrasies of a liberal cleric to a high-church Anglo-Catholic canon on his staff in the following words: "I know, I know, Paul Singletary has a remarkable gift for . . . self-promotion. He is grandiose at times and seems to have a great deal of trouble practicing the sort of humility that we are expected to demonstrate. Still, as Hooker says, let us not attempt to unscrew the inscrutable."

Hurray for Margaret Truman! We can be sure that few of her millions of readers understood her deliciously accurate allusion to Hooker's pleas for calm, patience, and letting sleeping dogs lie--and barking dogs bark. The great man lives on, however precariously, in the popular literature of the late twentieth century.

Worse than obscurity has been the degradation of Hooker's name and fame, resulting naturally enough from centuries of misinformation and ignorance about his life and work. It was, in fact, the corruption more than the neglect of Hooker that drove me at last to search for this remarkable man in order to rescue him from his tormentors.

I suppose that it is inevitable that Hooker would be confused, by otherwise literate people, with the prominent English Puritan and founder of Connecticut, Thomas Hooker, or the U. S. Civil War general, Joseph Hooker. It is less excusable when Exeter city guide books confuse him with his uncle, John Hooker, one-time chamberlain and historian of the city, or when the May 1995 issue of the popular English picture magazine, *Heritage/Realm*, repeats the slander about Hooker being a foolish man who was trapped into marrying his landlady's shrewish daughter.

Even more shocking to an academic like me is an entry in a recent issue of *A Concise Guide to Colleges of Oxford University*, promoting Hooker to the position of "bishop" in its listing of distinguished alumni. The post may or may not be one that he coveted, but he certainly never held it. More of a nit-pick, perhaps, is an error in the 1993 edition of the *New Illustrated History of Oxford*, listing Hooker as the "rector of Boscomb in Wiltshire" at a time when it has long been established that he was living in London and Bishopsbourne.

What finally drove me to write this book, however, was not intellectual chagrin but a painful personal experience. It happened this way.

About twenty-five years ago, my wife, Anne, and I were in Exeter visiting the magnificent twin-towered fourteenth century cathedral where Richard Hooker's family took him to services when he was a little boy during the reign of Mary Tudor. We fell in behind a gaggle of British and American tourists in the cathedral close, clustering around a guide in front of the only outdoor statue of Hooker in the world. This life-sized seated figure with book in hand and impassive scholarly aspect towered impressively over us as we looked up at his grand Elizabethan figure.

The guide apparently used the Hooker statue as a convenient landmark to gather her charges for a daily assault on the cathedral. She made no attempt to explain the sculpture before waving her willing troop on toward the church. To my delight, she was arrested in her progress by a Minnesota accent lingering behind with Richard Hooker: "Who's that up there?" Not surprised by what was surely the first question on many of her tours, the guide answered, "Uh, that's Mr. Hooker. He's one of our great religious men. Was a slovenly gent. Had a bad marriage, you know. Got her pregnant and her parents made him marry her. Then he was henpecked all his life by her."

A few chuckles from the group and then more history from the guide, warming to her familiar subject. "I'm not saying his wife was a 'hooker' at first, but she was one after she married him," she said, pointing up at that amiable face and pausing for effect.

"You Americans know what a hooker is, don't you? We don't have that word over here. It comes from your Civil War general Joe Hooker who encouraged women to follow his troops to improve morale, if you get my meaning. So they called them hookers. And, that General Hooker of yours--he was a direct relative of our Mr. Hooker here. So, you see, we have a lot in common."

Then the tourists, only mildly titillated by this tale, but not doubting its accuracy for an instant and prepared to repeat it back home in Chicago, Fort Worth, Cirencester, and Manchester, straggled on into the cathedral to hear God only knows what other tales of wonderful historical connection between English and American heroes.

I say "God only knows" because I did not continue with that tour. Instead, Anne and I remained at the statue until everyone was gone. Then I looked up again into that benign face and promised the ghost of my old friend Richard Hooker that I would put an end to these false tales and tell the true story of his life and his story.

My friendship with Richard Hooker began about fifty years ago when I joined the small group who comprise the fellowship of Hooker scholars. My tenure in that company was short-lived. As soon as my doctoral thesis had wended its way through Hooker's opus, *Of the*

Laws of Ecclesiastical Polity, in search of his theories on church-state relationships, I abandoned my study of Hooker's writings for a lifetime of other pursuits inside and outside the academy.

But over the years I was bothered by the knowledge that this important person never became part of the consciousness of the modern world in the manner of such other founding heroes as Luther, Calvin, Darwin, Marx, Freud. Yet Hooker's contributions to the fabric of our culture are only marginally less significant than theirs are. What is more, I have been haunted by the ghost of Richard Hooker himself, who would not rest until I had done my part to lift the obscuring veil from his life and liberate him from the incomplete, inaccurate, and biased--if sometimes charming--tales told about him for centuries.

Most of the picture we have had until now of Hooker's life and personality comes from a short biography written in 1664 by Izaak Walton, the famed author of *The Compleat Angler*. Although terribly flawed, this bit of hagiography[1] has withstood any complete attempt to take a fresh look at Hooker, partly because Walton has been so respected--even revered--by scholars and churchmen.

Hooker, Walton tells us, was a dutiful son, a brilliant lad, a pious student, a devoted teacher, a self-sacrificing and long-suffering husband, a beleaguered misunderstood preacher, a humble pastor, who gave his life to the tireless labor of writing so that the Church of England would have the spirit which he alone could breathe into her.

Not a wart anywhere.

Walton, and later chroniclers who copied and embellished his characterizations of Hooker, gave posterity such an unbelievable sanctified figure that the man became lost behind an icon of dove-like simplicity, personal purity, unimpassioned docility and unfailing judiciousness. No one could be that perfect and still be real, much less interesting to know. So Hooker ceased to be flesh and blood. He became a frozen symbol. His writings were all that remained alive. As Christopher Morris, a twentieth century editor of Hooker's works, put it, "Hooker . . . is the name of a book rather than the name of a man . . ."

---

[1] Hagiography is an early from of biography in which the subject is described in such a way as to illustrate moral virtues or evil qualities without any particular regard for the actual facts of the subject's life.

In fairness, Walton's portrayal of Hooker was altogether in keeping with the classical literary form that authorized using the subject being chronicled to exemplify virtue (or evil) and to teach civic and moral values. In a tradition as old and respectable as Homer and the authors of the Bible, biography was a means to promote a particular system of belief. The idea that writing the history of a person's life involved discovering and recording the facts of the subject's life through careful empirical research into the conditions of his rearing, education, social relations, individual accomplishments, and character development is a relatively recent understanding of how biography should be done. We can hardly fault Walton for not being ahead of his time. But neither is it necessary to continue to be intimidated by his reputation or to rely on him as a source.

I have been able to exorcise the intimidating ghost of Izaak Walton by utilizing the published research and helpful speculations of John Keble, C. J. Sisson, David Novarr, W. Speed Hill, and others who have either documented Walton's errors or suggested a more believable persona for Mr. Hooker, or both. I have allowed Hooker to give me his own clues about his character and personality by a close reading of his words, especially his sermons. Most of all, I have immersed myself for years in the environments and persons who most closely surrounded his life.

Hooker's relevance for our own time is evident when we see him for the person he really was: a creative, embattled Elizabethan philosopher-polemicist thoroughly engaged in the central struggle of his time, which was to discover and construct some moral and intellectual order amidst the apparent chaos of cultural transition from one age to another. He offered a broad and tolerant intellectual framework and religious spirit, which came to be known as Anglicanism--a middle way through the often violent and destructive thickets of religious and political debate.

More narrowly, but of great potential import to millions of Anglicans and Episcopalians in our day, is Hooker's relevance as the prophet of their tradition. The apparent absence of a founding human intellect and spirit for Anglicanism is a serious detriment to the rekindling of popular interest in this useful tradition of thought and practice. Unbeknownst to most of the seventy million members of Anglican churches spread through thirty-five self-governing church bodies in 164 nations, they are inheritors of a legitimating founding story to which they may turn for authenticity and inspiration. This is one of them. The good news here is that Christians who worship within the remarkably broad, tolerant, and welcoming Anglican tradition were not born of the sexual lust and political ambitions of King Henry VIII or the political and economic aspirations of a rising class of English gentry and merchants. Rather, these Christians were bred in that special seedbed of ideas, persons, and events which had its enduring liturgical expression in Archbishop Thomas Cranmer's *Book of Common Prayer* and came to fruition in the life and writings of a truly great and hitherto largely unknown person named Richard Hooker.

Since so much of Hooker's influence and persona are transmitted only through his own voice, I have allowed him to speak directly throughout the pages of this book. We will see him standing in the pulpits at the Temple Church, and St Paul's Cross in London, and hear again the famous sermons he preached--sermons that helped formulate the spirit of the emerging Church of England. We will follow him into the city streets, along the roads and rivers, and into the churches, homes, and college halls that defined his environment. We will watch him as he discovers his identity and formulates the ideas that were to fill his sermons and longer expository writings.

The Hooker we discover is a "poor boy" from a small village attending grammar school in Exeter in 1562; an Oxford undergraduate living on financial aid and trying to overcome inadequate academic preparation along with the horrific plagues, constant curriculum changes and student-faculty unrest of those years; a gifted teacher and tutor advising ambitious young men from powerful, wealthy families; a famous London cleric living near St Paul's Cathedral in one of the great merchant houses on Watling Street and walking through tumultuous and dangerous central London each day on his way to and from work; a sensitive husband of the daughter of a wealthy and prominent Londoner with good political connections; a perceptive, introspective person of peaceful disposition finding his way to fame in an age of bluster, extroversion, and novelty; a writer struggling with inner doubts and outer political pressures to write an honest explanation and defense of a new kind of Christian commonwealth--a broad and open community based upon reason, common-sense and toleration, a *Via Media*.

John Updike's charming description of the process of doing history, especially biography, in his 1992 book entitled *Memories of the Ford Administration*, describes the spirit of my own search for Richard Hooker. "History," he writes, "unlike fiction or physics, never quite jells; it is an armature of rather randomly preserved verbal and physical remains upon which historians slap wads of supposition in hopes of the lumpy statue's coming to life. One of the joys of doing original research is to observe how one's predecessor historians have fudged their way across the very gaps, or fault lines, that one in turn is balked by." (p.150)

Hooker, although not exactly lumpy, has been a slippery subject. Each time I thought I had hold of him, he escaped into some shrouded byway, away from the light of recorded history. But I was undaunted in my search and eventually found enough of Hooker on which to slap my own wads of supposition.

The Richard Hooker who emerges in these pages is neither the faceless author of a famous and influential book nor the pious sanctified icon of high-church Anglicans, but, I trust, a lively and believable Elizabethan personality fully endowed with the characteristics of active men and women of his time: quick-witted, urbane, intellectually acute, politically sophisticated, compassionate, vulnerable, sensitive, adventurous--a man to match the style and power of his words.

Like all writers, I am indebted to many people. To my friend and wife, Anne, I owe the most. She has been my partner for the past twenty years in research, editing, and a shared intention to bring Mr. Hooker and his ideas to life. To the late John Hallowell, Emeritus Professor of Political Science at Duke University, I dedicate this book as a token of my gratitude for introducing me to Hooker and, while he was about it, teaching me to appreciate the necessary relationship in any culture between religion and politics. I happily express thanks to Robert Smith, emeritus professor at Drew University, who taught me to think critically; to Hooker's seventeenth-century biographer, Izaak Walton, onto whose shaky shoulders I have tried to climb; to W. Speed Hill, the editor in chief of the *Folger Edition* Hooker's works who first encouraged my interest in doing a biography of Hooker; to Lee Gibbs, W. Brown Patterson, Stephen McGrade, Paul Stanwood and Egil Grislis, distinguished scholars all, who have in various ways encouraged and helped me over the years in my various efforts to put Hooker's life and thought onto paper; to distinguished church leaders who have encouraged me in these labors, including the Rvd. Dr Paul Avis, General Secretary of the Council for Christian Unity of the Church of England, the Very Revd. George Werner, President of the House of Deputies of the Episcopal Church USA, The Revd. Dr. David, Stancliff, Bishop of Salisbury (U.K.); The Rt. Rev. Paul V. Marshall, Bishop of Bethlehem (U.S.A.); to the Rev. Alan Duke, Hooker's present-day successor at Bishopsbourne in Kent, who has read critically relevant chapters of the manuscript; to English friends who have made helpful suggestions, including the eminent Exeter University historian, Joyce Youing; the Raleigh biographer, Reginald Wood; and the Dorset historian, Gerald Pitman. Many librarians have been helpful, especially Sheila Sterling of the Devon and Exeter Institution in Exeter, Suzanne Eward at Salisbury Cathedral, and Christine Butler, archivist at the library of Corpus Christi, Oxford.

Other friends who have been generous with their time, advice, and encouragement include the late Canon Frederick Tindal of Salisbury Cathedral and my good friends, Mary and the Reverend Peter Lewis of Amesbury in Wiltshire.

Last, but far from least, I express gratitude to Paul Burns, former managing editor of the distinguished English publisher, Burns & Oates (now an imprint of Continuum Books) which produced my earlier book upon which this one is based. Nearly a decade ago, Paul was willing to run the same risk run by Hooker's first publisher in 1593. He took a chance on a relatively unknown writer because he thought the subject was important.

In the final analysis, my principal thanks go to Richard Hooker himself. His footprints have been scarce and his appearances rare and often dimly lit but he has shown me enough of himself and his great spirit to make this biography possible.

About Sources And Citations

The primary sources used for writings by and about Hooker are W. Speed Hill, gen. ed., *The Folger Library Edition of the Works of Richard Hooker* (Cambridge, Massachusetts: Harvard University Press and Binghamton, NY: Medieval & Renaissance Texts & Studies, 1977-98), in seven volumes, cited in this book as *Folger,* and John Keble, ed., *Of the Laws of Ecclesiastical Polity,* 7th edition, by R. W. Church and Francis Paget (Oxford: Oxford University Press, 1887), in three volumes, cited in this book as *Works.* The Folger edition is the definitive choice for serious students of Hooker. Both are cited in this book.

I have sometimes modernized the punctuation and grammar of Hooker and his contemporaries when quoting directly in order to make their words more palatable to the modern reader. When paraphrasing from Hooker's writings, I have made every effort to remain faithful to his meaning and to retain the flavor of his writing by using key phrases and maintaining the syntax of the original text. (For faithful modern editions of all of Hooker's writings see my two recent works: *The Sermons of Richard Hooker* (London: SPCK, 2001) and *Richard Hooker on Anglican Faith and Worship: A Modern Edition of Book V of the Laws of Ecclesiastical Polity* (London: SPCK, 2003.)

For those wishing to pursue sources used for particular areas, a full bibliography is provided at the end of the book.

HOOKER FAMILY TREE

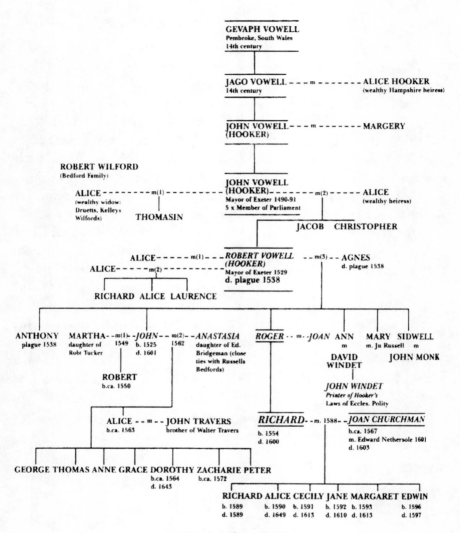

1. Hooker family Tree

Chapter 1

The Hookers Of Exeter

There has never been a birth-story for Richard Hooker. About all that has ever been known about his birth and earliest years is what his seventeenth-century biographer, Izaak Walton, and a few others writing generations after Hooker's death reported: he was born either in Exeter, or in Heavitree, a small village just outside Exeter, in 1554. He had a mother named Joan, a father named Roger, and a well-known uncle named John, who lived in Exeter. That was about it. Hardly an auspicious nativity story for the co-founder of a major religious tradition and one of the intellectual architects of the modern era.

Richard Hooker opened his eyes for the first time in late March or early April 1554, perhaps on Easter Day, 25 March. It is no exaggeration to say that Hooker was born into the midst of one of the most tumultuous, dangerous, confusing, yet formative periods in English history. With the advantage of hindsight and a cool eye on the long-term intellectual and institutional "results" of the period, historians have dubbed the religious changes of this era "The Reformation." But to those who lived through this rapidly changing and violent time, it was no 'reformation.' It must have seemed to more like a revolution.

The Hookers had come to Devonshire in southwest England from Wales in the fourteenth century to settle in and around the already ancient town of Exeter. They were descended from Gevaph Vowell of Pembroke in southern Wales. Gevaph's son, Jago, married Alice Hooker, a wealthy heiress from Hampshire. Thereafter, his male heirs, fancying the English name of Hooker, variously styled themselves Vowells, Vowell, alias Hoker, or Hooker.

The Vowell (Hooker) men were prominent in the life of Devon for nearly all of the fifteenth and sixteenth centuries. Richard's great-grandfather, John Vowell, was mayor of Exeter in 1490-91 and five times a member of parliament. His grandfather, Robert Vowell, the youngest of twenty children, survived them all to inherit the family fortune. He was a member of the Exeter ruling oligarchy ("the 24") and was named the first magistrate of the city in 1529. His son, Richard's uncle John, was the most famous Hooker of all, until posterity placed that mantle upon Richard.

Precisely where Richard Hooker was born and passed his earliest years we cannot know with certainty, but we can assume it was in the environs of Exeter. In the absence of birth records, it is tempting to adopt a circumstantial case that Richard was raised from infancy and perhaps even born in his uncle's ample homestead in Exeter. After all, in those days when the oldest son inherited most of the family estate, the oldest son (John, in this case), often felt obligated to help his less fortunate younger sibling (Richard's father, Roger, in this case), by supporting or even raising one or more of his less fortunate nephews or nieces. True, this social pattern was breaking down about the time of Richard Hooker's birth, but it was still often observed.

However, at the time of Richard's birth in 1554, John's first wife, Martha, had died and he had moved into much smaller bachelor quarters near his office at the guild hall in Exeter. He had neither the inclination nor the space to take in a young boy to live with him. The tempting notion that Richard spent his earliest years as part of the well-documented life of his prominent uncle in Exeter can be put to rest.

A decade later, in 1562, when Richard was eight years old and ready for school, his thirty-seven-year-old uncle was comfortably settled again in the historic family home on South Street, married to his second wife, Anastasia Bridgeman, a woman from a prominent family with close ties to those arch-Protestants, the Russells. John was now in a position to welcome his nephew into his substantial care and attention.

——— Hefa's Tree ———

There is no reason to doubt the tradition that Richard Hooker was born in Heavitree, a village about two miles outside Exeter, separated from the city by farmland, a few markets, and several dairies. Hooker's hometown claimed a gently hilly, wooded terrain near the River Exe. For centuries, the river teemed with salmon and provided easy access to more fish in the sea and to economic and social commerce with the rest of the world. An abundance of fresh water, rich agricultural land, good hunting grounds, and a generous bounty of easily quarried red-hued limestone ("Heavitree stone") added to Heavitree's importance as a suburb of Exeter.

In the seventh century, the first Christian church in Heavitree, St. Michael and All Angels, was built by the Saxons, who used the area as the capital of their Western Kingdom. They called the area "Wonford" and selected a special tree as a sacred place--a holy tree, "heaford treo" or "hefa's tree"--for proclaiming religious and secular law, issuing judicial pronouncements and executing criminals and enemies. This place, later "heavitrova" and finally Heavitree, eventually replaced Wonford as the name of Hooker's hometown.

The only hint of Hooker's early life in Heavitree is a street named Hoker Road, near St. Michael's church and within sight of that ancient yew tree, just a short two-mile walk from Exeter. Since it has long been a custom in this part of England to name streets for prominent persons and activities, it is plausible, even in the absence of substantiating records, to conclude that Heavitree's most famous son was born and spent his boyhood in a modest cottage near the place of this present-day one-block street of modest suburban homes.

As Richard grew from infancy to boyhood during these years of incredibly rapid and dangerous change, his family life was far from stable or secure. His father was absent most of the time. In the midst of instability in his family life and within the larger community, the boy found one reasonably constant and steady influence in his small world in addition to his mother--the parish church of St. Michael and All Angels. From his earliest years, Richard came to regard the church as the most reliable safeguard of his well-being, a feeling that would grow and sustain him throughout his life.

The historic role of a parish like St. Michael's as guardian of public welfare and enforcer of moral probity was being weakened by the eroding force of rapid change in church governance and worship requirements during the English Reformation: English Catholic under Henry VIII, English Protestant under Edward VI, Roman Catholic under Mary, "Anglican" under Elizabeth--all within three decades, scarcely more than a single generation. Despite the chaos and weakened church loyalty spawned by such confusion, the church remained the single most influential and effective instrument of social control in Heavitree and other small town and rural habitats in England during the middle third of the sixteenth century, as it strove mightily, if not always effectively, by means of pulpit exhortation and church legal jurisdiction, to retain and extend its influence over the moral behavior of the people.

——— The First Joan ———

Richard Hooker's mother, Joan, is lost to history. Like most ordinary people of her time, she can be viewed only dimly by inference from words and deeds of more famous persons who touched her life and left some record of their own activities.

Joan may be called one of the common people because, although connected by her relationship with Roger (probably as his wife) to the famous Hookers of Exeter, she was most likely a family "accident," the result of an unfortunate but typical liaison between the careless son of a prominent family and an available female of socially inferior status. Had she been a woman of any standing, that fact would have been recorded in the family genealogy which carefully lists all of the marriages and issues of this long family line. As it is, one genealogical chart shows the mere name "Joan" as Roger's wife, with no surname or family history. In another chart, no wife's name appears at all beside Roger's.

A "casual" relationship between Roger and Joan would not have been unusual in mid-sixteenth-century Exeter. What would be regarded just a few generations later as loose moral behavior was typical in the 1550s. This was a time with few effective social sanctions controlling sexual activity; birth control methods were primitive and ineffective; co-habitation without benefit of marriage was widespread; bigamy was not uncommon.

A double standard prevailed. The male was permitted--even expected--to have many lovers and to bring sexual experience to the marriage bed. His wife, unless previously married, was supposed to be a virgin at marriage and was to remain faithful thereafter. Formal church weddings were often disregarded in favor of a simple self-proclamation of marriage and the open fact of cohabitation. Not until a hundred years after Richard Hooker's birth were church ceremonies regarded as essential to a valid marriage.

There is no hard evidence that Roger and Joan Hooker were ever officially married. This may be explained by an absence of Heavitree parish records before 1555, or it may be that theirs was a marriage without benefit of clergy and church. Given the prominence of the Hooker family, if this were a serious relationship with intent by Roger Hooker to marry Joan with the approval of the family, the event would have been marked by at least a modest ceremony at the family homestead and recorded at St. Mary Major in Exeter, where church records for this period are extant.

It is especially noteworthy that John Hooker, ever the archivist, who carefully recorded nearly every event and person close to his family and career, never mentions such a marriage. Most revealing of all, Joan's famous son, Richard, avoids even the most fleeting reference to his mother. When Richard had his own daughters, he named them for the important women in his life, after the custom of the day. He chose as namesakes his mother-in-law, his best friend's mother, and other family members, but never his own mother, Joan.

The apparent absence of any other children resulting from the union of Joan and Roger supports the conclusion that she and Roger were not married long enough to produce a family, that she was in fact a poor and largely ignored wife, living for the most part, outside the protection and security of the Exeter Hookers, and that she either died or disappeared shortly after Richard's birth or while he was still a small boy. It is, of course, possible that Joan bore the usual child a year and that none survived. It is also possible that her peripatetic husband simply ignored his conjugal responsibilities.

Although we do not have records of Richard's birth and early childhood, we do know that, by twentieth-first century standards, childbirth in mid-sixteenth century England was often a horrendous experience for both mother and child. Richard, who was among the fortunate eighty percent of newborns to survive this trauma, suckled at Joan's breasts, which were probably protected by lead nipple shields. He would have been wrapped tightly in swaddling cloth and perhaps hung on a hook on the wall to be kept out of his mother's way and safely away from household vermin. He probably slept in the same bed as his mother or siblings, if he had any.

As he grew older, Richard would have joined his mother at meals consisting of an often inadequate diet of spoiled food eaten from poisonous pewter plates (made with lead) and water often polluted by human and animal excrement. They lived in what we would regard as a grim domestic environment where malnutrition, dysentery, rickets, bodily deformities, corporal punishment, and death abounded.

Neither Richard nor his mother bathed, cleaned their teeth, or changed their clothes often. Soap was a luxury. Even by the standards of those days when cleanliness was not the high virtue it would later become, the English, and especially English women, had a reputation among Europeans for being among the dirtiest and smelliest of God's creatures. There is no reason to think that the modest household in which Richard Hooker was born and where he spent his early years would have exhibited an unusually high standard of domestic health and welfare.

Death, not love, was the most reliable member of the family circle when Hooker was a small boy. The grim reaper visited his cold touch on infants, children, mothers, and fathers. Those children, like Richard, who survived the early years of life--and only about sixty percent lived past the age of five--were usually packed off in their early teens to live and work elsewhere as apprentices in some trade, or to live with a more affluent relative, or simply to fend for themselves. If Richard had not shown early signs of unusual intellectual promise, he would have been sent away from home to serve as an apprentice in some trade.

Richard's attitude toward his parents and other elders was one of abject obedience. If he displayed any independence of spirit, not to mention rebellion, the custom of the day allowed for whippings and floggings from the earliest age of childhood, both at home and in school. This was the accepted means to break the will of children and civilize them.

Still, in Richard's case there is reason to believe that, owing to the comparatively decent social standing of his father, his childhood was relieved of the more oppressive features of lower-class family life in Heavitree. He may have been that rarity--an only child, in an age when women normally had as many children among whom to divide attention and affection as their health and fecundity permitted. If this was the case, Richard was the sole recipient of maternal attention.

Although Richard Hooker never mentions his mother in his writings, doubtless because her early death or disappearance left him with no memory of her, he reveals in his life the characteristics of a person who as an infant and small child had been loved and cherished. There was little of the harsh, cruel, loveless, mean-spirited, cynical intolerance in him that characterized so much of the religious and political writing and living of his day and might well have marked the character and style of an unloved or unwanted child.

This, of course, is speculation. But it is a conjecture that helps to explain the exceptional grace and generosity of spirit that overshadows the occasional flash of temper in Hooker's responses to what he saw as religious and political extremism.

The first Joan Hooker may not be lost after all.

— Roger Hooker: "A man very expert & skyllfull" —

Richard Hooker's father, Roger, was, for the most part, an absentee parent. But, Richard was not bereft of strong male influences throughout the course of his life. As we shall see, he had a number of influential and supportive surrogate "fathers" to stand in for his missing birth-father. In his youth, there was his powerful Uncle John and his uncle's influential friend, Bishop John Jewel of Salisbury. Later, there was a reliable succession of helpful father figures: his Oxford tutor, John Rainolds; his father-in-law, John Churchman; his ecclesiastical patrons, Archbishops Edwin Sandys and John Whitgift; and, finally, his companion at the end of life, the Dutch theologian, Adrian Saravia.

Roger Hooker was away from home during most of his son's boyhood in Heavitree and Exeter. Later, when Richard was off at college and, later still, residing as an adult in London, Roger was living permanently in Ireland. Despite their lifelong separation, Richard was probably aware of his father's many exploits and accomplishments. Roger may have had at least an indirect impact on his son's character, even as an absent father.

If we speculate that Richard received his characteristic gentle and compassionate nature from his mother, then in his father he surely had a model for the courageous, self-confident, adventurous, imaginative, and non-parochial spirit apparent at key points in his life and typical in his writing style. The father expressed this liveliness in deeds, the son in words. Not surprisingly, the son's influence upon posterity was the more lasting.

Absentee fatherhood was not unusual in sixteenth-century England. Men like Roger Hooker were forced to seek their fortunes where they could find them--and a host of Devon men found them far from home on the continent or in Ireland. As a son who was not the principal beneficiary of the Hooker family inheritance, Roger had to make do with the leavings of the family estate and the good will of his more fortunate brother, John. In his case, the leavings were modest but not insignificant: one quarter of his father's "goods moveable and not" and a percentage of his father's interests in the local tin works.

Because so little is recorded about Roger Hooker, we glean what we can about his life by inference from the better-chronicled famous families with whom he found employment after he left Exeter and Heavitree to seek his fortune. These included men and women who played prominent roles in the politics of the age: the Challoners, Blounts, Courtenays and Carews. A look at the activities of these remarkable families tells us something about Roger Hooker and, at the same time, provides further historical background for his son Richard's life.

Our first glimpse of Richard's father through the veil of nearly half a millennium is in 1562, by which time Richard was probably living much of the time at his Uncle John's house in Exeter. Roger, having left Exeter a short while before, was serving as steward on the staff of Sir Thomas Challoner, a prominent statesman, scholar, and poet. As steward in such a large and important household, he held a responsible position, supervising a large staff, purchasing supplies, keeping inventories of family possessions, often managing finances and serving as secretary to the head of the family.

Roger's employer, a Yorkshireman with extensive family estates in Buckinghamshire, was Queen Elizabeth's ambassador at England's most important diplomatic post, the court of King Philip of Spain, then located in Flanders. Challoner's only surviving son, Thomas, became famous later in the century for introducing into England the use of alum in dyeing wool and leather with madder, a process he had observed in Italy as a young man and that was later to revolutionize the English woolen industry. That Roger found such respectable employment in so prominent a family as the Challoners reveals much about his ingenuity, talents, and effective use of Hooker family connections. He might not have been the model husband and father, and he may at times have mismanaged his own finances, but he was enterprising when it came to securing good positions for himself.

Sometime after his service with Sir Thomas, probably about 1566, when his son Richard was twelve years old, Roger became steward in one of the most famous and influential families of sixteenth-century England, the Blounts (Barons Mountjoy). The story of the Blounts and their relatives the Courtenays of Devon, in whose lives and legends Roger was caught up, reads like a piece of romantic fiction. There were illicit love affairs with kings, claims to the throne, religious and political intrigues at court, confinements in the Tower, executions for treason, plots to restore the Pope to England. Thee employers of Roger Hooker were involved in just about every dangerous and important event that took place during the reigns of Henry VIII, Edward VI and Mary I.

The Hookers In Ireland

In 1568, on the recommendation of his brother, John, Roger Hooker was employed by the powerful Carew (often pronounced Carey) family of Devon. As reward for help in conquering much of Ireland, Henry II had granted the Carews extensive holdings in southern Ireland, in Munster County, called the Kingdom of Cork. This grant was the basis for John Hooker's friend Peter Carew's claim to Irish lands eight generations after the fact--a claim that was to shape the life of Richard Hooker's father and, to a lesser extent, his uncle.

In the Spring of 1568, Peter Carew engaged his friend John Hooker, then chamberlain of Exeter, to come to Ireland as his agent. John had two major assignments. The first was to investigate records in order to substantiate Peter's title to the Irish lands. The second was to survey the political and social terrain preparatory to Peter's coming over to set up a permanent household in Ireland. Carew wanted John to build a solid legal case that he could lay before the new Munster council before he came himself to make good his claims and settle his family on his vast estates in Ireland.

On 26 May of 1568 John sent his employer, who was still at home in Devon, a good-news-bad news letter. The good news was that John could make a plausible legal case for the Carews' rightful ownership of the lands they claimed. Furthermore, he could report that the lands in question were extensive and beautiful to behold and that the present "owners" (tenants) were disposed to be friendly and welcoming toward Peter. The bad news was that Peter would need to bring plenty of hard cash, most household goods and certainly all luxury items if he wished to set up house and live in any decent style on his Irish holdings. And he would need a reliable steward to manage his household affairs in Ireland.

The ideal person for that assignment, John told his friend, was none other than his enterprising younger brother, Roger. Here are John's words about his brother--Richard Hooker's father:

> And, forasmuch as an expert man in these things may do you pleasure here, I have thought to recommend to you one who was sometime servant and steward to Sir Thomas Challoner, ambassador in Spain. He is a man very expert and skilful as also to his said master profitable, of whose praise I would speak as I have heard, if he were not my own brother. He now dwells with the old Lady Mountjoy, and for loyalty and faithfulness I will not refuse to give bond as much as I am able to. If your worship and my lady shall so think it good, I have given order to my wife to send for him. I trust he shall please you both in such sort as you wish.

This remarkable letter--one of only two extant contemporary descriptions of Richard Hooker's father--gives warrant both of John Hooker's affection and regard for his brother and of Roger's considerable experience and talent. Only in his early thirties at the time, and with a son he scarcely knew soon to enter Oxford, Roger Hooker had already served two of England's leading families and was about to enter the service of a third.

In short order, Peter Carew hired Roger Hooker as his steward in Ireland. Roger quickly passed muster with the Carews. Within a year he was running the family estate at Leighlin and was fairly launched on the final and most successful phase of his eventful career. In due course, Sir Peter's claim was upheld and he was given the title of Baron of Idrone. He was appointed captain of the government's garrison at Leighlin Bridge within his new barony with the understanding that it was his responsibility to provision the fortress and provide most of the soldiers necessary to subdue the insurgent Irish.

Roger's part in making good Carew's responsibility to defend the Queen's Irish holdings provides us with a rare view of his career in Ireland. In August of 1569, he was left in charge of Carew's homestead, called the Queen's House, at Leighlin. The Irish rebel, Piers Butler, was laying siege to the house and Roger had insufficient soldiers and supplies to hold out for long. He wrote a frantic letter to Sir Henry Sidney, the English commander in Dublin, requesting immediate assistance. The rebel's, in Roger's words, had attacked with thirty horsemen and a large cadre of "carne" (foot soldiers) who had just, in Roger's words, "spoiled the whole town of Leighlin, taken one hundred marks in property, burned seventy houses, killed nine men, and burned four children."

Roger appeals for reinforcements. He understands that the Lord Deputy may have some fifty soldiers at Dublin and requests that they be sent to him as quickly as possible. "My Lord Deputy left about 100 carne to guard the town and county but none to guard the house which has only twelve men among the servants."

Roger concludes: "Thus, my Lord, I humbly beseech your honor to consider our estate here and send us your men that are there, and they shall have victuals provided for them [so] that they shall not want."

His letter is filled with the urgency and immediacy of an event as it is happening. We are there with him as he fights to protect his new master's household from the assault of his arch-enemy, Piers Butler. Roger's assurance of provisions available to supply Sidney's forces shows that he recognized that his master would be obligated to provide supplies (and men) to defend Leighlin and repulse Butler. His pleas for help from Sidney also provide a glimpse of the tenuous, fluid alliance between the West country adventurers like Carew and the queen's policy in Ireland--an ambitious policy of subjugation, with too little commitment of resources to carry it out.

Roger Hooker remained in Ireland for the rest of his life, involved directly and indirectly in many of the aforementioned adventures that carried his employer through so much of the tumultuous history of Ireland in the latter decades of the century. The only view we have of Roger in these later years of his life is in his clerical position of dean of Leighlin parish. He was appointed to that post in 1580. There is no record of his having been ordained. The Lord Deputy simply used his broad powers of appointment to reward Roger for faithful service with this clerical living at Leighlin.

At some point, while he was Dean of Leighlin, Roger was "seized," along with "Master Wood, one of his chapter ... and carried off with Feagh McHugh as a prisoner by Maurice Kavennaugh of the Garquil." Although the details of this incident are not known, one can easily deduce from it Roger's continued involvement in the Irish wars and the ongoing adventure and danger of his life in Ireland.

Roger Hooker died at Leighlin sometime before Michaelmas in 1582, at about the age of forty-six. His son Richard was still teaching and pursuing his doctorate at Oxford. Given the constant movement of persons close to the Hookers back and forth between Devon, London, Ireland, and Oxford, it is probable that father and son were at least dimly aware of one another's whereabouts and achievements.

We can only lament that Richard Hooker never really knew his father. Roger was truly a remarkable man--one of a type in Elizabethan England--a man of favored lineage but essentially disinherited by primogeniture and thereby neither quite a gentleman nor a privileged burgher. We may safely picture him as an engaging, enterprising, courageous, quick-witted, risk-taking adventurer. He exploited his family connections and his own good mind to find a place for himself during a long, exciting career as courtier, steward, secretary, aide-de-camp, soldier under arms and church administrator. His was the life of a sixteenth-century adventurer who ranged far from home and family in pursuit of his own destiny.

Chapter 2

School Days

Grammar School

By the time Richard entered grammar school in 1562, the violent frenzy of the early Reformation in Exeter and elsewhere in England was subsiding. An astute monarch,Elizabeth I, was safely ensconced and had already begun to affirm her supremacy over all rivals, clerical and secular. For the rest of the century and for all of Hooker's adult life, the political and religious battles of the day would be waged under the visage of this long-lived Renaissance prince. The machiavellian virgin Queen and her superb chief ministers, especially William Cecil and Francis Walsingham, would keep the lid on or, to use the nautical metaphor Elizabeth would have preferred, provide a stabilizing rudder for the ship of state so that England might successfully complete its tumultuous transition from medieval to modern life.

1562 was a fateful year in Richard's life. His father had left home for good to find his fortunes elsewhere, having recently begun his peripatetic career by serving as steward to Sir Thomas Challoner, England's ambassador to Spain. Richard's uncle John, as we have seen, had moved back to Exeter, after sojourns at Oxford and Strasbourg, to take up his family inheritance and assume his position as a leading citizen of Exeter. John had married his second wife, Anastasia Bridgeman, and settled into the family homestead which he had leased a decade earlier. By this time, Richard Hooker's mother may have died, although there are no records to confirm this. It is just as likely that she lived on in modest circumstances in Heavitree, rarely seeing her absent husband and sharing more and more of her young son's life with her prosperous brother-in-law and his family in Exeter.

Each morning, a few minutes before 6, the eight-year-old Richard entered the Exeter City Gate after a 20 minute walk from Heavitree. He found his way to his schoolroom in a recently renovated hall located on the ground floor of a building on Trinity Lane (today's Musgrave Alley), just a short distance from St. Laurence Chruch on High Street.

Enrollment was low during his years at school, owing to the unfunded scholarships for poor boys. Only about a dozen students spread out comfortably on benches meant to accommodate nearly three times that number. Most of Richard's classmates had attended the preparatory "petty schools" or had enjoyed the benefit of private tutors. Richard's father may have taught him his ABC's. (His mother was probably barely literate and his uncle was not living in Exeter during his earliest years.) He had to work industriously to overcome his poor academic preparation and prove to the master that he could do the work. Fortunately, he was blessed with an excellent mind and a determined spirit. He was a bright, precocious, even brilliant boy. If he had not been, he would almost certainly have been apprenticed out somewhere to learn a trade, like other boys in his social situation.

Young Hooker may have been rich in intellectual potential, but otherwise he was a poor boy. Without his uncle's financial support and political influence, he would probably not have entered grammar school at all. That he was poor was obvious to Richard from his first days at school. He began attending classes shortly after his eighth birthday, just as his new classmates, ranging in age from eight to about twenty-five, were returning from their traditional twelve-day Easter recess, full of excited tales about good times on family country estates, attending fairs, riding ponies, roaming about in well-appointed town houses, having lessons with expensive tutors, enjoying trips to far away places like London, buying expensive clothes, feasting at sumptuous family banquets. As Richard listened to their social chatter, observed their rudeness to the master and endured their rowdy behavior in school and out, he soon realized that he had little in common with these privileged and badly spoiled lads.

Fortunately for Richard, all students were required to wear a school uniform, providing him with a at least a superficial cloak to hide his social inferiority. Uniforms, like all costs of education, including books, were supposed to be provided free of charge by the dean and chapter at the cathedral. If this had been so, there would have been more poor boys like Hooker in the school. But the Queen's *Injunctions* requiring such support, like those of her royal predecessors, went largely unheeded by the church leaders in Exeter.

2. John Hooker

In the event, it fell to each student's family to pay the schoolmaster from their own pockets. Uncle John would have had not only to pay Richard's tuition, but also buy him the cloak, waistcoat, breeches, cap, stockings, shirts, shoes, and handkerchiefs that made up the prescribed attire of an Exeter school boy. In later years, John would see to it that his nephew had access to the books, paper and other supplies he needed to pursue his studies. Some of the books, such as William Lily's *Latin Grammar*, Nicholas Udall's *Flowers of Latin Speaking*, Foxe's *Book of Martyrs*, Erasmus's *Colloquies*, Cicero's *Epistles*, Ovid's *Metamorphises*, Aesop's *Fables*, various writings by Virgil, Horace, Juvenal and, of course, books by leading reformers like Calvin and Peter Martyr, plus the authorized editions of the Bible and Prayer Book, would likely have been in John's personal library for use by his own children.

Although he may have been poor in his own eyes and those of his peers, Richard was fortunate to be increasingly under the influence and protection of John Hooker, one of the most important father-figures in his life. Among the attributes he probably absorbed from his uncle's prosperous household were a sense of ease in the presence of rich and powerful people, an interest in the great political and religious issues of the day, a bias in favor of the more moderate, practical, and peaceful- -as opposed to ideologically extreme--solutions to the divisive public issues of the day.

The most immediate and direct influence of John on Richard was that he rescued his talented nephew from his obscure origins in Heavitree and facilitated his formal education, first at school and later at college, an education that would give shape and stamp to Richard's character and philosophy.

The Exeter Latin (Grammar) High School which Richard attended had an ancient provenance. Earliest records date it from 1332 when Bishop Grandison endowed a grammar school in Exeter and described how it was to be run. Twelve students were to be chosen, two each from Barnstable, Totnes, Exeter, Cornwall; three from among the choristers at the cathedral and one from Erniscomb parish, whose lands the bishop used to create the scholarship endowment fund. The weekly support of 5d was to be paid from the endowment to support each scholar in the prescribed five-year course of study.

The academic exercises occupying Richard Hooker and his fellows at the nearly 350 grammar schools throughout the country in the 1560's was not much different from the medieval curriculum of two hundred years earlier. Latin was the language of learning, instruction and discourse. At many schools of the day, the boys were forbidden to converse in any other language during school hours. Latin was learned as a spoken language by memorization and recitation of the speeches (colloquies) of Erasmus, Vives and others. Later, students graduated to Cicero's *Epistles*, then on to the works of Ovid, Aesop, Horace and others, always using only the original Latin.

In time, Hooker learned to copy out whole sections of the Latin masters and then incorporate them into his own original Latin compositions. The *trivium* (logic, grammar, rhetoric) was the heart of the curriculum. Even here, Latin was the language for mastering these traditional disciplines. As a consequence of so much emphasis on Latin, the writing and public declamations of literate adults (including Richard Hooker) in Elizabethan England would be characterized by a formal and elaborate style that was full of copious imagery, stately rhythms, strained metaphorical flourishes, exaggerated rhetoric and a kind of artificiality that that often seems stilted to our ears and eyes.

Apart from Latin, grammar, logic and rhetoric, the primary emphasis of the formal program at Hooker's school was religious study and moral instruction. Unlike a few of the wealthier grammar schools, such as St. Paul's or Merchant Tailor's in London, which were beginning to offer some Greek and even a bit of Hebrew along with music, geography, mathematics, history and some modern foreign language, Richard's school stuck to the traditional medieval curriculum. As its name implied, the Exeter Latin High (Grammar) School emphasized Latin and grammar.

Religious studies were grounded in the modern reformed theology of the English Church. Gone were the texts of the important Catholic Fathers, replaced by reformers like Erasmus, Luther, Calvin, Beza, Bullinger, Martyr, Foxe, and Jewel. Hooker and his classmates learned very little theology. Long prayer-times were observed as a part of each school day. Students were required to copy out and memorize extended sections of holy scripture and then recite them in class.

Richard and his fellows were also required to attend church services at the Cathedral every Sunday and on all holy days. He took notes during the sermons. On Mondays, he might be unfortunate enough to be one of those called on to summarize the sermon and then recite sections verbatim from memory. If he failed to do this to the master's satisfaction, he could be severely punished.

Throughout its history, the Exeter Latin High (Grammar) School was under divided church control. Either the bishop or the archdeacon at Exeter selected, licensed and paid the salary of the headmaster, but the school building was owned and maintained by the dean and chapter. Since bishop and chapter were usually at odds about this, as about most matters, the question of who really controlled the school was unresolved. In the breach, the headmaster frequently had his own way and operated independently of clerical control. That the school was located outside the cathedral close served further to separate it from church authority.

Although surviving records are scarce, it is clear that Hooker's school had acquired a good reputation by the time of the Reformation. Over the centuries, the school's endowment fund, which was part of the St. Johns Hospital Foundation, was a favorite charity in the bequests of wealthy persons. A surviving note in cathedral obituary books shows a gift of ten marks in 1457 from one Laurence Bodyngton, who was "late master of the Grammar School of the city of Exeter." A nineteenth century scholar of English grammar schools doubted "whether there is a single Will ... in which a legacy to St. John's Hospital is not contained."

A severe blow to the school was inflicted in the 1530's when Henry VIII dissolved the local monasteries, taking St. John's Foundation endowment and with it the school's scholarship fund. At the time, there were nine supported students at the school, costing the endowment 15.12s, plus 8s per week for each student's maintenance. In its impoverished condition, the school now fell on hard times from which it did not recover until long after Hooker's day.

Many of the students in Hooker's class were undisciplined sons of the nobility and gentry, headed for careers at court, or as landed gentlemen, or as world travelers and soldiers of fortune, or all three. These boys, many of them in their middle to late teens, had neither the need nor the desire to pursue the traditional medieval curriculum of England's better grammar schools. As a result they were often hell-raisers who disrupted the more serious academic pursuits of such classmates as Richard Hooker. Richard, on the other hand, represented the more traditional type of grammar school student who was headed for college and then a career either in the church, the government, or the university. Not necessarily of wealthy or noble parentage, his type of student usually had a patron who recognized his academic potential and covered his costs.

The sharp dichotomy in the student mix, in age and social class, was an accelerating characteristic of the education that was to follow Richard Hooker from grammar school in Exeter on into his educational experience at Oxford. The medieval church-supported institution, with its emphasis on training bright young men of modest social backgrounds for careers as clerics, educators and bureaucrats, was changing during Hooker's life. The emerging pattern was one of secular schools and colleges responding to the career needs of budding businessmen, scientists, lawyers, doctors and internationalists who came from families wealthy enough to pay for more modern and practical courses of study.

The disciplinary methods used by Hooker's teachers were, by later standards, severe, regardless of the need to stem the tide of rowdiness among students of such varying ages and interests, all living for ten hours a day in one room. The most common punishment in Richard Hooker's day occurred when the master laid a rowdy or inattentive boy over a bench or against the back of a classmate and beat his bare bottom with a bundle of birch branches until he bled. Another typical punishment was to strike the young offender on his hand or mouth with a flat piece of wood, called a ferule, that had a hole in the middle of it. This invariably raised a painful blister.

In a day when children were punished severely at home by whippings for even small offenses, such treatment at school was not only tolerated but often encouraged by parents and community leaders. By early in the next century, however, when pressure was strong in Exeter for a new free school, an exposé of conditions at Hooker's alma mater raised an outcry against both the poor instructional quality and the persistent beatings of students. Such excessive cruelty, it was charged, encouraged students to truancy so that their parents either had to keep them home or let them run wild in the streets.

In Edward VI's reign, in the late 1540's, the Bishop and the chapter, financially weakened by the plundering of their resources under the Protestant "reforms" of both Henry and Edward, were failing to provide adequate support either for salaries or building maintenance. The King issued an injunction requiring the bishop to pay the headmaster a minimum annual wage and provide him with a house. The headmaster would now be permitted to charge his own fees to students in order to supplement his small salary. In return, the master was required to pay the chapter an annual rent of five pounds for use of the school building. The chapter was enjoined to support twelve poor students but these royal injunctions were ignored.

Under Queen Mary, nothing was done to advance the state of the school. Queen Elizabeth specifically required the Cathedral to strengthen the school and expand its service. She ordered that under-educated vicars enroll at the school. She also commanded that the master and his students attend morning prayer daily. Elizabeth was no more obeyed in these matters than her brother Edward had been.

The once proud Exeter grammar school had indeed fallen on hard days by Richard Hooker's time there. Increasingly, primary education was regarded as a civic rather than a church responsibility, especially as the demand for education rose in the face of declining church ability (or willingness) to provide it for growing numbers of prospective students. At first, the monarchs, as noted, tried to assume some responsibility for regulation. But their reach was longer than their grasp. By Richard's time, the local city fathers were taking a major interest in primary education and attempting to wrest control from the Cathedral.

An example of this process of change from religious to civic control of primary education in Exeter occurred in 1561, shortly before Richard was admitted. The school building was in bad repair. Once again, the chapter had failed to heed the demands of parents and city fathers to fix the building. The headmaster, Mr. Williams, had paid the chapter his rent, which was supposed to be used for repairs but nothing was done. In frustration he appealed to John Hooker, chamberlain of the city, for help. Richard's uncle responded with characteristic alacrity and organized what we would call a capital fund-raising drive. The result was a great success. As John put it, "The high school in this City by a common contribution at the request of Mr. Williams the schoolmaster and by the labor and industry of the writer hereof was rebuilt, sealed, scraped and plastered."

Richard's preparation at the Exeter Latin High School was barely adequate to equip him for Oxford. He was attending grammar school at the very end of a long era in the history of England's primary education--the era of church control and medieval curriculum and pedagogy. The new educational era which was to take definite shape in the next century was only beginning to emerge--just strong enough in its earliest impact to disrupt the old educational order but not yet sufficiently clear and authoritative to provide a clear pattern for the new learning and discipline.

As in other aspects of Richard Hooker's life, so with his primary education, nothing is more definite than the disorder, change and decline in quality of the educational institutions on which he and others in his day depended for support and development; or at least so it seems with the perspective of four and a half centuries. For Richard himself, attending school in Exeter was simply the first great adventure of his life.

The Bridge To Oxford: John Jewel Of Salisbury

We know that young Richard Hooker demonstrated promise as a student while at grammar school in Exeter because a leading intellect in the Church of England, Bishop John Jewel, at nearby Salisbury Cathedral, adopted him as one of the talented young men he helped advance educationally.

The celebrated Bishop's "discovery" of Richard Hooker came by way of Jewel's association (probably a friendship) with Richard's uncle. These two prominent Devonians had struck up a relationship far from home in Strasbourg during the exile that had seen many like Jewel flee before the persecutions of Catholic Mary Tudor. Why John Hooker, who was not a cleric, or even a devoutly religious person, joined the nearly eight hundred Protestants seeking refuge in Switzerland and along the Rhine in Germany is not at all clear. Perhaps he was just a wealthy young man seeking excitement. Perhaps he had been deeply affected while at Oxford by the teachings of the influential Italian reformer, Peter Martyr

(Pietro Matire Vermigli) and subsequently joined other young men in following Martyr into exile. Jewel's motives for flight were not, as we shall see, at all obscure.

When the two men returned from Europe to seek more secure fortunes under the new Protestant queen, their paths may have crossed a number of times. Jewel had visited Exeter in 1560 as head of the Elizabeth's commission on religious conformity. No doubt John had extended his personal support and hospitality to the Queen's emissary on that occasion. Then sometime in 1567 or 1568 John Hooker had a problem with which he thought his friend the bishop of Salisbury could help. John's nephew, Richard, was doing so well in his studies at grammar school that the headmaster thought he should go on to college to continue his studies. Which college should he attend? Who would sponsor him for admission and pay for his education? Richard's parents could not help. His father was in Ireland and his mother, assuming she was still alive, had no resources. The boy's future was in his uncle's hands, as it probably had been for years.

John would not have needed any help to secure a place for Richard at Exeter College, Oxford. Admission there was virtually assured to a recommended student from Exeter. But John preferred to send his promising nephew to Corpus Christi College, Oxford. This institution, not Exeter, had been endowed, with the financial help of Bishop Oldham of Exeter, and was well regarded by the Protestant leaders in the city. John also preferred Corpus to Exeter College because of its progressive ("liberal") curriculum and its Calvinist leanings. Most of all, he liked Corpus because his friend John Jewel had spent his own early career there as scholar, fellow, and lecturer. When asked his opinion, the good Bishop recommended his own college for Richard. (John later sent his sons Robert, Zachary and Peter to Corpus Christi, and may have attended there himself for a short time in the early 1550s, though there is no reliable evidence for that.)

Izaak Walton reports that John Hooker actually took Richard and headmaster Williams to Salisbury for a private interview with Bishop Jewel to seek his patronage. The Bishop was apparently so impressed with Richard that he gave some money to his parents and to the Headmaster for the boy's support and promised to keep an eye on him as a candidate for later admission to Corpus Christi. While it is always wise to be skeptical about Walton's accounts of such events, the essentials of this famous story are probably reliable. It is plausible that John Hooker would have asked John Jewel for help in evaluating his nephew's abilities and in assisting with his educational placement and expenses, and it is just as likely that the Bishop would have delivered what was asked of him. Jewel was by this time a well-known supporter of promising young men like Richard Hooker.

Jewel's subsequent request that President William Cole at Corpus Christi take a personal interest in John Hooker's nephew and that John Rainolds, already the most brilliant fellow at Corpus, serve as Richard's tutor, would have fallen on receptive ears at the college. After all, the entreaty came from their most prominent alumnus. The fact that Jewel had been expelled from Corpus for refusing to attend Mass in the college chapel during Queen Mary's reign would only have added to his luster with the current Puritan regime at the college.

Jewel loved his college but was critical about what he rightly regarded as the deteriorating educational quality there, and at Oxford generally. As early as 1560 he wrote to Peter Martyr describing the university as "sadly deserted; without learning, without lectures, without any regard to religion." The colleges at Oxford, he said, were "falling into ruin and decay" and "filled with mere boys and empty of learning." Nonetheless, it is safe for us to assume that the Bishop remained a loyal son of Oxford, and was happy to recommend a bright and serious lad like Hooker for admission to his college.

John Jewel was at this time arguably the most influential and respected theological polemicist writing and preaching on behalf of Queen Elizabeth's reformed Church of England. He is important in Richard Hooker's life story not only because he facilitated the beginning of Hooker's career, but also because he was a hero to Hooker and served as a role model for much of his later thinking and writing.

During his years of exile in Zurich with other reform clerics like Peter Martyr, Jewel was infused with a brand of radical Calvinism that would soon be labeled "Puritanism." During the so-called "Elizabethan Settlement" of religion, which Jewel would help to forge, there were two major kinds of "Puritan" in England. There were the radical and impatient militants on the far left (Archbishop Parker called them "precisians"), many of whom, whether or not they were open about their true intent, were bent on overthrowing the entire religious establishment, root and branch: the episcopacy, the *Book of Common Prayer* and, for some, the Queen as head of the Church of England.

Then there were the more moderate Puritans, most of whom I would call emergent Presbyterians. These Protestants sought radical liturgical change and major reform in church polity, but within an established Church of England. Some of them said they would retain the episcopal polity but in truth most in this group preferred, if they did not openly advocate, the Presbyterian discipline of consistories of clergy and lay elders.

Distinguishable from these Puritan Protestants were the emergent Anglicans, such as John Jewel, Edmind Grindal, Edwin Sandys, and later John Whitgift and Richard Bancroft who presaged the high Anglicanism of Archbishop Laud and the Caroline devines in the seventeenth century.

What united the emergent Anglicans and usually distinguished them from the Puritans and most other Calvinists were: (1) insistence on an established Church ruled by bishops and headed by the crown; (2) use of the *Book of Common Prayer* and the *Bishops' Bible* as opposed to the more popular *Geneva Bible (t*hese "anglican" books expressed a middle-ground in biblical interpretations and liturgical expressions, somewhere between Rome and Geneva); (3) a tendency to view scripture as the primary but not the only authority for faith and practice, holding that reason and religious custom were two other important sources of God's revelation; (4) a preference for the synoptic Gospels rather than Paul's Epistles; (5) an emphasis on the incarnation, the passion and the resurrection as central theological and liturgical themes, with concomitant stress on the importance in worship of the sacraments and common prayer rather than preaching; (6) a tendency to stress man's awe and wonder before the holiness of God, and a concomitant aesthetic inclination, as contrasted to the Puritan emphasis on man's sin and God's judgment.[2]

---

[2] The terms "Puritan," "Presbyterian," and "Anglican" were not commonly used until the seventeenth century. For sake of clarity, I have used these expressions, as well as such terms as "extreme" or "advanced" Calvinsim to refer to religious groups and ideas that were in process of developing into more permanent institutions during the second half of the sixteenth century.

In the dynamic and often confusing Elizabethan drama of emergent Anglicanism--a story with the misleading title of "Elizabethan Settlement"--John Jewel stood near the beginning. He would not always be comfortable with what was required of him in a church headed by a monarch and peopled by a citizenry still holding strong preferences for traditional Catholic forms and practices. But he remained loyal to his Queen, struggling for all the reform he could get and heading down a pragmatic "middle road" that would make advanced forms of Calvinism as acceptable as possible within the established Church of England. In so doing, he presaged Richard Hooker who appeared at the end of Elizabeth's reign to clarify and authenticate this *via media* that would come to characterize the Anglican tradition for centuries to come.

In November of 1559, on the eve of his consecration as Bishop of Salisbury, Jewel preached the most famous sermon of his career. This came to be called "The Challenge Sermon," because in it he threw down the gauntlet to Catholics and Catholic-leaning clerics and laity in the English church at home and abroad. He attacked all of the major ingredients in Catholic faith and doctrine including the supremacy of the pope, use of holy communion in one kind only for the laity, private mass, and the doctrine of transubstantiation. His sermon, made it clear that the Church of England intended to be a part of the Reformation--a church freed from association with many of the major doctrines and practices of Roman Catholicism.

In 1562, Jewell wrote, or was the principal author of, *The Apology for the Church of England*, and in 1565 he wrote his *Defense of the Apology*. These works, sponsored by Elizabeth's chief minister, Lord Burghley, became the official theological and scriptural defences of church doctrine and practice and were regarded, much as Hooker's works would be later, as manuals for instruction to be kept and read in all cathedrals and colleges of the realm. Jewel's *Apology* was immediately regarded as a definitive statement of church belief and practice and it was placed in every parish, hailed by Calvinists and Lutherans abroad as the hallmark document of English Protestantism.

Like John Calvin, and his own mentor, Peter Martyr, Jewel saw the secular prince as God's agent for preserving order on earth and held that he could only be resisted when he was tyrannical or anti-Christian and then only in a passive way. Outwardly, full obedience was owed, even to a tyrannical ruler. In expressing this view, Jewel was vindicating his own behavior in changing his outward obedience to fit changing royal requirements for the church, while, as he would have it, remaining true inwardly to his basic (Puritan) convictions.

Toward the end of the century, Richard Hooker addressed the same problem in a different guise. This time the issue of disobedience to the monarch was raised by the writings and actions of radical Puritans and separatists who had become nearly as outspoken as the Catholics had been earlier. Calvinist extremeists like Thomas Cartwright would assert, to Hooker's consternation, that obedience to the queen was limited by her obedience to God's Word, which would be interpreted, of course, by the Puritan clergy.

Unlike many of his colleagues, Jewel was not an absentee bishop. He was resident at Salisbury, preaching regularly and working tirelessly to strengthen the performance of the clergy and to reform the worship life at the cathedral and throughout his diocese and was especially committed to improving the quality of the clergy through better education. To that end, he assisted promising young men like Richard Hooker to find their way to Oxford before ordination.

John Jewel died in the midst of his pastoral rounds in 1571 at the age of fifty. His legacy to the Church of England is noteworthy. Seen in proper context, he was second in importance, in the sixteenth century, only to Cranmer and Hooker (and perhaps Whitgift) among the founders of what was later to be called Anglicanism. That he was of such importance was recognized by Hooker himself in one of his rare extant references to any person who had been a part of his own life. In Book II of the Laws, he said of his first patron and supporter that Bishop Jewel was "the worthiest Divine that Christendom hath bred for the space of some hundreds of years."

Chapter 3

Leaving The Nest

The Road To Oxford

In the fall of 1569, at about the time his father was under siege by the troops of Piers Butler at Leighlin Bridge in Ireland, young Richard Hooker was making his way along the old road from Exeter to Sherborne in Dorsetshire, perhaps on a good horse from his uncle's stable. It was the first leg of his long journey to Oxford.

John Hooker may have given his nephew a departing lecture on the dangers of road travel. Ever since the monasteries were dissolved back in the 30s, the roads had been filled with so-called "rufflers." These out-of-work beggars and thieves who had once been supported by the monks now roamed freely, menacing decent folks. There were also the roving bands of former soldiers and sailors who had been mustered out with their ragged "uniforms" and little else--rogues who lived now in the forests along the sides of the road, coming out at night to prey on travelers. These assorted "footpads" and "high lawyers" were tipped off about good "marks" like Richard by the ostlers in the stables at roadside inns.

Richard would have no trouble so long as he did not stop to talk with strangers unless they were outfitted as men of means or as scholars, like himself, and did not enter ale-houses or inns along the road as these places were frequented by all manner of scoundrels and swindlers. Instead, he should put up only at religious houses or at inns in towns where the letters his uncle had given him would serve as introductions and he must get off the road well before dark.

The fifteen-year old boy would surely have stopped to say good-bye to his mother on his way through Heavitree, if she was still living. He would want to show her his new clothes and tell her not to worry. He would tell her that Uncle John had given him a little spending money, and that Bishop Jewel's influence would assure him aid and protection at college. Even if Richard did not visit his mother, the few minutes of his long ride would take him by his old cottage. More than a twinge of nostalgia would slow his pace as he passed by the almshouses, the brewery, St. Michael's Church and the other familiar landmarks of his early childhood.

The rest of Richard's trek to Salisbury was unfamiliar, even frightening. A boy alone traveling this road for the first time in the year 1569 would be more than a little startled by encounters with vagrants and beggars who haunted the long spaces between towns. He had never before encountered such as the "pillards," "cranks," "clapperdudgeons" and other varieties of panhandlers who worked their wiles on unwary travelers with their clever but often false tales of illness, physical abuse and all manner of personal misfortune.

Despite any warnings his uncle may have given him, Richard would be unprepared for the shock of encountering so many vagrant women on the road: the "morts" and "dells" who may have approached him with their offers of adult entertainment off in the bushes alongside the road right now, or an hour or so later at a nearby inn. These were usually unfortunate women, unmarried or abandoned by their husbands. They sold their favors for a few pence, some scraps of food or a bit of clothing. Some of them, the boy could tell, were true "doxies"--professional whores who shilled for their pimps, "king-of-the-road" rogues. These so-called "upright men" waited at the nearest inn to fleece the latest unsuspecting traveler seduced by their doxies.

Richard, no doubt wide-eyed, wary and not a little intimidated by his first day's adventure on the road, would have managed the sixty-mile trek across the rolling hills of east Devon, through the villages of Honiton, Chard, Yeovil and finally on into Dorsetshire, where he may have had his first night's lodging in the busy market town of Sherborne. Here, after a journey of nearly twelve hours, the tired but excited lad would have his first view of the great tower of Sherborne Abbey, well before nightfall.

To garner something of the flavor of Richard's journey to Oxford, we might imagine, not improbably, that he stopped for the night at a fine Sherborne Inn, the Julian. This was a popular traveler's hospice where his uncle could conveniently have arranged his lodging. The

Julian was easy for the lad to find, just off the main road at the top of Cheap Street, next door to the George Inn. The Julian's ostler took the horse from the weary teenager and led it off for a rubdown, some oats and a well-earned rest. Although the inn was crowded, advance word of Hooker's arrival would have assured him at least a small truckle bed upstairs, perhaps near a window facing the back garden. He would sleep cheek-to-jowl with as many as thirty other guests in the upper hall.

It is unimportant that we do not know whether young Richard Hooker actually stayed in Sherborne on this first night of his great adventure on the road. What is important is that he certainly had some such experiences broadening his horizons while making his solitary way toward a new life at Oxford. We may be sure that he would have been too excited about the final leg of his ride to Salisbury and his meeting with Bishop Jewel to tarry long at whatever place he may have stopped for his first night on the road. If it had been Sherborne, then one may imagine him casting a final backward look at the lovely town as he began the thirty-six mile trek along the north rim of the beautiful Blackmore Vale, through the hilly town of Shaftesbury, and finally into Wiltshire and Salisbury. By mid-afternoon, he had left his horse in Bishop Jewel's stables and handed over the letter of introduction from his uncle to one of the bishop's servants.

Bishop Jewel may have been away from Salisbury visiting parishes, in his on-going effort to support the clergy and improve their performance. He endangered his frail health in these persistent and tiring perambulations. If he were not at home, the Bishop probably had left instructions that Richard was to be welcomed into the small company of young scholars he housed under his protection and tutelage at the palace, and be provided with a mount for the rest of his trip to Oxford.

It is unlikely that Richard tarried long in Salisbury. For what was left of the day he probably looked briefly into the great cathedral and was appropriately overwhelmed by its soaring, stately beauty. Then, perhaps, he ventured briefly into the town outside the sturdy walls of the close. Someday he would return and spend more time here, especially in this splendid cathedral, but for now his attentions were fixed on what lay north of here at Oxford.

As he rode out of Salisbury in the early morning and paused to look back at the disappearing cathedral spire, Richard could not imagine that twenty-two years later he would be appointed a subdean at this beautiful cathedral. Nor could he guess, as his journey took him near the churches at Netheravon and Boscombe, that one day he would have the livings of prebend at one and rector at the other.

Shortly after sunrise he may have passed through the important and already ancient abbey town of Amesbury where he would have stopped briefly and accepted the abbey's hospitality of water and oats for his horse and a pint of ale for himself. A short detour would bring him to a site he had probably been advised not to pass by: Stonehenge. These spectacular megaliths were then, as now, a place of wonder and pilgrimage for travelers who had various theories about their significance. The giant stones had been placed here by one of the earliest peoples in Europe, as long ago as three thousand B.C. For young Hooker, on this autumn morning, whatever else Stonehenge might signify, it afforded a good place to rest his horse and himself during the long climb up the Boscombe downs.

An easy day's ride would have brought the boy to Marlborough by suppertime. A letter of introduction from Bishop Jewel would secure him a welcome, a meal and a bed. A second day on the road saw the lad through the heavily wooded county of Oxfordshire and within reach of the university by mid-afternoon. One can almost feel the fifteen-year-old boy's excitement as he walked alongside his horse over the small bridge spanning the narrow Thames, and caught his first sight of the tall tower of Oxford's Christ Church. His apprehension at being so far from home and entering an entirely unknown world, easily transmits itself over nearly four and a half centuries.

The town of Oxford was not much smaller in population than his native Exeter. But Richard would notice at once that it had a very different tone and texture from his hometown. As he turned into the high street, he would have sensed that this was a university city. Like all such places before and since, its character was colored, if not dominated, by the needs, serious and frivolous, of those demanding, annoying and talented prima donnas who inhabit places of higher learning.

By the time Hooker arrived in 1569, most of Oxford's six thousand residents were actively engaged in supplying goods and services to the colleges. Amidst the impressive academic buildings and tall church steeples, Oxford was a working-class town alive with the sounds and smells of brewers, bakers, butchers, weavers, fish mongers, prostitutes, taverns, haberdashers, masons, carpenters, property managers, rent collectors and similar persons of professional and administrative skill. These men were usually citizens of the town working at the university or at one of its colleges.

Quickening his pace his pace in search of Corpus Christi College, Richard observed the most dramatic and obvious evidences that he was in a university town: large college buildings lining the streets and alleys, one after another. In Exeter, the dominant buildings, apart from churches, had been places of commerce and civic power: Guild Hall, Tucker Hall, Bedford House, the palace. But here the architecture proclaimed learning and study. All along the high street was a superfluity of impressive collegiate halls: Lincoln, Brasenose, All Souls and, at the end of the street, the magnificent Magdalen College, exemplifying the ornate architectural style of Edward IV's mid-fifteenth century reign.

Up on Broad Street, Richard saw the recently renovated university-wide buildings: the library, the law school and the school of theology. Walking through narrow alleys, he crossed High Street, passed in front of the early fourteenth-century Oriel College and turned left onto narrow Merton Street. At last he stood in front of his new home, Corpus Christi College.

Throughout his first quick tour of Oxford there was much more than collegiate architecture to amaze this provincial innocent. There was the excited chatter of older scholars and fellows coming in and out of college gates, the frenzy of new students carrying their belongings into the halls, the horses and coaches kicking up dirt as they transported men dressed in the colorful livery of wealth and power. There was energy here, a pervasive sense of excitement, even urgency, that seemed to Richard to be saying: "You have arrived; this is where important things happen."

This spirit of Oxford, of which young Hooker sensed only the external aura on this autumn afternoon, was a dynamic and unsettled spirit charged with the excitement of rapid change, fired with danger and violence and filled with the promise of new ways of living and thinking. This was the Oxford he would come to know and draw inspiration from--a center of learning, teaching, public disputation, writing and preaching, where powerful intellectual and spiritual forces conflicted. The complex, confusing and sometimes dangerous cross-currents permeating Oxbridge for the two centuries we call the "Renaissance" and the "Reformation"--a misleading shorthand for the complicated and intertwined events that historians have often described as "movements" shaping the "modern" era.

Ever since the middle of the fifteenth century, English scholars had studied in the Italian scholastic centers at Florence and Venice and then returned to Oxford and Cambridge to spread the new humanism, with its emphasis on Greek and Roman classical language, literature and philosophy. Such scholars as William Grocyn, Thomas Linacre, John Colet and Richard Fox, founder of Corpus Christi College, were the intellectual progenitors of modern Oxford. Their humanistic perspectives represented a major threat to the medieval metaphysical orientation of the academic status quo.

These scholars were followed by the giants of the English Reformation who came to the universities in the sixteenth century and taught a similarly threatening radical individualism in religion, men like Erasmus, Thomas More, Peter Martyr, John Rainolds (Hooker's mentor) at Oxford; William Tyndale, Martin Bucer, Thomas Cartwright at Cambridge.

To be sure, there had been a temporary setback for these new humanist and Protestant emphases at Oxford and Cambridge during Queen Mary's reign from 1553 to 1558. Cardinal Pole was installed as chancellor at Oxford. He replaced most of the Protestant humanists at the universities with a cohort of Catholic medievalists, mainly Spanish clerics. The grisly burning to death in front of Balliol College of the three most famous Protestant martyrs of the English Reformation, Bishops Latimer and Ridley, in 1555, and the aged Archbishop Cranmer, in 1556, brought the agony and danger of this revolutionary age close to home for a generation of Oxford students and faculty.

In the generation before Hooker's arrival, Oxford had shown both Protestant and Catholic tendencies, whereas Cambridge had become predominantly Calvinist. There were strong Catholic elements among the fellows at New College, Corpus Christi, Trinity and St. Johns on into the end of the sixteenth century and beyond. In June of 1551, for example, during the heat of Reformation fervor in England, the President of Corpus Christi, Robert Morewent, and two college fellows were imprisoned in Fleet Street for continuing to use the traditional Catholic service in the college chapel.

Despite this backsliding of religious and intellectual reformation at Oxford, when Queen Mary died and Queen Elizabeth ascended the throne, the church bells of Oxford tolled in jubilation. The long and uneven movement from medieval to modern education resumed, the curriculum increasingly reflecting the more humanistic emphases of the Renaissance. The enclosed and self-sufficient secular colleges replaced the medieval religious halls. Education for undergraduates steadily supplanted graduate studies as the major emphasis. In sum, the Reformation and the Renaissance, in somewhat cautious and conservative forms, had returned to Oxford in plenty of time to greet the arrival of Richard Hooker in 1569.

Young Hooker, of course, had none of these intellectual and historical themes in mind as he walked about Oxford on this autumn afternoon, about to take his first steps through the gate of Corpus Christi and into his new life. Before entering the quad, he may have noticed a well-worn path between Corpus Christi and Merton and turned onto it, finding himself at once in a delightful pasture. To his left the fields extended as far as he could see. Sheep grazed nearby. A large area had been cleared as a playing field. If he turned his head to the right, he would see, at the end of the path rising magnificently through the late afternoon haze, the beautiful tower of Christ Church. Here, just behind his college, was a lovely pastoral retreat, only steps from the noise and bustle of Oxford. How lovely and peaceful, he may have thought. No doubt, he would spend many hours here in the months and years to come, drinking in the quiet beauty of wild blue harebells and violets growing in profusion amongst yellow cowslips and wild daffodils in the spring, and Mary-buds, daisies and hemlock weed in the autumn. A young man with no real place to call his own, Richard would sense at once that he had found a true home at last here at Oxford.

—— Corpus Christi College ——

Finally, it was time to walk through those college gates. Hooker could delay the inevitable passage no longer. Back up the path and onto Merton Street, a left turn, a few steps, and there he was. The expanse of clean, plain, four-story brick wall with simple arches, and tracery and crenellated topping, was in front of him. The defining moment of his life was at hand.

Richard passed through the fortress-like gate tower rising several stories above the roof line and entered an entirely new world. He carried with him the name of an important Devon family, the blessing and patronage of one of England's most distinguished church leaders and his own considerable intellectual potential. What he lacked was the close family support, emotional and financial, which would have given him the self-confidence and economic security enjoyed by many of his classmates.

As he walked into the college gatehouse, with its splendid oriel and fan-vaulted roof, he had his first glimpse of the quad. But before entering the enclosure, he found stairs leading up to President Cole's office in the gate tower. He climbed those stairs toward his future, tightly gripping Bishop Jewel's letter of introduction.

President Cole had just completed his first year at Corpus Christi. The Queen herself had had to force the fellows to accept him as their head. They were a conservative lot. Such strong Catholic sympathies he had not expected. The fellows had gone so far as to defy the queen by electing the papist sympathizer, Robert Harrison, as their president. The Queen had sent for the college Visitor, Bishop Horne of Winchester, who had the authority to force Cole's installation as president. Later that year, the Queen's favorite, Robert Dudley, Earl of Leicester, in his role as university chancellor, had come to the college, examined all the fellows and dismissed some of them as "romanists." The exodus of college fellows to the Roman Catholic centers at Louvain, Douai and Rheims had begun and would most likely continue until Dudley could weed out the recusants and other papist sympathizers.

A zealous Puritan, Cole knew that his life in exile had been much calmer than it was here in the groves of academe. Then, he had been with friends in Zurich, Geneva, and, later in Strasbourg, working with Peter Martyr on the translation of the Geneva Bible. He could not have imagined that his tenuous beginnings as college president were just the prelude to thirty stormy years at Corpus Christi. Despite his good relations with most students, he would often have ample reason to be grateful for the unfailing protection of the queen's chief ministers. They managed to ward off the unending and often justified attacks of the college fellows who rebelled at his inefficient and sometimes corrupt management of college affairs.

What did Cole think about Richard Hooker, this latest protégé from Bishop Jewel? He knew that young Hooker satisfied the major statutory requirements for admission to Corpus Christi: his age, at fifteen, was at the average for admission and the certificate from Exeter Latin High School gave some promise that he possessed the necessary proficiency in grammar and logic. This would be tested shortly as would the boy's ability to compose verses. Still, Cole probably worried about Hooker's admission on several counts.

First there was the matter of the legitimacy of his birth. There was a strict prohibition against admission of illegitimate boys, since they could never be eligible for ordination. Cole wondered why this boy's father was not involved in his sponsorship for admission? Who was his mother and who were her family? Apparently, his uncle, John Hooker (hadn't he been a student here briefly back in the 1540s?) had helped support Richard. However, even he was not in the picture at this point but somewhere in Ireland with Peter Carew, Cole had heard. Fortunately, the Hookers were from a good line of Devon folk, and, with John Jewel as sponsor for the boy, Cole was reassured on the matter of genealogy.

Another and more immediate problem faced William Cole. He had no openings available for a regular student from Exeter at this time. Only twenty baccalaureate candidates could be in residence, twenty-seven at most. There was a quota for each diocese and counties named in the statutes of the founder, Bishop Fox: five from Winchester; two each from Exeter, Bath and Wells, Lincoln (Fox's birthplace), Gloucester and Kent; one each from Durham, Lancaster (co-founder Bishop Hugh

Oldham's birthplace), Wiltshire, Bedford, Oxford and seven from other counties where the college owned property.

Even if the boy in front of him were to pass the qualifying tests, Cole could not admit him officially as a degree candidate because there was simply no opening for Devon at this time. The president may not have realized that he would not be able to find an opening from Devonshire for Hooker even after Richard had completed his degree requirements, four years later. At that time, because the college wished to name Hooker a "disciple," an honor reserved for gifted students, they had to use an opening available from Hampshire. Even at that, Hooker was by then over the sacrosanct nineteen-year age limit for matriculation. The only exception to this rule was for older students coming from outside the university who had the special permission of the president.

To qualify for that exception, it is likely that Hooker had to withdraw from the university in late 1573, when he had completed his degree requirements, so that he could be readmitted, probably on Christmas Eve, 1573, just a few months shy of his twentieth birthday. Almost immediately upon readmission, he was made a disciple and awarded his B.A. degree. Thus, one of Oxford's most illustrious graduates and one of England's greatest intellectual figures almost failed to get his undergraduate degree.

President Cole had a third problem facing him as he considered Hooker's qualifications. Here was a boy, well-recommended and probably qualified for admission but without the means to cover the cost of a B.A. degree. This amount could run anywhere from £50 to £100 over the thirteen-term (four-year) period. Although not completely without resources--Corpus rarely admitted the destitute--this boy was clearly not one of that new breed of wealthy full-paying students (commoners) who brought needed revenues with them as they entered college.

Hooker's needy condition, although less typical than in the past, was still not unusual for Corpus applicants in the 1560s. Many of his classmates were poor bright lads like himself headed straight for ordination and careers in the church. President Cole was well aware that the role of Oxford and Cambridge, since their founding in the middle ages, had been to educate such young men and to support them while in college through various forms of church patronage.

But exactly where would Cole find financial aid for this needy student, especially when he had no opening for him as a scholar? True, Bishop Jewel seemed to be guaranteeing the five mark minimum annual income for Richard, but this would hardly cover the boy's expenses. Cole decided to resolve Richard's financial-aid problem by registering him either as a chorister or a clerk. That way, he could admit him on a probationary basis and give him a chorister's clothing allowance. Richard could then study alongside the regular scholars as soon as his tutor stipulated that he was doing well enough in composition and grammar. The college would provide room, board, livery and a small stipend of one mark (13s.4d.) for spending money until Richard finished his B.A. degree, just as it did for the regular scholars.

In the meantime, on the strength of Bishop Jewel's recommendation, Cole decided he would apply for a Nowell grant for the boy. His friend Alexander Nowell, Dean of St Paul's, administered his brother Robert's trust fund to support "poor" boys like Richard. Cole and Nowell, both ardent admirers of John Calvin, had been friends together in exile abroad during Mary Tudor's inhospitable reign. He would apply to his friend for twenty shillings from the Nowell Trust for Richard's first year at college.

Put in early twenty-first century terms, young Richard Hooker sitting in Cole's office in the gate house at Corpus Christi College on this autumn afternoon in 1569, was a rather poor, although not impoverished, boy of promise from the provinces whose rich relatives (and their friends) were using their influence to gain him admission to a good college on a small scholarship. His existence as a student would always be precarious, requiring outstanding academic performance to maintain and secure financial aid from as many sources as possible. He would become what educators in a later century would term an "over-achiever" in order to prove himself worthy to his professors and to the college's "financial aid office" which arranged his package of grants, gifts, work assignments and loans. His immediate family, as we have seen, gave him little support either financially or emotionally. At a young age, he was on his own.

The college quadrangle that Richard now entered would become the physical and emotional matrix of his life for the next fifteen years, and his intellectual fulcrum until he died in 1600. He was one of those persons who were to find a home at college, whose psyche would be formed primarily by the cloistered academic environment and who would discover in great literary figures, living and dead, and in fellow students and scholars, the personal relationships, and emotional support he often found lacking elsewhere. The comforting enclosure of this monastic-like quadrangle, secure and protected behind the great gate tower and surrounded on all sides by an unbroken inward-facing wall of college buildings, would have been immediately reassuring to him. A young man who had not known the security of a stable family might well hope that here at last was a safe haven. Nor would Hooker's reaction to Corpus Christi College have been unique. The college had been intentionally designed, both architecturally and academically, to create just the effect it was having on him.

The school had been founded in 1516 by Richard Fox, Bishop of Winchester, with substantial help from his friend, Bishop Oldham of Exeter. Fox was a well-educated man and a leading advocate of the new "Renaissance" learning. He had studied at both Oxford and Cambridge and held a doctorate in canon law from the University of Paris. At various times in his career he was Bishop of Exeter, Bath, Wells, and Durham. In 1501, he became Bishop of Winchester, then England's wealthiest and most prestigious see. When Henry VIII became king in 1509, only Cardinal Wolsey outranked Fox in power at court.

This was the man who created the very special college where Richard Hooker was now enrolled. Fox's original notion had been to found a monastic school for the Benedictine monks at Winchester. But his friend, Bishop Oldham of Exeter, convinced him that the new king might soon be dissolving such monastic establishments and that he had better create a secular institution, on the model of Magdalen College founded sixty years earlier by his predecessor at Winchester, Bishop Waynflete.

Oldham himself was a confidant of Henry VII's, having served as chaplain to the king's mother, He was a wise and prophetic man who helped Fox create at Corpus Christi the prototype for what Americans centuries later would know as the undergraduate "liberal arts college." The Bishop of Exeter urged Fox to follow his own strong instincts and build a college which would break the medieval mold and embody the new learning, an educational environment where students would study a more practical (humanistic) curriculum designed to produce an educated clergy. Instead of living in separate halls in town, attending lectures and studying in the traditional state of lonely and impoverished isolation, students should reside and study inside college walls where they could have close interaction with one another and their teachers. A free-standing school was envisioned with its own curriculum, faculty, dormitories, library, chapel and professorial quarters.

Bishop Oldham is reported to have said to Fox: "Shall we build houses and provide livelihoods for a company of buzzing monks, whose end and fall we may ourselves live to see: no, it is more meet and a great deal better that we should have care to provide for the increase of learning for such as by their learning shall do good in the church and the Commonwealth." Oldham was as good as his word. He endowed the new foundation with a handsome gift of 6000 marks (£4000 pounds). He had been planning to make a large donation to Exeter College, the traditional beneficiary of the see of Exeter, but he was piqued by a personal affront from college authorities to a friend named Aiken and so gave his gift to Fox's new venture instead.

Not only did Fox, with Oldham's support, design a college that in its innovative physical layout would invite close interaction between students and their teachers, but he also inaugurated a revised curriculum and a new pedagogy that extended and expanded the radically different style of learning that had been started earlier, in a small way, at Magdalen College. He used the happy metaphor of the "bee garden" to describe the learning environment that he envisioned for Corpus Christi, referring to his ideal "as a certain bee garden, which we have named the College of Corpus Christi, wherein scholars like ingenious bees, are day and night to make wax to the honor of God . . ."

In Fox's garden, the principal gardener was the "herbalist," a professor of arts and humanities who would teach Cicero, Horace, Virgil, Pliny, Ovid, Juvenal. The second herbalist was the professor of Greek, who would lecture not only within the college but to the entire university. His task was to introduce the young student "plants" to the ideas of Homer, Aesop, Hesiod, Demosthenes and, of course, Aristotle and Plato. So important was the study of Greek language and literature in Fox's educational scheme that he established at Corpus Christi Oxford's first endowed professorship in Greek, a complement to his two other endowed professorships in humanities and theology.

39

The "bees" who buzzed about Fox's academic garden carrying life-giving pollen from plant to plant were chosen from among the college fellows. Named "tutors", they represented the most important and radical innovation of all. Their task was to assure, by the closest possible interaction with students, a healthy development of the precious seedlings entrusted to their care.

Within a few years Richard Hooker himself would be among the most effective "bees" in Bishop's Fox's collegiate garden, serving as tutor to the grandnephew of the martyred Archbishop Cranmer and the son of no less a personage than Edwin Sandys, Archbishop of York. That powerful Elizabethan cleric and his amazing son were each in their turn to have a defining impact on Richard's life and career. But these events belonged to a future of which the boy had no inkling. Today, he was looking anxiously for his own tutor, a young man only four years older than himself who had just completed his A.B. degree. Like John Jewel before him and Richard Hooker after him, John Rainolds had made the journey up from Devon to be pollinated in Richard Fox's bee garden and then, in turn, had become one of Fox's most prolific bees.

———— John Rainolds ————

John Rainolds, although not yet twenty, was already one of the most prominent figures at Oxford when Richard Hooker first knocked on his door in the fall of 1569. In securing the precocious and irrepressible Rainolds as Hooker's tutor, Bishop Jewel knew what he was doing. Rainolds had already made a name for himself, not only for his abilities as a scholar and public speaker in the oral disputations that were part of academic requirements, but also as a thespian. In 1556, he had performed a female role in a play called *Palamon and Arcite*, derived from Chaucer's *The Knight's Tale* which was performed before the queen. Life at Oxford and Cambridge was regularly enlivened during Elizabeth's reign by such dramatic productions, although stodgy Oxford was less prone than Cambridge to allow the more modern and increasingly popular vernacular plays.

Later in his career, when Rainolds had become a more zealous Puritan, he tangled with the dramatist William Gager concerning morality plays. Rainolds condemned much of contemporary drama, and especially the practice of female impersonation. Not surprisingly, his youthful indiscretion was remembered and thrown back in his face. By this time, he had become such a notable Puritan that, in 1592, the Queen herself admonished him for prudity and hypocrisy and for what she called his "obstinate preciseness."

By the time Hooker met Rainolds, the tutor's undergraduate shenanigans were behind him and he was well on his way to becoming one of Oxford's leading scholars and public figures. Within a few years, he was appointed to the most prestigious faculty post at Corpus, Reader in Greek. Four years later, when he presented Richard for an A.B. degree, Rainolds was one of the college's leading orators, debaters and most outspoken proponents of the Puritan Reformation. He was hard working and hard driving, a scholar and a voluminous author.

Rainolds' impact on Hooker cannot be exaggerated. Richard's Protestant theology, although never so rigidly Calvinist as Rainolds', owes much to the influence of his tutor. Under Rainolds' direction, Hooker studied Greek language and literature, and--so important for the powerful and persuasive style of his later writings--classical rhetoric. His close familiarity with the great religious reform theologians of the day also owed much to his tutor.

Before his career was over, Rainolds would be Oxford's leading Protestant radical, a key figure along with Hooker's cousin, Walter Travers, and others, in the important Oxford Presbyterian Conference of 1587. In 1599 he was elected President of Corpus Christi, and a few years later was the principal initiator of the so-called King James version of the Bible, a project that probably originated in his rooms at Corpus Christi. He would also serve as a Puritan representative at the important Hampton Court Conference, convened by King James I in 1604, and one of the most widely read and heard Puritan writers and speakers of the day. Oxford might be generally conservative on religious issues compared to Cambridge, and Corpus Christi especially so, but Richard Hooker's mentor, John Rainolds, was one of the university's few flaming Calvinist radicals.

Rainolds, who made a formidable impression upon his peers, would have seemed an almost overpowering figure to the boy from Exeter. His piercing dark eyes were set in a long thin face extending from a high forehead down to a short sharply pointed beard, and gave quick evidence that here was a high-strung and brilliant young man who did not suffer fools easily. Hooker would learn soon enough that his tutor was a scholar and teacher nonpareil, a man of immense erudition and massive resources of memory, with an eye for detail and a disposition of high seriousness.

One of Rainolds' first concerns was to ascertain if his new charge was ready to begin studying for his degree in the present term. Richard might need remedial work in grammar and composition before he could begin with logic. Rainolds was aware that Hooker's school at Exeter had only a fair reputation. It was no St. Paul's or Merchant Tailor's. As soon as Richard was fully qualified in grammar, Rainolds would see to it that he got a spending allowance. In the meantime, Richard's room and meals would be underwritten by the college. Extra money for his support could be had by drawing on the college loan chest and there would probably be at least 100 marks there to draw on by the beginning of the school year.

In the event, Richard probably roomed for a time with his tutor. Corpus was crowded. As many as twenty-five scholars, about twenty rich commoners and as many as ten younger clerks and choristers like Hooker, competed for limited space. Rainolds would have taken the larger of two beds, the one nearest the hearth, while assigning Richard a smaller one farther from the fire. Richard untied the bundle he had carried from home and laid his few possessions out on a table. He most likely had a pillow, a small carpet, a few extra items of clothing, a knife, a cooking pot and several books, including, perhaps, an advanced grammar and copies of Jewel's *Apology*, Calvin's *Institutes* and Bullinger's *Catechism*. He would need to buy other items: chamber pot, wash basin, candle holder and candles, curtains for his small unglazed window and, most importantly, a mattress.

Life would be more comfortable for Richard here in this upper floor room with his tutor. It might be drafty and cold in winter but the small hearth would be some relief. He would not have to endure the awful dampness of the rooms below where there was only a dirt floor and no heat at all. Richard would be expected to clean the room thoroughly every day. Since there were no servants to perform this service at Corpus, the younger lads did the work, just as their tutors and the other fellows had done before them.

One of the first items Rainolds would have discussed with young Hooker was the long list of the college rules governing most aspects of student life. For example, he must rise in time for 5 a.m. Matins in the chapel every morning and must never, ever, miss chapel. The penalties for unexcused absence were severe. Required logic classes would start promptly at 6 a.m. Rainolds would give Richard regular and mandatory written and oral examinations on his studies but he would have to walk over to Magdalen for more preparatory work in grammar and composition. He must, though, never walk out of the college gate to go to Magdalen or anywhere else alone, but must always go with one or more fellow students. If he disobeyed this, or any other rule, whoever discovered him in the transgression was obliged to report the infraction at the annual Holy Week assembly where all the delations (accusations) were presented. Stiff punishments were administered within two weeks of that assembly.

It was, in fact, easy to slip in and out of the gate and go into town on one's own. Many of the commoners (rich boys) did just that. They loved to go whoring, drinking, and carousing and many of them got away with it. In some of the other colleges they even assaulted the college officials who attempted to discipline them. But, if any regular Corpus students were caught off campus on their own, they would be in serious trouble. In a letter written later in life Rainolds recalled his moral and social prescriptions for Oxford students. He specifically forbade drinking, pleasures of the flesh, card-playing, dancing, football-- "a beastly fury"--or lewdness, or any dramatic productions that displayed the foregoing vices, or lovemaking, or violence. Here was a man worthy of the name "Puritan."

Listening to his tutor's orientation instructions, Hooker may have wondered if Corpus Christi was stricter about class and lecture attendance, participating in disputations and taking examinations than most of the other colleges. No doubt, Rainolds informed him that they were fortunate not to have been at Corpus back in Bishop Jewel's day when students had to rise at 4 a.m. and when missing a lecture or a disputation could mean a loss of meals and a public whipping. Those were harsh days. The health of many a student was wrecked, including, quite possibly, that of the good Bishop himself. Nevertheless, Jewel thought Corpus had lost much of its academic and moral discipline in recent years to such a degree that he worried about the college's loss of quality.

On more mundane matters like vacation time and meals--issues of primary interest to new students--Rainolds informed young Hooker that once he was officially admitted as a scholar he would be entitled to take up to twenty days a year as vacation time. When he became a fellow, like his tutor, he would be allowed forty days but they would do him no good unless he had travel money to get home or wherever he wished to go. The Nowell Trust could help with that. Perhaps his uncle or Bishop Jewel would send money for vacations.

Concerning meals, Richard learned that two were served each day and, quite likely, he would be one of those who served meals. Although we have no evidence of the fact, it is not unlikely that Hooker's college job was to join other choristers, clerks and probationary undergraduates working in the kitchen or dining hall in order to help pay for his expenses. The main meal was dinner at 11 a.m. Supper was at 5 p.m. The food at Corpus, Hooker would soon learn, was plentiful but not much varied and certainly not so fine as at some of the richer colleges, where fellows dined on fish, game, fowl, cream, wine and good ales. Here, supper would usually consist of cold meats, oatmeal, pottage (cereal), bread and cheese. Dinner might include a piece of mutton or beef at each table along with bread, cheese, butter and beer.

As Richard was arranging his few possessions in his section of Rainolds' quarters, he tried on the collegiate gown that he would wear over his clothes every day and everywhere. When he became a scholar, he would acquire a new gown, more elaborate. This would announce that he was moving up in the world. Then, as a fellow, he would wear an even better one, larger and of finer fabric. If he failed to wear the robe while he was an undergraduate, he could be punished by the college administration with strippes (whipping), or by being barred from the dining hall or by confinement to his room. More rules!

By the time Rainolds finished his oral orientation, Richard was well aware that Corpus Christi was a place where education and moral discipline were serious matters. He had joined a close-knit community that paid attention to study and was earnest about teaching and learning. They were few in number here, an intimate and well-disciplined society. Most of the teaching fellows had been undergraduates at Corpus, making for an ingrown fellowship. Each student was paired closely with a fellow so that the older members of the foundation monitored the behavior, academic and social, of the younger members.

John Rainolds may have guided Richard on a tour of the campus during his first days at Corpus. As the two walked out into the quad, Richard would notice how compact and self-contained his new world was. The small unobstructed cloister was open to the sky but was otherwise a secure enclave surrounded by college buildings. On the west side a two-story structure housed most of the fellows and regular scholars, usually two to each living chamber. On the east side of the quad was the great hall that housed the refectory and was the center for all important college events including the annual reading of the founder's statutes, receptions for visiting dignitaries, major college and university lectures, disciplinary hearings, graduation ceremonies and any other function requiring a large space.

On the north side of the quad were the tower, containing the entrance gate, the president's quarter and the rest of the chambers for fellows and scholars. At the far end were the library--the crown jewel of Fox's "bee garden"--and the chapel, with its nave extending well outside the quad itself. Behind the library and chapel was another enclosure that held the president's garden and commons area.

No structure marred the open space of the college quad in 1569 and recreational activities were sometimes allowed here. In earlier years of stricter Puritan governance, all sporting activity had been forbidden. Queen Elizabeth was more tolerant. Archery and tennis were allowed. (In fact, the first tennis at Oxford was played in the Corpus quad.)

Within a few years, however, by the time Richard had joined his tutor on the staff, they and everyone else at the college would be subjected to a major impediment to tennis or any other sport in this space. A large statue dominating the interior of the quad was erected by one of their colleagues, Charles Trumbell. This unusual structure, just inside the gate, was to become the college landmark: a tall pillar with a perpetual calendar and the colorful arms of Bishops Fox and Oldham on its sides, a sundial clock near the apex and the college emblem (a pelican) at the top. The pelican is pecking its breast for fresh blood to feed her hungry chicks, a symbol of Christ shedding His blood for His children.

3. Bishop John Jewel

The library was the showplace of the college and one of the marvels of Oxford. Richard had never seen its like. No less a person than the premier humanist of the age, Erasmus, who had had a strong impact on the college's founder and whose influence permeated the curriculum, had predicted earlier in the century that the library at Corpus Christi would become one of Oxford's leading attractions. And he was right. By Hooker's time, the college probably had the most complete classical collection at Oxford, one of the best Reformation libraries and the finest holding of Greek manuscripts.

Many of the books were not chained. (In the medieval period and well into the sixteenth century, books were regarded as so valuable that they were literally chained in the reading rooms of libraries so that they could not be removed.) To allow books to be taken from the library was most unusual at Oxford or anywhere else. Obviously, the intent at Corpus Christi was to allow a freer circulation of books and manuscripts into the rooms of fellows so that they and their undergraduate charges might have convenient access to them at all hours of the day and night.

The college founder had contributed over 150 volumes to begin the library, a princely collection in his day. The first president of the college, John Claimond, a prominent scholar lured by Fox from Magdalen where he had been president, contributed about the same number, mostly valuable Greek and Latin texts and commentaries. (Claimond had the distinction of admitting the man who would be the first famous graduate of Corpus, and some would say the most renowned of all her sons, save Richard Hooker and, perhaps, John Jewel, John Rainolds, and John Keble. This was Reginald Pole who would become Archbishop of Canterbury and papal primate of England during Mary Tudor's reign.) Another important donor of books had been Thomas Greneway, the unpopular "papist" president with whom Rainolds had had bitter disagreements during his early student days. Greneway had resigned under fire just a year before Hooker's arrival on campus but he left behind as a gift to the college a fine collection of theology texts.

In addition to the nearly four hundred volumes in the college library, many of the fellows had personal collections in their chambers, some of which held more than one hundred volumes. These also could be borrowed if one were on good terms with the owner.

The college chapel, a two-story building located directly opposite the library, was one of the original buildings, dating from 1517. The beloved first president of the college, John Claimond, was buried here. A striking eagle-shaped brass lectern and a beautiful altar piece, ascribed to Rubens, may have caught Richard's eye when he first entered the chapel and can still be seen there today.

As Richard concluded his first campus tour, he came at last to the great college hall. This room was the largest at the college, wider and longer than either the library or the west building. Its beautifully carved hammerbeam roof was similar to the fan vaulting in the tower entrance. The clean whitewashed plaster walls were adorned with painted hangings; the long trestle tables were arranged neatly around the central hearth; the floor was richly carpeted; and beautiful stained-glass windows commemorated Bishop Fox, various college benefactors and the Queen. At the far end of the room a raised dais held the high table where the president, vice-president, reader in theology and doctors and bachelors of theology all sat, along with any distinguished guests or visiting lecturers. The elevated table to the right of the high table was where the M.A.s and Greek and Latin readers ate; and, at the upper table to the left, would sit the other fellows, probationary fellows and chaplains. The scholars and disciples sat below at the other tables in the hall.

The steward had his own table on the side of the hall near the buttery, where food was kept before it was served by the clerks and choristers. A small door nearby led to an adjoining kitchen, located in a courtyard with its own gate to the street for deliveries. The kitchen was the earliest college building, built even before the chapel or library. (Richard Fox was a practical man.) The bursar and accounts clerk sat at the table with the steward and helped him oversee the meal and make sure the dining rules were obeyed. Oh yes! There were rules for behavior in the dining hall also! One of the most important was that only Greek and Latin would be spoken during the meal. English was strictly prohibited.

At some point during the repast, one of the fellows would read from the Bible. After the meal, there would be a short homily on the Scripture reading, usually delivered by the president or one of the fellows. Then a large ornamental two-handled silver loving cup would be passed around and all--or at least those at the head table--would share a draught of wine before everyone quietly left the hall. No loitering for conversation was allowed. Eating was not considered a social occasion at Corpus Christi.

Thus oriented, did Richard Hooker, in this or some similar fashion, take his first tentative steps into the collegiate environment that would nurture his spirit shape his character, and define most of his intellectual perspectives for the rest of his life.

Chapter 4

The Oxford Years

—— Life As An Undergraduate ——

During Hooker's first few days at Corpus Christi, his tutor examined him in grammar and composition and determined that he was not far enough advanced in these subjects to begin college-level work in logic. Rainolds sent young Hooker to Magdalen College each morning, along with several other clerks, choristers, and under-qualified students, to master basic skills that he should have acquired in grammar school.

Although the work in the college preparatory program at Magdalen was similar to what Richard had been studying during his last year at the Exeter Latin High School, the learning environment here was different. The pace was faster, expectations higher and better discipline was maintained in the classroom--a relief, no doubt, from the near pandemonium that had often reigned in his schoolroom at Exeter.

Before the first term was over, Rainolds reassessed the situation and determined that his pupil, ready or not, should proceed with the regular first year in logic. Whatever problems Hooker might be having with his grammar and composition, he would need to get on with the logic if he hoped to move toward his degree in a timely manner.

Writing did not come easily for Richard. Putting his carefully developed thoughts into clear English prose was a struggle. How ironic that this lad, who was destined to be an exemplar of English prose, was initially so lacking in basic writing ability that he was not fully certified in composition until the eve of his baccalaureate degree four years later. Even then, Rainolds probably had to look the other way insofar as Hooker's writing skills were concerned in order to recommend him for a degree.

Even as a mature writer of masterful sermons and theological works, Hooker's friends often found it necessary to correct his composition and spelling. Probably his mind raced too rapidly for his hand to keep pace. Fortunately, he never lacked friends and admirers willing to help improve his writing, both while he was in the process of composing his major works and after his death. In addition to his tutor and his two prized students, Edwin Sandys and George Cranmer, this small host of sympathetic "editors" would include such notables as Henry Parry, Lancelot Andrewes, Nicholas Eveleigh, Henry Jackson and John Spenser. All but Andrewes were his contemporaries at Oxford, where a lasting bond was forged between these men and the brilliant if under-prepared lad from Exeter.

During Hooker's four undergraduate years and in the decade following when he stayed on at Corpus as a fellow, he lived through upheaval of every sort. The most obvious disruption was the sheer growth of the university, with all of the attendant annoyances: overcrowding, shortages of everything from food and housing to qualified teachers and the general mess of constant construction.

The most terrifying disruptions of college life in Hooker's years were the dreaded epidemics that periodically ravaged Oxford. Bubonic plague, malaria, typhus and influenza were common in this overcrowded city of filthy streets, polluted streams, and swampy terrain. Efforts by city and university officials to control by legislation the unsanitary conditions that they understood to be one of the causes of these terrible diseases usually failed, partly because of inadequate police surveillance and lax enforcement of sanitary regulations. Garbage and human waste were routinely dumped into the streets and rivers. Privies were built along the edges of streams, if not suspended directly over them.

Oxford town reeked of human and animal offal. Butchers slaughtered animals in their shops and then disposed of the remains in local streams, from which brewers and bakers drew water to make some of the staple beverages and food supplies for residents. Students and others were packed into unsanitary and overcrowded rooms. The marshy city was a fertile breeding ground for the vermin that made the plague such a horrible part of Hooker's student years at Oxford.

There were no effective treatments for the plague and other epidemic diseases. Officials could only try to evacuate as many people as possible. Those who could afford the cost and had some place to go simply left. Most of the colleges maintained a country retreat somewhere out of town where as many as possible of the professors and students took refuge.

The plague ravaged Oxford intermittently for six years beginning in 1571, just two years after Richard's arrival, and ending when it reached its peak in 1577, the year he was made a probationary fellow. In that year, the pestilence infected over six hundred persons in one night, killing some three hundred within a matter of days. This catastrophe was attributed by many pro-Catholic Oxonians to God's retribution for the conviction and punishment of one of their number, a local bookbinder named Rowland Jencks. Jencks was condemned by the Oxford assizes to have his ears cut off for speaking against the Queen and the Church. Immediately after the sentence was carried out, the plague struck again and more people began to die. Some Calvinists saw this as a kind of black magic performed by the antichrist as revenge for the just punishment God had meted out to their Catholic foes.

The plague and other epidemics were not merely ingredients in a theological debate between Catholics and Protestants for those who, like the seventeen year old Richard Hooker, were struck down by one of these dread diseases. If we may trust Walton's testimony, Hooker was very ill for a time during his undergraduate years. He would have shivered with fever in his small bed in his poorly heated room at Corpus Christi, probably during the early winter of 1571. No doubt, he feared for his life as some of his fellow students sickened and died, their diseased bodies carried off in the city's death carts. During those dark days, Richard would have remembered that his own father had been orphaned when his grandfather and grandmother had perished in the plague that struck Exeter in 1538.

Once stricken, it was imperative that he leave Oxford as soon as possible. Rainolds could arrange to have him transported as far as Salisbury, where Bishop Jewel would see that he was cared for and, if necessary, returned home to Devon. As Walton tells it, the Bishop lent Richard a horse and gave him a small purse of two ten-groat pieces (a little less than seven shillings) to cover his expenses for the rest of his trip home to Exeter. Hooker apparently made the trip safely back to Exeter, retracing the route he had taken two years earlier. He probably remained at home, at his uncle's house, for several months, recovering from his illness and waiting for word that it was safe to return to

Oxford. To finance his trip back, Richard would have needed help from his uncle, at least in the form of endorsement for another grant from the Nowell Trust.

However upsetting plagues were to the life of an Oxford student in those years, a more fundamental disruption was the rapidly changing composition of the student body. Richard had had evidence of this when he first walked into Oxford and caught sight of those flashy rich boys, some of them with their own servants in tow, and all of them with money to burn. These young men, called "commoners," included his Devon contemporary Walter Ralegh, who was at this time a student just across Merton Street at neighboring Oriel College. These sons of wealthy fathers were often glamorously, if not gaudily, attired (contrary to college regulations) in the finery of their social class--a far cry from the traditionally prescribed medieval monastic garb of mendicant scholar-clerks like Hooker.

Richard learned quickly that, no matter what John Rainolds had told him about the need to obey college regulations, these new lads could break the dress codes and other rules that governed personal expenditures, lecture and chapel attendance and all the rest with impunity because the money and influence of their parents protected them from serious punishment. With each passing year, Richard noticed that such rules were being relaxed for everyone in the face of pressure from these new students and their influential parents.

Often housed outside college walls and living a far more boisterous and rowdy lifestyle than traditional students, these wealthy commoners had generous allowances from indulgent fathers--money for adolescent carousing in the streets of Oxford. Far from depending on scholarships, clerical patrons and teaching fellowships, as Richard did, they paid their own way for educational costs and room and board. They were a most welcome new source of income for the colleges.

President Cole was as aware as any of his counterparts (then or now) that rich parents meant not only full-paying students but excellent prospects for large capital and endowment gifts. One need only stroke a few parental egos and be careful not to ruffle feathers and plumes by too strict an accounting of infractions of the rules by the progeny of the wealthy.

4. Corpus Christi Quad

5. John Rainolds

As long ago as 1458, Magdalen College, the school with which Corpus Christi had always had close relationships, signaled this radical change in the composition of Oxford's student body by allowing a limited number of the sons of "noble and powerful" persons to be admitted "at their own expense, or that of their friends." But this was viewed as an exception. It was not until shortly before Hooker arrived at Oxford that the practice had spread to most of the colleges and become a trend. By the end of the sixteenth century, rich boys outnumbered the poorer lads by a six to five margin. The majority of the new students were not being trained for the clergy. Most of them were not even completing their academic work, merely attending university for two or three years to acquire the necessary polish and prestige of having "gone up" to Oxford and Cambridge.

Hooker soon learned how to appreciate and accommodate persons from different social backgrounds who had radically different career aspirations from his own. Within this closed community of shared collegiate experience and tradition, Hooker, as we shall see, was like many poor college boys in all generations who forge the friendships and acquire the shared bonds of loyalty to alma mater that provide the contacts with wealth and power necessary to advance their career prospects and move them up the social ladder.

Whenever there are fundamental changes in the social complexion of student populations, challenges to traditional curricular and pedagogical canons and patterns of collegiate governance will not be far behind. This was as true in Hooker's sixteenth-century Oxford as it has been in the schools and colleges of Britian, America, and Europe during the social and political upheavals of the twentieth century. Before Hooker's young eyes, the form and content of Oxford, indeed, its very mission was in the process of radical change. The focus was shifting from educating ministers and scholars for the church to preparing the sons of wealthy and socially important families for careers in government, law, business, trade, natural science and medicine, or simply to providing the broad education in the arts, languages and sciences deemed necessary for the life of an informed and cultivated gentleman.

Although this change in educational purpose took more than a hundred years to complete, most of it occurred during the sixteenth century. When it was over, nearly every aspect of collegiate life was altered, including the curriculum, teaching methods, governance and bases of financial support. Nothing less than a revolution in education was underway at Oxford during Hooker's time. All the strain, conflict, and confusion of such change was evident during his fifteen years there as student and professor.

As Richard and John Rainolds planned Hooker's course of study, they plotted a twelve year academic program: four years for the undergraduate degree, another three for the M.A. and at least six more for the doctorate. Rainolds told his charge that there would be little he could accomplish during the four year undergraduate program. The important learning would begin in the masters and doctoral programs when he would study theology, philosophy, metaphysics, history and languages. In the meantime, he would do preparatory studies in grammar, logic, rhetoric, geometry, music and astronomy.

Hooker's mentors in grammar were Priscian, Linacre, Virgil, Horace and Cicero. For rhetoric, Aristotle was his master, along with Quintilian and Cicero. In logic, he drew upon Porphyry, Agricola, Aristotle and Boethius. For arithmetic, he examined texts by Boethius, as well as two contemporaries: Tunstall and Frisius. He studied geometry in the company of Euclid. For astronomy, there were the writings of Johannes de Sacro Bosco and Ptolemy. He learned his Greek from Homer, Euripedes and Plato, and his history from Plutarch, Sallust and Caesar's *Commentaries*. In music, he drew, once again, mainly on Boethius. (His *De Institione Musica* was a somewhat obscure and difficult text that viewed music as a branch of mathematics and was of no value for practicing musicians but it was regarded as useful for learning music theory and may have played a part in stimulating Hooker's lifelong interest in music.) In the months and years ahead, Hooker became familiar with these writers and others who comprised the great classical canon of his college, principally Homer, Euripides, Plato, Horace, Pliny, Plutarch, Sallust, Julius Caesar, Virgil, Terrence, Plautus, and Ovid.

He took his courses one at a time, spending four to six weeks studying each text and then moving on to another. In this manner, he could concentrate fully on each writer before changing to another subject. Between the readings and examinations on them given by his tutor, Richard attended "disputations" and lectures.

The basic curricular outline into which Rainolds fit Richard's studies was the time-honored medieval format consisting of: the *trivium* of grammar, logic and rhetoric; the *quadrivium* of arithmetic, astronomy, geometry and music; and the *three philospohies* (reserved largely for the doctoral candidates) of moral philosophy natural philosophy, and metaphysics. As Rainolds knew, the emphasis was shifting within each of the three main branches of the curriculum toward the more "relevant" subjects. Within the *trivium*, Hooker did most of his work in rhetoric and grammar, although logic was still required for one year. Among the philosophic subjects, metaphysics now received less emphasis than natural and moral philosophy. And the *quadrivium* was now emphasized more than in the past. In later years, Rainolds would urge Hooker to study the "newer" languages of Greek and Hebrew as well as more Latin, still the scholar's choice.

Richard Hooker never satisfied all of the curricular requirements that his tutor laid out for him at the start of his academic career. There was a shocking lack of interest in enforcing the traditional academic canon. The new breed of upper-class students had little interest in studies designed to produce religious scholars. They had no intention of staying in college long enough to complete the curriculum through the doctorate--some twelve years!

Even among the more traditional students like Hooker, who had to make some effort to take as much of the required curriculum as was available, the standard fare was being modernized. Subjects like logic were generally viewed as less relevant than rhetoric, although Hooker excelled at both. Among Socrates' disciples, the utilitarian Aristippus commanded a more enthusiastic response from faculty and students than the idealist, Diogenes. The early church Fathers and medieval theologians were being gradually supplanted by the more exciting modern religious reformers: Luther, Calvin, Beza, Melancthon, Zwingli and, of course, the influential Oxford Visiting Professor of Divinity, Peter Martyr (Vermigli).

To one degree or another, everyone at Oxford felt the impact of curricular and pedagogical change. College fellows often failed to deliver the prescribed lectures, preferring to speak on more modern topics or none at all. Students frequently skipped lectures. This did not necessarily mean that serious students like Hooker learned less than their medieval predecessors, only that what they studied and how they did it was often radically different from earlier times. Filling the gap left by fewer lectures was a new pedagogy based on reading books and being examined on their content.

The more affluent boys crowding into Oxford and Cambridge could afford to buy the books used by their professors as a basis for lectures and tutorial sessions. The students could read the material for themselves, often without benefit of a professorial lecture. At Corpus, Hooker, as we have seen, had an excellent library readily at hand for his own use and many of the fellows had their own personal book collections. Passively listening to lectures, taking notes and then regurgitating professors' ideas in public exercises was a mode of learning being replaced by reading and informal discussion. The eye and the mouth were replacing the ear as primary sensory organs for learning. Nowhere was this trend more advanced than at Corpus Christi.

More than anything else, what should fill both eye and mind, according to Hooker's tutor, was the ideas of John Calvin and his followers. Rainolds advised Hooker that whenever he had any difficulty resolving a theological or moral issue, he should follow the judgment of John Calvin. Peter Martyr was also recommended as a good guide to follow. That dynamic teacher had left Oxford by Hooker's day, but Rainolds lent Richard his notes on Martyr's lectures and told his student about Martyr's important ideas. Aristotle was urged on Hooker as the best authority in interpreting the pagan writers but even here, when in doubt, he should always turn to Master Calvin.

Rainolds urged his students to take careful notes on Calvin's *Institutes*. It would not be sufficent merely to summarize the ideas contained therein. Hooker and his fellow students must also record their own understandings of Calvin's method of thought--the logic of his arguments. Only by learning how to interpret the ancients and the Fathers of the Church in the light of holy scripture, and then scripture in the light of Calvin, could Richard hope to become a wise and learned Christian scholar.

When Hooker and his fellow students were not reading and analyzing texts and being examined on them, they did attend some lectures. They preferred the intramural presentations given by scholars hired by their own college. These men taught more appealing and immediately relevant subjects like law, medicine, and the "Renaissance" languages: Greek and Hebrew. The individual colleges could offer such lectures because their growing affluence provided funds to endow their own professorships. Corpus Christi was in the forefront of this trend with the early establishment of well-endowed lectureships in Hebrew and Greek. Little wonder that students whould choose to take these popular subjects rather than attend the often boring and repetitious statutory university lectures.

The lectures Hooker attended supported a host of new courses given outside the required curriculum. These included such non-traditional subjects as literature in translation, modern history, geography, biology, magnetism, chronology, practical morality, manners and courtesy. Among the most popular of the new subjects was modern political theory, including introductions to such works as Machiavelli's *Prince* and *Discourses*, Thomas More's *Utopia*, and Sir Thomas Smith's *Republica Anglorum*. There is evidence in Hooker's writings that he had become familiar with such thoroughly modern thinkers while a student at Corpus Christi.

An important part of Richard's academic regimen, in addition to lectures, books, and examinations, was participation in periodic public performances called "disputations" and "exercises." These public debates were designed to test abilities in logic, grammar and metaphysics. Through these oral demonstrations, Hooker gained proficiency in the scholastic mode of argumentation prescribed by Peter Abelard, the early twelfth century French philosopher who was still standard fare at Oxford. It was a method that had been used for centuries and would one day be reflected in Hooker's sermons and writings.

The disputations were a cause of daily excitement. The chapel bell heralded each debate and sent students hurrying into the college hall to see and hear their classmates perform. The exercises tested abilities in logic, except on Fridays when they might be on grammar, moral philosophy or rhetoric. Three or four participants performed in each disputation. A senior student (respondent) would begin the debate by setting forth a proposed subject, presenting the issues involved, and offering an interpretation of the problem. Then one or two other seniors (opponents) would attack this argument. After that, students in the audience (arguers) might join in with their own opinions. Finally, another senior student (replicator or moderator), who had been presiding over the whole affair, would give his analysis, offer conclusions and either shower abundant praise or heap scorn on the various participants.

During his early years, Hooker, as was the custom, merely attended the disputations as an observer. Because Rainolds was so keenly interested in dramatics and public presentations, he required Richard to attend as many of these events as his schedule permitted. The most important disputations in a student's career were called "exercises." For the senior scholars, these were career highlights--formal full-dress affairs attended not only by the fellows but by such dignitaries as the chancellor, members of parliament, the court and, on rare occasions, the Queen herself.

At some time between 1573 and 1575, Hooker received news of an event that would fix the course of his career. The Bishop of London, Edwin Sandys, wanted him to serve as tutor to his second son, also named Edwin. The boy came up to Oxford at about age fourteen and probably moved into Rainold's room with Hooker for a time. It is safe to assume that, wishing to please the bishop of London, the college soon found Hooker his own room, with adequate space therein for the Bishop's son.

Hooker was well aware that this opportunity to become closely involved with the influential Sandys' family could only help his career. His first clerical patron, Bishop Jewel, had died only two years before. This quickly, he now had the prospect of a new supporter at the highest level of the church. He might dare to hope for a good post if he had to leave Oxford. As Bishop of London, Sandys held the third most important post in the church. He was a prime candidate to replace Edmund Grindal at Canterbury. Surely, this was the most exciting news Richard had had since his uncle had first told him he would be attending Oxford.

It is probable that Bishop Jewel had recommended Richard to Bishop Sandys sometime before Jewel's death. The two had been close friends and colleagues for many years. John Rainolds, already a well-known scholar and teacher, would also have been consulted as to who was best qualified to tutor the bishop's son, and he too would have recommended Hooker. To have so impressed Rainolds that he would make such a recommendation to Bishop Sandys is clear evidence of Hooker's outstanding performance as a student.

This young Edwin Sandys, whom Richard mentored, nurtured and befriended for the next four years, later would become one of Hooker's closest friends, one of the most formative influences on his career and the most important facilitator of Hooker's reputation as the major apologist for the Anglican reformation of the Church of England.

When Richard had completed nearly all requirements for his undergraduate degree, sometime late in 1574, he participated in a full-dress event, called the "Lenten" or "determination" exercise. Along with other candidates, he presented himself on the Saturday before Ash Wednesday, called "Egg Wednesday," for a disputation in which he was a respondent to propositions presented by a fellow, or an advanced undergraduate, who then would evaluate Hooker's performance for intellectual attainment and religious orthodoxy.

When Hooker had finished his presentation, at least nine of the senior bachelors present voted "yes", the number required for him to be accepted as an M.A. candidate and allowed to proceed on to a three-year course of study, primarily in moral philosophy, metaphysics and natural philosophy. Aristotle would be his primary guide for the next several years.

———— An Oxford Don ————

In 1577, after three years of graduate study, Richard was "incepted" as an M.A. at a public ceremony where he received his degree insignia. He then was admitted by the vice chancellor as one of Oxford's masters of arts. Before the ceremony, he was required to make a scholarly oration called a "declamation" in the hall at Corpus Christi. This requirement, applauded by Erasmus as an excellent means to sharpen rhetorical skills, was an innovation at Oxford in the sixteenth century that had been taken from an ancient Roman practice.

Unfortunately, there is no record of Hooker's oration or of the response to it. Given his rapid rise in the church shortly thereafter, it is safe to assume that his was a stellar performance. After the declamation exercise, Richard made a formal "supplication" for his M.A. by visiting the masters at each of the Oxford colleges personally and asking them to certify him as qualified. This was easily accomplished, for he was by then well-known throughout the university as a promising candidate. His final step was to make a formal "deposition" to the vice chancellor as to his qualifications.

Why all this fuss to get a masters degree? Because an Oxford master of arts was automatically a voting regent of the university and a junior member of the faculty. As such he was expected to enter one of the graduate schools and pursue advanced studies for his doctorate. He was also expected to engage in disputations, tutor undergraduates, accept lecture assignments, preach at Paul's Cross in London, when asked to do so and generally enter into the full academic life of Oxford as a permanent and responsible member of England's intellectual elite.

The late 1570s were busy times for Hooker. He took his master's degree in 1577 and became a probationary fellow in the same year. Also in that year the son of another distinguished family was entrusted to his tutelage. This was George Cranmer, grand-nephew of Archbishop Cranmer, author/compiler of the *Book of Common Prayer*, who had been martyred at Balliol College in 1556. George took his B.A. in 1583 at the age of about fifteen--a testimony to his genius, Hooker's ability and, no doubt, considerable relaxation of academic standards at the college.

By the end of 1578 Hooker had shepherded Edwin Sandys through the undergraduate requirements at Corpus. In the meantime, Bishop Sandys had been advanced to the post of Archbishop of York. At the age of twenty-four, Hooker had a grateful parent sitting in the second highest seat in the Church of England.

In August of 1579 Hooker took holy orders as a deacon in the church. The following month he was made a full fellow at the college. These two highlights occurred shortly after an important meeting with President Cole in midsummer of that year. On that occasion, Cole informed Hooker that the university Vice Chancellor, Leicester, with approval of Secretary of State Francis Walsingham would be appointing him to serve as *de facto* Regius Professor of Hebrew at Oxford, a very high honor indeed. Eloquent testimony to Hooker's ability and reputation as a scholar and linguist!

Thomas Kingsmill, over at Magdalen, had been the university's Regius Professor of Hebrew before Hooker had arrived at Oxford in 1569 but he had been too ill to present lectures for many years. Kingsmill would keep the official title of Regius Professor but Hooker would deliver the lectures in Hebrew and be designated Deputy Professor. The professorship carried a stipend of £40 a year. Hooker would receive only a small portion of that, about six shillings. The teaching obligation was to deliver four lectures a week beginning at eight in the morning. The topics usually covered holy scripture, with a healthy dose of grammar worked in along the way.

Hooker must have exulted in this appointment. What professional academic person would not be proud of such an achievement? He was rapidly becoming a star at Oxford. However, Richard may not have felt quite so proud of himself when he read, at about this time, his former student Stephen Gosson's book. The book, published in 1579, was entitled *The School of Abuse Containing a Pleasant Invective against Poets, Pipers, Plaires, Jesters and such like Caterpillars of a Commonwealth.* It recalled Hooker's undergraduate days when he, Gosson, Sandys and Cranmer--all under the strict disciplinarian influence of John Rainolds-- had joined in a self-righteous attack upon much of popular contemporary drama, music, poetry, and other forms of entertainment. On reflection, Hooker may now have thought that those traveling companies of players, jesters, musicians and jugglers that visited Oxford from time to time were harmless enough. Perhaps some of their performances were not to his taste but he probably no longer wanted to be counted with Gosson as one of those rigid moralists who would condemn these pleasant diversions.

Earlier in this eventful year of 1579, Richard had the considerable satisfaction of welcoming his cousin Zachary (Uncle John's son) as a student at Corpus. The now well-seasoned Oxford don, who had come so far from the poverty of his own beginnings as a poor relation of the Hookers of Exeter, must have felt considerable personal gratification as he showed his fifteen-year old cousin through the college buildings and, we assume, gave him the inside story on how to succeed at Corpus Christi.

In the following year, Hooker, now near the height of his academic career, was summarily tossed out of Corpus Christi. He had committed the crime of supporting the political ambitions of his colleague, friend, and mentor, John Rainolds. One may well wonder what cousin Zachary thought of that. As a Hooker, he was probably as proud of his cousin as his father John would have been. The Hookers seemed to have a special affinity for taking stands, notable even in those times when it seemed that nearly everyone was in the midst of some kind of public moral posturing.

For Richard to be expelled was not a singular event at Oxford in those days. Political and religious controversy were regular fare at the universities throughout the years of the English Reformation. Corpus Christi was scarcely two decades old, for example, when its second president, Robert Morwent, was imprisoned for a short time for his religious beliefs during the reign of Edward VI. Morwent was a diplomat and businessman with a great love of learning who had been selected by Richard Fox himself to head Corpus in 1537. He successfully steered the College through dangerous crises occasioned by radical changes in government policies during his twenty-year presidency under Henry VIII, Edward VI and Mary I. His crime was that he had continued to use the Roman worship service in the College Chapel during the Protestant reign of Edward VI.

Thomas Greneway, who headed the college from 1561 to 1568, was also accused of being a romanist. In addition, it was claimed that he was guilty of immoral personal behavior: cavorting with whores, being drunk in public, singing bawdy songs and stealing college funds. In his defense, Greneway accused others of hiding the chapel vestments and silver from the royal authorities and said that the charges against him were intended to cover up these misdeeds by his accusers. It was a tumultuous era at the college, as elsewhere at Oxford.

By Hooker's time on campus, the worst features of the political disruption were subsiding, but troubles did not end entirely. President Cole, as already noted, took office the year before Richard arrived only through the forcible intervention of the Queen's ministers. He was destined to have a stormy presidency, the event that included Hooker's expulsion being only a minor episode.

The expulsion incident is, however, important to our story because it involved a conflict between John Rainolds and another senior fellow, a Catholic sympathizer named John Barefoot. The two were rivals for the college presidency, a post they had reason to believe William Cole was about to vacate. Each man and his supporters lobbied the university chancellor, the Earl of Leicester, for his support. Barefoot had a good case because he was already Vice President of the college and could expect support from Leicester's older brother, Ambrose Dudley, Earl of Warwick, whom he was serving as chaplain. But Leicester supported Rainolds, a fellow Calvinist of advanced stripe. Cole put an end to the dispute by deciding not to resign the presidency after all. (He remained in office for another tumultuous nineteen years.)

An angered Barefoot then used his authority as Vice President to expel his rival Rainolds from the college, along with four other fellows who supported Rainolds' candidacy. One of these was Richard Hooker. Rainolds wrote to Sir Francis Knollys, in October of 1580, complaining of "the unrighteous dealing of one of our College [Barefoot] who has taken upon himself, against all law and reason to expel out of our house both me and Mr Hooker and three other of our fellows, for doing that which by oath we were bound to do."

Within a few weeks of their expulsion, Hooker and his colleagues were restored by the Chancellor to their places at the college. In frustration over Cole's failure to leave the presidency, both Barefoot and Rainolds soon departed from Oxford for greener pastures. Barefoot became Archdeacon at Lincoln. Rainolds left Corpus in 1586, not to return until he was named President in 1598. In a letter to his old rival Barefoot in 1594, Rainolds said that he had left the college because "dissensions and factions there did make me so weary of the place."

During his nearly eight years as a doctoral candidate, Hooker completed most of the required studies in Hebrew, Bible, Patristics (Church Fathers), the Reformation theologians and, of course, Greek. Despite the fact that many of the statutory requirements could easily be waived, because required lectures were frequently not even offered, it is safe to assume that Richard attended and participated in all courses available to him. He listened to lectures in theology based not only on the traditional texts but also on Luther's treatments of Genesis, Habakkuk, Psalms, Galatians and Corinthians, as well as Philip Melancthon on Genesis, Proverbs, Romans and Martin Bucer on many books of the Bible.

Throughout her reign, Queen Elizabeth and her high-ranking ministerial "scouts" at Oxford were on the lookout for promising candidates to preach at St. Paul's Cross, the famous open air pulpit in London, and to fill the important clerical posts of the realm. They were looking for men who could express with force and conviction the emergent middle-of-the-road position of the Church of England. Hooker displayed the desired qualities in his lectures and disputations: a sound grounding in classical, biblical, and modern thought (the attributes of a Renaissance scholar); a capacity for making an argument and defending it (a homiletic talent) and, what the Queen prized above all, a predilection for moderate reformation in religious practice within an established church headed by the crown--a church to be marked not so much by purity of doctrine as by a welcoming spirit of compromise, inclusion and accommodation among a variety of acceptable religious positions—in a word, a *via media.*

The day was not far off when Hooker would be on his way to London to preach at Paul's Cross, and, later, to accept the Queen's appointment as the Master of the Temple Church at the Inns of Court in London. He might never have received such preferment, despite his connection to Bishop Sandys, had he not been regarded by his peers and betters at Oxford as a man of special talent and promise. As his colleagues and students encountered Richard performing in a public disputation or debate, delivering a formal lecture in Hebrew, teasing and testing them with drills in logic--his favorite subject--informally discussing a Greek writer, arguing with them about what he saw as the excessive claims of some of Calvin's English disciples or simply listening patiently to their own ideas, they recognized in him exceptional qualities of mind and spirit.

What were these attributes that the professors, students, and colleagues who lived and studied with Hooker on a daily basis at Corpus christi found so appealing? He had an uncommon ability to see beyond the immediate issue at hand to more important and enduring truths amidst the passionate polemics that characterized most of the intellectual discourse of the day. He also had the capacity to organize vast quantities of disparate and apparently confusing material into a clear and convincing synthesis. No doubt he had a knack for avoiding the academic pedantry so common at the time. Hooker was already proficient at seeing the practical truth of a matter and he could argue convincingly, even passionately, for broad common-sense accommodation of apparently conflicting views. Perhaps most attractive was his moderate tone in argument and his modest, even reserved, personality which was most appealing at a time when nearly everyone around him was howling with such passionate intensity! Little wonder that his intellect was admired and his counsel sought.

Another quality which endeared Hooker to many of his academic colleagues was that he posed no real threat to them. His relative poverty and lack of social polish meant that he probably could not compete effectively with them for the best positions outside the university. How easy to befriend, support and admire this brilliant but quiet academic who was blessed with a sharp wit, a rhetorical flair, and a grand passion for order and rationality. Noblesse oblige!

As Hooker moved beyond his master's degree toward what he hoped would be a permanent career as an Oxford fellow and don, he knew that the apogee of his university career, the goal toward which he was expected to strive, the meal-ticket that would eventually assure him of promotion, was the doctorate in divinity. He had already spent seven years at Oxford and looked forward to at least seven more years of tutoring undergraduates, reading, taking notes, attending lectures, engaging in disputations and presenting formal lectures of his own before earning his final degree.

Hooker never received his doctorate. This failure was, for him, as it has always been for career academics, a defining fact of life. He remained at Oxford for almost eight years after receiving his M.A. These were probably the happiest years of his life. He fully intended to earn his doctorate and spend all of his career at the university. When he left, it was not because he disliked the professorial life. There can be little doubt that he abandoned Oxford primarily for financial reasons, lacking the independent means to continue his studies and to survive at a suitable standard of living in an environment that could not--or would not--provide decent salaries for most of its professors.

Like most of his M.A. colleagues, Hooker was stymied in his quest for a doctorate by the distraction of having to earn his keep by tutoring and lecturing, when he should have been doing his own scholarly work. Eventually, he was lured away from the university altogether by the promise of a preferment outside the academy. Hooker's stipend as a university fellow was only a third more than the pittance he had received as an undergraduate, three marks (£2), rather than two. His clothing allowance was only slightly higher. Even as a senior (doctoral) fellow he could earn only four marks per year. As a university lecturer, the most he could hope to make was a total of about £10, including all stipends and allowances. If he were fortunate enough to secure another position outside the university or to be offered a clerical benefice that would pay him a total of more than £5 a year, he would have been required to resign his fellowship altogether.

In the face of what must have seemed a financial conspiracy ranged against him, it is not at all surprising that Hooker, like most of his pre-doctoral colleagues, did not remain at the university long enough to complete his final degree. The average tenure of a fellow at Corpus Christi in Hooker's time was only about five years.

To say that Hooker had financial needs as a graduate student is not to say that he was destitute. Certainly there were scholars at Oxford in more dire financial straits than he. He was fortunate, as we have seen, to have received a number of grants from the Nowell Trust administered by the Dean of St. Paul's in London. In a special gesture of support, which demonstrates the continuing interest of John Hooker in his nephew's well-being, Richard received from the city of Exeter an annual sum of £4, beginning on 29 September (Michaelmas) 1582. By formal resolution, the mayor and chamber, "Agreed that Richard Hooker, the son of Roger Hooker deceased, and now a student of Corpus Christi College in Oxford shall have the yearly pension or annuity of £4 to be paid quarterly, and the said payment to continue as long as it shall please this house, and the first payment to begin at Michaelmas next."

This generous financial assistance from home more than doubled Hooker's stipend as a college fellow. But it came late in his Oxford career, after he had already suffered years of genteel (at best) academic poverty. Even with his stipend as Deputy Professor of Hebrew and funds earned as a tutor, Hooker's financial situation was far from enviable. His only recourse was to cut back on his study time and earn extra money by tutoring undergraduates, thereby delaying progress on his doctorate.

Tutoring undergraduates was not merely a matter of supervising their studies. It also involved serving as their guardian, responsible for overseeing all aspects of their lives, *in loco parentis*. Tutors, often called "creancers," were employed by the college, not the university. One of their most important functions was to assure that allowances and other funds coming to their student charges were deposited in their accounts, paid to the college for fees, and doled out as periodic allowances. A tutor was the parents' agent at the college, responsible for watching over all of the personal affairs of their sons--their own private "dean of students."

Fathers and patrons usually selected a tutor with the same care used in picking a college. Each college understandably took similar care to offer its best fellows to serve in this role. As we have seen, when John Jewel helped his friend John Hooker choose a college for Richard, his first concern was to select what he felt to be the best one-- Corpus Christi, Oxford. His second consideration was to identify the prime tutor. He chose that already famous young Puritan scholar, John Rainolds. A generation later, when Edwin Sandys, Bishop of London, wanted the finest possible tutor for his son, he chose Richard Hooker, by then one of the outstanding fellows at Corpus.

Tutoring was a demanding role that left Hooker less time and energy for pursuing his own studies. However unfortunate this diversion to undergraduate mentoring may have been for the scholarly attainment of many graduate students at Oxford and Cambridge, it did produce the most profound change in teaching and learning methods taking place in Hooker's Oxford years: the transition from the lonely-scholar mode of the medieval clerk-student to the tutorial mode characterized by personal interaction between a student and his mentor. By 1576, every student at Oxford was required to be registered in a particular college and to be under the tutelage of a fellow.

Nowhere at Oxford was the tutorial method more integral to a reformed undergraduate education than at Corpus Christi. As one of the "bees" in Bishop Fox's "garden," Hooker was aware of his role as a facilitator of a new pedagogy that focused on improving undergraduate learning, rather promoting advanced scholarly attainment. In addition to a strong tutorial relationship, Fox's pedagogy called upon tutors, like Hooker, to administer written examinations covering lectures and readings. This in itself was a radical departure from earlier tradition and another example of the replacement of eye for ear in the learning process. Book reading, note taking and exam writing, instead of listening to lectures and taking public oral examinations, were becoming the stuff of academic life. This change put a heavy burden on the tutors.

From the perspective of college bursars, the tutorial system presented both a problem and an opportunity. The problem was to find an adequate supply of qualified tutors to manage this labor-intensive one-on-one faculty-student relationship. The opportunity was to tempt needy graduate students with small stipends for teaching and superintending undergraduates. Here was a ready supply of cheap labor. Graduate students, then as now, were willing to toil for a pittance as tutors, graders, lecturers, counselors, and house proctors. Administrators could then spend their available funds to attract and hold senior lecturers and scholars who were too important to "waste" on undergraduate teaching.

Almost everyone benefited from this new system. Undergraduate students received better instruction from readily available and personally involved tutors than they had under the old system where they sat in large lecture halls listening impassively to scholars who probably did not even know their names. Colleges could admit and effectively educate larger numbers of full-paying students. Only the tutors--the graduate students who would never have the time to complete their studies and become full professors--were the losers. Even they might be better off, in the long run, by being forced out of the academy into more rewarding careers in other fields of endeavor.

———— An Emerging *Via Media* ————

As mentioned earlier, the primary religious and intellectual influences on Hooker at Oxford came from his tutor, the staunch Calvinist, John Rainolds. Yet Hooker would one day become a leading enemy of extreme Calvinism. To explain this, we must recall that, despite the influence of Rainolds, Cole and a few other fellows at Corpus Christi, the general religious leaning of the college and of Oxford at large during Hooker's years was Catholic. Repeated efforts by the queen and her ministers to root out Catholics were only partially successful despite strict requirements, including the 1578 Convocation that specifically required all undergraduates to receive instruction in the reformed faith and mandated study of Calvin's *Institutes*, the *Heidelberg Catechism of 1563* and Jewel's *Apology*.

Chancellor Dudley continued to talk of "secret and lurking papists" who "seduce your youth and carry them over by flocks to the [Catholic] seminaries beyond the Seas." The problem, he felt, was the lack of enough required instruction in the reformed faith. In 1586, a new lectureship in theology was created to remedy this default. (None other than John Rainolds was appointed to fill the chair.)

Hooker was surely influenced by this strong residual Catholic presence at Oxford. In his earliest extant sermons, and in most of his later writings, we notice a tolerant attitude toward Roman Catholics, an emphasis on free will as opposed to Calvin's rigid determinism and a balancing of Scripture with reason and the patristic tradition as sources of God's divine revelation--all debts to Catholic humanism. Perhaps Oxford's basic religious conservatism (and Hooker's), in the face of the more radical elements of the Reformation, should come as no surprise. After all, one of the founding spirits of sixteenth-century Oxford, and especially Corpus Christi, was the Catholic humanist, Desiderius Erasmus, as his work was filtered through his friend Bishop Fox. This brand of Christian humanism was quite comfortable with a reformed Roman Catholicism.

It is not mere speculation to regard Oxford as the seedbed for Hooker's later opposition to Calvinist extremists. There was a specific influence in Hooker's later years at Oxford that moved his ideas away from Rainolds and toward a more moderate position. This was the Spanish theologian, Antonio (del Corro) Corrano, who lectured and served as a catechist in many of Oxford's colleges and halls between 1579 and 1591. Corro was a former Catholic monk who had come to England to preach to Spanish Protestants in London. Both Cecil and Leicester were early patrons and secured him the post of lecturer at the Temple Church in London, where Hooker would one day serve as master. While at the Temple, from 1571 to 1579, Corro was castigated by Hooker's immediate predecessor, Master Richard Alvey, for preaching free will and for "speaking not wisely about predestination." Corro presaged Hooker in such ideas, and in preaching tolerance for Roman Catholics, from this influential London pulpit.

Corro questioned the twin pillars of Calvinism: predestination and justification by faith alone. He advocated toleration and reasonableness in resolving religious differences. For his ideas he was accused of heresy and denied a doctorate of divinity at Oxford in 1576, owing largely to the strong opposition of Hooker's mentor--by now Oxford's arch-Puritan--John Rainolds, who accused Corro of being a hypocrite for subscribing to the *Thirty-nine Articles.*

In his teaching and writing Corro stressed man's free will and natural reason. Arguing against what he saw as the extreme determinism and judgmentalism of many Calvinists, he urged brotherly love and compassion, rather than creedal confessions and strict biblical interpretations. His ideas are clearly reflected in Hooker's later sermons at Paul's Cross and the Temple Church. In fact, Hooker's opponent, Walter Travers, accused Hooker specifically of promoting a doctrine "not unlike that wherewith Corranus sometimes troubled the church."

Hooker undoubtedly spent hours with Corro discussing these issues in his chambers at Corpus Christi and elsewhere at the university. Oxford's new Deputy Professor of Hebrew, troubled by what he saw as the excesses of Catholics and Calvinist extremists alike, would have found welcome balm in the sweet reasonableness of the Spaniard. It is tantalizing to speculate as to with whom Hooker sided when John Rainolds urged his friend, Lawrence Humphrey, President of Magdalen, to oppose the move then afoot to grant a degree to Corro. Rainolds told Humphrey that he was afraid that Corro would "raise such flames in our University as [only] the Lord knows whether they shall be quenched."

Another moderate at Oxford who probably influenced Hooker, and who was also opposed by Rainolds, was Corro's fellow Spanish scholar, Francesco Pucci (1540-1593). Pucci earned his M.A. at Oxford in 1574. In his teaching, he flirted with the idea of universal salvation for all who believed in God. He professed the same sort of broad tolerance and brotherly love that Corro taught. Like Corro, Pucci had the kind of winning personality that led such scholars as Rainolds to fear that he was gaining the hearts of too many students. Hooker's tutor was influential in having Pucci expelled from the university in 1576.

Rainolds' influence on Hooker was thus moderated by the ideas of Corro and Pucci. In turn, Hooker passed on his own more conservative brand of Calvinism to his pupils, Sandys and Cranmer. They became even more ecumenical than Hooker. In his *A Relation to the State of Religion*, (1605) Sandys would one day argue that the Roman Church had so many positive features that it might even serve as a model for Christian unity and, furthermore, that even the pope might be saved.

During Hooker's years at Oxford, the university was debating, accommodating, and absorbing the vast intellectual and social challenges represented to traditional learning, piety and social order by the twin influences of the Renaissance and the Reformation. Individual colleges often differed sharply from one another in religious and intellectual tone, Corpus Christi being among the more humanistic and Puritan. But even at Corpus, the agents of change, exemplified by men like John Rainolds, did not go unchallenged by the voices of traditional Catholic learning and piety.

With hindsight, a convincing case can be made that during this period Oxford was the seedbed for an emergent middle theological ground between Puritanism and Catholicism. Advanced forms of Calvinism provided the leaven which worked the old patristic system into a new synthesis. Richard Hooker, a son of Oxford, was destined to provide the most complete and influential formulation of that new *via media* that we call Anglicanism.

6. Archbishop Edwin Sandys

Chapter 5

Leaving The Academic Cloister

— Bishop Sandys —

7. Drayton Beauchamp Church

There were six "father figures" in Richard Hooker's life. Each had a profound influence by appearing at a critical stage to rescue him from current predicaments and send him forth in new and more promising directions. Three of them, John Hooker, John Jewel and John Rainolds, had seen him through childhood and college. The fourth was the powerful Archbishop of York, Edwin Sandys, who first touched Richard's life when he sent his son to live and study under his guidance in about 1574. In placing such trust in young Hooker, Sandys had acted on the advice of his friend, Bishop Jewel. Once again, friendship among powerful men had formed a network of support for Hooker, as one handed him on into the patronage of another.

Sandys was so pleased with Hooker during the years of his tutelage of Edwin that he facilitated offers of advancement for the Oxford don. The first of these came in 1584 when the thirty-year old Hooker had been a fellow for about seven years and Sandys had been Archbishop of York for nearly a decade.

By this time, despite the recent largess of the Exeter city fathers, Hooker was feeling the pinch of a tight personal budget and the fatigue of his long struggle to finish his doctoral program while tutoring undergraduates. The offer of a living, called "compounds of first fruits," at Drayton Beauchamp parish in nearby Buckinghamshire was welcome indeed, as was the opportunity presented at about the same time to preach at Paul's Cross in London and thereby to taste the promising world of church politics on a national level. Bishop Sandys, who was a great favorite of the Queen and her chief minister, Lord Burghley, was most probably behind these early extra-mural appointments. With such friends in high places, Hooker's future seemed bright.

Few Elizabethan clerics cut such a colorful figure in the saga of the English Reformation as the surprisingly unsung Edwin Sandys. Hooker's first clerical patron, John Jewel, had been at heart an intellectual--delicate, sensitive, sometimes indecisive, often enigmatic. How different was Jewel's friend and fellow Calvinist, the robust, courageous, straightforward and altogether unbending Edwin Sandys.

The Archbishop of York was cut from the same cloth as other heroes of the English Reformation on both sides of the religious divide. Some of these stalwarts, such as the Protestants Cranmer, Ridley and Latimer, and the Catholic Thomas More, went to the stake for their faith. Sandys, as we shall see, came close to being martyred under Queen Mary. Queen Elizabeth found him a bit too warm-tempered and cocksure for her Machiavellian tastes. Possessed as he was of intemperate proclivities and at the same time, being married (perish the thought!) probably stayed the queen from naming this remarkable man Archbishop of Canterbury in 1575. Even so, she did give him both of the other two most powerful posts in the church: Bishop of London and Archbishop of York.

During the reign of King Edward VI Sandys' star had been in the ascendancy, a sure sign of his advanced Calvinist positions. When the sickly King died on 4 July 1553, Sandys went so far as to preach and write against Mary Tudor's succession and to support the efforts of Lord Northumberland and others to seat the Protestant Lady Jane Grey on the throne. Jane was crowned Queen in London on 10th July. For his support of her cause, Sandys was made a bishop. Within days, however, the tide turned for Mary Tudor, not so much, perhaps, for her Catholic religion as because she was the rightful heir. Northumberland turned coat and declared for Mary. He was imprisoned just the same, as were Lady Jane and many other Protestant leaders. Both Northumberland and the erstwhile Queen Jane were subsequently executed.

Sandys was arrested almost at once and taken off to be imprisoned in the Tower of London. On Mary's coronation day, his jail door was left open and he was encouraged to walk out. He refused, saying that to do so would be a tacit admission of guilt. He remained in the Tower for twenty-nine weeks before he was removed to the jail at Marshalsea to make room for other notable traitors, including Ridley and Cranmer, soon to be martyred at Oxford for their faith. While in the Marshalsea, Sandys received an offer to be forcibly liberated by Sir Thomas Wyatt, son of the poet of the same name, who was then leading a rebellion against Mary in the streets of London, a rebellion that represented the only serious threat Mary ever faced. Fortunately for Sandys, and for the later career of Richard Hooker, the Bishop had the good judgment to decline Wyatt's offer of rescue. He was not convinced, he said, that the rebellion was really God's will. (God's will or not, the Wyatt rebellion failed and it leaders executed as traitors. A close call for Sandys!)

After Sandys spent another two months in prison, his friends convinced the Lord Chancellor, Stephen Gardiner (who was also Bishop of Winchester), to support his release so long as he agreed not to leave the country and to post bonds to that affect. Ever firm in his convictions, Sandys declined the offer. Thanks, but no thanks. "I came a free man into prison, and I will not go forth a bond man ... and if I be set at liberty, I will not tarry six days in this realm if I may get out. If therefore I may not go free forth, send me to the Marshalsea again, and there ye shall be sure of me." Eventually Sandys was released. He fled the country with the authorities in hot pursuit, having many adventures as he made his escape, now hiding, now running, almost being captured after betrayal by supposed friends. At last, in May of 1554, with his would-be captors close behind him, the future Bishop made his way to

Antwerp at just about the time newly-born Richard Hooker was getting used to the bright sunlight of spring days in far off Devon.

When Elizabeth ascended the throne, Sandys returned to England at once, arriving in London on the day of her coronation. She put him to work on a commission to review and reform the Prayer Book. By the end of 1559, he was installed at Hartlebury Castle as the Bishop of Worcester quickly becoming a leading figure in the Queen's campaign to root out Catholicism in England. At Hartlebury, Cicely Sandys gave birth to a second son, Edwin, who would be Richard Hooker's student and lifelong friend. In 1570, the Queen installed Sandys in the third most powerful clerical post in the realm: the See of London. His friend and fellow exile, Edmund Grindal, had held that post and now was granted the number two bishop's chair, Archbishop of York. In just five years Queen Elizabeth's first Archbishop of Canterbury, Matthew Parker, would die leaving vacant the number one See. Grindal would move there and Sandys would go to York. Ecclesiastical musical chairs!

Throughout all of the troubled years of his career in the church, Sandys' attention remained fixed on the major priority of his vocation as a bishop: the improvement of the clergy. Too many ministers were poorly educated, inadequate as preachers and careless in their conduct of worship services. The Bishop's attraction to Hooker and his advancement of him in the church was born primarily of his zeal to find men of such high quality and see that they were placed in important clerical positions. Sandys was also responsible for his son Edwin's being made a prebend[3] at York and probably wished that his son would pursue a clerical career. If so, he would be disappointed.

It is likely, however, that young Edwin urged his father to regard instead his own teacher, Richard Hooker, as a more likely prospect for advancement in the church. His own interests lay elsewhere: in the law, politics, and world commerce.

---

[3] A prebend is a cleric who receives a stipend from a cathedral and is often a member of the chapter of that cathedral.

——— Pastor At Drayton Beauchamp ———

In the summer of 1584, Richard Hooker, having proved himself to Archbishop Sandys as a promising candidate for preferment in the church, was offered the living at St. Mary's parish in the village of Drayton Beauchamp, near Alesbury in the shadow of the forested Chiltern hills amidst the sheep-grazing fields of central Buckinghamshire--a scant twenty-five miles east and a bit north of Oxford.

Probably Hooker resided in the rectory at Drayton Beauchamp only periodically on weekends and other special occasions. He was, after all, a don at Oxford and this was only a part-time position. Still, this was his first pastoral assignment and he must have been delighted to express some of his ideas outside the academy. What can be said of his life there? To begin with, this was a quiet and peaceful environment--a dramatic change from the noisy, crowded, contentious and sometimes violent life in Oxford. The new rector was unused to rural living. Now a mature man of thirty, he had spent all of his life so far, except for his early years in Heavitree, in urban environments surrounded by the human chatter and excitement of intellectuals, clerics, merchants, artisans and politicians. Now his companions were a few farmers and shepherds, a handful of landed gentlemen, some occasional drovers driving flocks to London from as far away as Wales or the border lands along the Severn and flocks and flocks of sheep. His surroundings were bucolic, restful, conducive to contemplation, prayer and writing.

The commodious rectory at St. Mary's was more than adequate for the needs of the young bachelor, who spent at least some of his time away from the parish, not only at Oxford but also in London. He probably endured at least one of the annual "stephening" celebrations held at the rectory. This local custom required that on St. Stephen's Day the minister welcome his parishioners into his home for a feast, at his expense, of all the cheese and ale they could consume. (This tradition at St. Mary's lasted well into the nineteenth century.)

While at Drayton, Hooker had a brief opportunity to clarify and organize his thinking on a number of important controversial subjects. Here at peaceful Drayton he could try out his ideas in sermons, some original and some refined from lectures and sermons previously delivered at Oxford. We may see what the Hooker scholar C. J. Sisson describes as "the beloved figure" of Hooker "stooping in the pulpit to say his word to the congregation, turning from one group to another in intimate address, from the young men and to the fathers, to the matrons, to the sisters and to the little ones too, with great tenderness [when he says]: 'Sweet babes, I speak it even to you also.'"

From his extant writings dating from this time, especially those using a favorite sermon text, the Letter of Jude, it is possible to hear his very voice speak on some important issues of the day:

How We Know Our Enemies

"Let us first examine the description of the worldly and carnal men, the reprobates, who wrongly honor and dishonor, credit and discredit the words and deeds of others according to what they have or what they lack. If a rich and well-attired man comes among us, though he be a thief or murderer or whatever the condition of his heart, so long as his coat be purple or velvet, everyone rises up and all of our reverent solemnities are to little effect. Even among us, a person who truly serves God will be condemned and despised if he is poor.

Do not marvel if in the last days you see people with whom you live and walk arm-in-arm laughing at your religion and blaspheming that glorious Name whereto you are called. Thus it was in the days of the patriarchs and prophets. Are we better than they?

These mockers among us are those who use religion as a cloak to put off and on as the weather requires, those who shall hear the preaching of John the Baptist today, and tomorrow agree to Herod's decision to have him beheaded; those who will worship Christ while all the time planning some massacre in their hearts; those who kiss Christ with Judas and betray Christ with Judas. These are the mockers. As Ishmael the son of Hagar laughed at Isaac who was the heir to God's promise to Israel, so shall these mockers laugh at you as the maddest people under the sun if you, like Moses, choose to suffer affliction with the people of God rather than enjoy the pleasures of sin for a season. And why do they mock you so? Because, unlike you, God has not given them the eyes to see nor the hearts to conceive the abundant rewards awaiting you in the promise of salvation.

As atheists, these mockers cannot help but be beasts in conversation. Why do they remove themselves from God's love in this way? Why do they take such pains to abandon and put out of their hearts all taste, all feeling, of religion? They do so because only thus can they give themselves over to lust and unclean behavior without feelings of inner remorse or guilt. Being mockers of God, these people are of necessity followers of their own ungodly lusts."

——— How We Know Our Friends ———

"We know the righteous by their admiration for Christ's Apostles. These were men not only of poverty but of little learning. Yet how fully replenished they were with understanding. They were few in number yet how great in power. They were contemptible in worldly goods yet how strong in spirit, how wonderful.

So that you may better see what all this division and separation among members of the church means, we must understand that the great multitude of true believers, however dispersed they may be from one another, are all of one body, of which Christ is the head, one building, of which He is the cornerstone. As members of this body, they are knit together. They grow into men of perfect stature. As stones of the building they are coupled and used to become the temple of the Lord. They [are that] which joins Christ to us is His mercy and love towards us. That which ties us to Him is our faith in the salvation revealed to us in the Scripture--the word of truth--that which unites and joins us to one another so that we have but one heart and soul in our love.

Thus, those who are inwardly in their hearts lively members of this body and polished stones of this building, coupled and joined to Christ as flesh of His flesh and bones of His bones are linked and fastened to each other by the mutual bond of His unspeakable love towards them and their uncontrived faith in Him. No one can tell, of course, if another is deceitful in his profession. No one can tell who is a true believer and who is inwardly unbelieving; no one can tell, except God whose eyes alone behold the secret disposition of all men's hearts."[4]

---

[4] For readable texts of Hooker's sermons, see the author's, *The Sermons of Richard Hooker: A Modern Edition*, cited in the Bibliography.

Hooker would preach this message again and again throughout his life: only God can tell who among us is saved and who is damned. We have no right to judge one another.

—— WHY WE MUST NOT JUDGE ONE ANOTHER ——

"We whose eyes are too dim to behold the inner person must leave the secret judgment of each to the Lord, taking everyone as he presents himself and accounting all as brothers and sisters, assuming that Christ loves them tenderly so long as they continue to profess the Gospel and to join outwardly in the communion of the saints. At any time that they outwardly fall away from and forsake either the Gospel or their church membership, then there is no harm in calling them what they are. When they separate themselves from us, they are judged not by us but by their own actions.

So what if these evil ones seemed to be the pillars and principal upholders of our faith! What is that to us? We already know that angels have fallen down from heaven. If these men had been truly of us, they would have stood more certain than the angels and never departed from their place. As it is, we should not marvel at their departure at all. Nor should we be weakened in our faith by their falling away.

I have already told you that we must beware not to presume to sit as little gods in judgment upon others and, as our mere opinion or fancy leads us, rashly to determine if this man is sincere or that man is a hypocrite. They themselves make it known by actually separating themselves from us. Who are you that you take it upon yourself to judge another beforehand? Judge yourself! God gave you the infallible evidence whereby you may at any time give true and righteous sentence upon yourself. We cannot examine the hearts of others. We may, however, examine our own hearts."

An issue that Hooker could not avoid as his career moved into its public, political phase, was the status of Roman Catholics in England, the theology of the Roman Church and the status of the pope. His stand on these issues, beginning to take shape during his later years at Oxford and his time as rector at Drayton Beauchamp, would become one that was too sympathetic toward Rome to win him much favor with church authorities and would, in fact, become a major impediment to his advancement to high positions in the church. But, at this point in his career, Hooker was still as staunchly anti-"Romanist" as the most advanced Calvinists in the Queen's church, although his tone suggests a merciful response to Catholic excesses and a defensive stance regards Rome's attacks on the reformers rather than a frontal assault of his own on Catholic doctrine.

——— On Papists ———

"Here I must, as an aside, advertise to all people who have the certainty of God's holy love within their breasts, how unkindly and injuriously our own countrymen and brethren [the Roman Catholics] have dealt with us. They have acted as if we were the evil-doers of whom St. Jude speaks. They never cease charging us with either schism or heresy or plain and clear apostasy, as though we were the ones who had separated ourselves from Christ, utterly forsaken God, quite renounced heaven, and trampled all truth and all religion under our feet.

To those who accuse us of schism and heresy, we have often shown that our church is founded on what is written in law and the prophets and that we are obedient to God's voice telling us to leave sinful Babylon [Rome] and cleave to the everlasting covenant of God with His people. You Jesuits and papists listen to me. You ought to know that the only head of God's church is His Son. Of course it is true that He is the mystical and unseen Head of the church. But so is it true that Christ has given the visible headship of each congregation of His church to whomever of David's sons the Holy Ghost selects to go before them and lead them into their several pastures, one in this congregation, another in that one.

No pope or papist will ever be able to prove that these Romish bishops had supremacy over all churches by any word that is in scripture. Even the children in our streets laugh them to scorn when they use the phrase, 'thou art Peter' to prove their case. Yet this is the sole basis for the opinion held throughout the world that the pope is the universal head of all churches. But Jesus never said this. All He said was *Tu es Petrus*, You are Peter. But, not being able to overcome the words of Christ which forbid His disciples from behaving like worldly princes, this man of sin has risen up and rebelled against his Lord and to strengthen himself has crept into the house of most of the noble families in his country and taken their children from infancy to be his cardinals.

Beloved in Christ, let us hourly and heartily bend our knees and lift up our hands to heaven, each in his own chamber and all of us together openly in our churches, and pray for this pope. Let us do this even though he has laid a solemn sentence of excommunication against our country, even though he and his scholars, whom he has stolen from our very midst, have falsely charged our gracious Lady, the Queen, and the rest of us with abolishing prayers within the realm, allowing sacrilege in God's service, being unfaithful to God by putting a strumpet in place of a virtuous ruler, abandoning fasting, abhorring confession, disliking penance, liking usury, finding no good in celibacy. According to these charges, all who are under our religious care are not only worse off than when we received them, but corrupted as well."

Clearly Hooker believed that the head of state should be he the administrative head of the national church, to which all citizens must belong. In this he was a medieval thinker, unable to grasp, much less adopt, the merging modern idea of separation of church and state. For him the only viable question was which prince should govern the English church, a foreign potentate in Rome (or elsewhere) or an English ruler. This is not to say that Hooker was unaware of abuses of the church by secular monarchs or uncritical of such practices. He consistently urged as high a degree of independence from government authority for the church as possible and, as we shall see, even flirted with the idea of passive resistance to monarchs who abuse their authority.

One of Hooker's favorite texts, which he certainly used at Drayton Beauchamp as he did later in his preaching career, was from the Old Testament prophet, Habakkuk, who expressed so well his own discomfort over the hatred and judgmentalism that marked much of church life in his day. Hooker saw Habakkuk as a kindred spirit. He often cited him in his sermons and tracts. He found some consolation in recalling the ancient but oh so timely words of this prophet:

How long, O Lord, have I cried to thee unanswered? I cry violence!, but thou dost not save. Why dost thou let me see such misery, why countenance wrongdoing? Devastation and violence confront me; strife breaks out, discord raises its head, and so law grows effete; justice does not come forth victorious; for the wicked outwit the righteous, and so justice comes out perverted.

I will stand at my post, I will take up my position on the watchtower, I will watch to learn what He will say through me, and what I shall reply when I am challenged. Then the Lord made answer: Write down the vision, inscribe it on tablets . . . The reckless will be unsure of himself, while the righteous man will live by being faithful; as for the traitor in his over-confidence, still less will he ride out the storm, for all his bragging. . .

Self-righteousness, prideful certainty, noisy confrontation, condemnation of those who in other times and other places practice their faith differently from us, judging who is saved and who is not--these, for Hooker, were the threats to Christ's church. Those who speak and act thusly, he believed, do so contrary to the spirit of scripture, the dictates of reason and the accumulated wisdom of Christ's Apostles and the Fathers of the church.

By the time Hooker left Drayton Beauchamp for London in 1585, his ideas on the issues of the day were not yet fully formed, especially those concerning the Roman Catholics. But he had the essentials well in mind. And the fire was lit in his spirit.

Paul's Cross

Richard Hooker had every reason to be nervous on the Sunday morning in the late summer of 1584 as he walked, possibly in the company of young Edwin Sandys, into the churchyard of St. Paul's Cathedral in London. This was the most important day thus far in Hooker's professional career, the day for which all else may be seen as prologue. In just a few minutes, he would stand alone on the Paul's Cross platform and look out upon an audience of some of the most powerful people in England. They would listen to him speak on a controversial subject. (What subject in those days was not controversial?) They would take his measure and then his future might well hang in the balance.

This outdoor pulpit in the churchyard of St. Paul's Cathedral was filled from time to time by leading fellows at Oxford and Cambridge who were invited to preach there by the Bishop of London. It was nothing less than the national platform for exposition and discussion of public policy and religious doctrine, especially from the viewpoint of the crown and the established church. From this place, royal proclamations were intoned, new sovereigns welcomed, heretics and traitors condemned, military victories and royal marriages celebrated and important sermons preached. It was here, on public festival days, that Cathedral clergy, regaled in all the pomp and color of their various offices, read prayers and preached before a mixed audience of royalty, nobility and commoners. Paul's Cross was what Thomas Carlyle called "The Times newspaper of the Middle Ages." At the end of the twentieth century we would see it as a media center, a marketing mecca, the source of the latest official news, the TV cable news network of Hooker's day.

It could be risky preaching here at the Cross. Hooker would have heard tales of that infamous Sunday in 1558, just two weeks after the Queen's ascension, when Bishop Christopherson of Winchester, a renowned papal sympathizer, had preached a sermon here that had angered the new Queen. He was brought before her and examined on his sermon. Not satisfied with the bishop's responses to her questions, Elizabeth had him summarily imprisoned in the Tower of London. Clearly, this could be a dangerous pulpit.

Despite any such danger associated with preaching at the Cross, Hooker would have been delighted at the opportunity to speak from this famous pulpit. He would now have wide public exposure for his ideas. And he would enjoy the opportunity to see a bit of London at the Bishop of London's expense. The free lodging at John Churchman's house, provided at the Bishop of London's request, and the forty-five shilling preacher's stipend, made for a welcome holiday. Hooker was no doubt pleased that Bishop Aylmer had chosen the Churchman's as the place to put up his guest preachers this year. Staying there provided an opportunity to talk with Mr. and Mrs. Churchman about their poor William's brief time with him at Oxford. How tragic to lose their son to sickness, possibly the plague, and so soon after the deaths of their little girls, Katherine and Sara.

Richard Hooker stood in front of the octagonal wooden structure, with the huge wooden cross atop its lead-covered roof. Then he mounted the few steps and took a seat in the center of the platform to compose himself before his fateful moment arrived. In those few moments of anxious reflection, he focused on the challenge that lay immediately before him. He knew that this outdoor pulpit had been a place of high drama in the church and nation since the early fourteenth century, a potentially dangerous cauldron for distilling and exposing explosive political and religious ideas, a place to influence public opinion. It was also the crown's official pulpit, what U. S. President, Teddy Roosevelt, would have called England's "bully pulpit."

He may have recalled stories that Bishop Jewel had told him years ago of his own experiences preaching here. Those were the heady early days of Elizabeth's reign when the task of Paul's Cross preachers was to denounce papal sympathizers and argue for a Calvinist reformation of the English church. Giants like Nicholas Ridley and Miles Cloverdale had held forth from this very platform. Jewel would have taken special delight in recounting tales of the most dramatic events at the Cross: the very first sermon of record in 1330 when the Chancellor of St. Paul's, William de Brenham, preached on the excommunication of Lewis of Bavaria, the selling of indulgences by Archbishop Courtenay in 1387 to finance the rebuilding of Paul's Cross, the great day when Thomas Cranmer defended the proclamation declaiming Henry VIII to be the rightful replacement for the pope as head of the church in England, the unforgettable "Of the Plough" sermon denouncing the greed of the rich and mistreatment of the poor by that Reformation firebrand, Hugh Latimer--the same man who had once preached at Exeter and stayed in uncle John's house. Then there was the day in late November of 1553 when Elizabeth Barton, the "holy maid of Kent," along with a small group of friars and priests, was tied onto a scaffold high above the Cross and forced to listen to a sermon condemning her supposed revelation from God of the King's misdeeds, including his divorce from his most

Catholic Queen Catherine, before the maid and her little band were executed at Tiburon a few months later.

Hooker knew that from the time of Henry VIII this open-air pulpit had been the most rudely disrupted and confrontational public platform in the realm. Here, Sunday after Sunday, ordinary people had mingled with the powerful and the literati to hear a preacher like himself proclaim religious doctrine and policy. The crown's policy was supposed to be pronounced from here, but often a nonconforming preacher would slip through the scrutiny of the Bishop of London. Then they would later have to bear the wrath of the monarch.

More often, the official position espoused from the pulpit would be hooted down by jeers from a disapproving crowd or disrupted by loud uninvited rebuttals from someone on the benches or even in the galleries. At the very least, a preacher at Paul's Cross could expect rebuttals in speeches, sermons and written publications following his sermon, no matter how well prepared he was or how careful he tried to be in his research and argumentation.

No doubt Hooker hoped that his own remarks would not provoke too much controversy. After all, his intent was to plead for an end to conflict in the church. He would condemn only those who sought to make trouble. In fact, much of what he had to say had been pronounced from this very pulpit by Archbishop Whitgift less than two years previously. Certainly, Hooker's preaching style would not normally provoke antagonism in his listeners. He is not known to have embellished his thoughts with much oratorical flair. His sermons stood on their own internal logic and were persuasive on their merits, aided only by the use of rhetorical devices woven into the written composition. He rarely employed either dramatic gesture of hand and head or excessive modulation of voice. To be well rewarded, a listener would have to give attentive ear to Hooker's carefully chosen words.

Richard Hooker stood up at last. He took several steps forward, placed his sermon text on the lectern, and looked out over the churchyard, dismissing from his concern the now largely inattentive crowd of talking and walking Londoners behind the benches. He slowly drew his gaze in toward the forms, where many occupants were still turned away from the platform, visiting with one another in small clusters and paying no attention to him.

There is no surviving text of Hooker's Paul's Cross sermon but it is quite certain that one of its central themes dealt with the doctrine of predestination as it was expounded by the more extreme English Calvinists of the day like his cousin, Walter Travers. This view, that Christ died only for the chosen "elect" (supralapsarianism) and that this group usually turned out to be those of Calvinist persuasion was one that Hooker rejected as too rigid and self-serving. In any event, he would argue, we have no way of knowing who is and who is not one of the "elect." Only God knows that. We must take as elect those who believe that they are, attend church and generally seem to be trying to live their lives according to Christian principles. This more tolerant and inclusive view of salvation was to characterize Hooker's thinking for the rest of his career and position him as a leading opponent of the dominant Calvinism of the day.

"Devastation and violence confront me," Hooker read his favorite Old Testament writer, Habakkuk, from his copy of the authorized *Bishop's Bible*. "Strife breaks out, discord raises its head, and so law grows effete; justice does not come forth victorious, for the wicked outwit the righteous and so justice comes out perverted."

Hooker closed the Bible. He noticed that several of the inattentive barristers from the Inns of Court sitting on the front bench had stopped talking and were looking up at him. He looked down at his manuscript and began to preach.

> Who is responsible for the strife, the controversy, the disorder, the dishonesty, the hatred, the violence that threaten to destroy all law and justice and all peace in our country? Are you? Am I? Is Rome? Is Mr. Calvin? Is the Church? Is God? Who is at fault here?

Many more people sitting on the benches, in the galleries, and on the lawn looked toward the pulpit now. This did not sound like the usual fare from Oxford: a dry recitation of theological axioms and proofs, or the endless citation of scriptural texts to support the charges and countercharges of religious opponents. Maybe there would be some excitement this morning after all.

8. Paul's Cross

Hooker continued to read out his sermon from his manuscript. He was no extemporaneous spellbinder like Walter Travers. Hooker knew that Travers had made a name for himself as an exciting and compelling preacher at the nearby Temple Church. Travers employed the new "London" style of preaching so popular among Puritans. These preachers memorized their sermons so that they would appear to be speaking extemporaneously. They made generous use of gestures and voice inflections, as if they were actors in one of the stage plays then popular in the city. Hooker disdained this sort of staged performance from the pulpit. He thought it was better suited for children in the nursery than for instructing adults. He was confident about his own preaching style. His material was organized and well-documented. More importantly, he was sanguine about his ability to move others with the logic of his argument and the power of his words. His rhetorical flair had been well-honed in all those Oxford disputations where he had sharpened his use of metaphor, simile, epigram and a host of other rhetorical aids. He had had wonderful models at Oxford, including John Rainolds' famed lectures on Aristotle. He was no newcomer to the public platform. He had mastered the art of persuasion.

He continued to preach.

The fault for all of this terrible conflict and chaos among us lies in our zeal to set ourselves up as judges of one another. In the name of holy scripture, in the name of the Fathers of the Church, in the name of Master Calvin, in the name of God himself, some of us condemn others of us as damned, as cut off from salvation. We proclaim ourselves to be righteous, to be saved by God's predetermined election of us.

Who are we to know what God has pre-ordained? By what awful authority do we declare that God had by His pre-election cut off all of our Christian forebears who lived and worshipped in the only church they knew, the Catholic church of Rome, and then condemned them to a certain damnation?

He continued to elaborate an irenical message of toleration, cooperation and inclusiveness which sought to enfold even Catholics within its forgiving embrace.

> Because the church of Rome is corrupt and mistaken in many of its teachings does not mean that all members of that church today or in past generations are cut off from God's tender mercies because of God's supposed pre-ordination of their damnation. Is it not more reasonable for us to assume that by their ignorance of the holy word, which a corrupt church had withheld from them, and by even that small portion of true faith given to them, they are by God's grace, saved?
>
> Wherever we differ strongly on matters of God's plan and intention for His people, to the point of disrupting the public peace and order of our realm and church, and where the scripture is silent or unclear, should we not use the light of our God-given reason to point us toward His intention for us? And do we not have evidence that we are close to that divine intention when discord ceases and a tolerant and accepting accord prevails in our mutual relations?
>
> A reasonable interpretation of scripture and an examination of the history of what God had revealed to His Church throughout the ages have shown us how wrong we are to presume to judge one another. We are asked to forgive and accept as we have been forgiven and accepted. We proclaim the damnation of other men at the peril of our own souls. We must stop this judging and damning one another in God's name, as though it were His eternal will we are proclaiming and not our own presumptuous self-righteousness.

Richard may have looked up from his manuscript at this point and seen a number of men in the gallery squirming uncomfortably in their chairs and several barristers on the benches in front of him taking notes. No doubt about it, there would be some strong reactions to this sermon. Hooker wondered what his patron, Archbishop Sandys, would have to say about his failure to take the strict Calvinist line and damn all Catholics. Too late now. He continued from his text.

> Some among us have based their condemnation of our Roman brothers and others with whom they find fault, including the Galatians of old who practiced circumcision, on God's eternal decree of reprobation which they believe predetermined the damnation of such persons. Then they look to the same high place to find the cause of their own pre-election to salvation and blessedness.
>
> Granted that both the Galatians and the papists were and are in error. From this does it follow that God ordained such error, that He is the author of evil and sin in the world? We mistake holy scripture if we find therein the proof that our God is the cause of our ignorance and sin.

Hooker continued.

> Surely, holy scripture does not teach that God wants us to destroy His church by condemning or electing one another in His name. We in this realm are one Christian commonwealth with one sovereign prince as head. As citizens of this commonwealth we are all members of one English Church. That church is founded upon God's truths as revealed in His scriptures and to His church over the ages.
>
> Our religion is reformed in the spirit of Master Calvin, but not in slavish obedience to him or his followers.
>
> All English citizens are welcomed as members of the church so long as they conform outwardly to the forms and customs of our religious practice. We do not presume to search the hearts and souls of church

members to discern their innermost thoughts and intentions. That is the providence of God alone.

God save our gracious queen. God save us all.

Hooker stopped speaking. He was probably greeted with a few cheers, mingled with some hoots and boos, perhaps the latter predominated. The more extreme Calvinists would not have been pleased by what they had heard. He was learning a hard lesson. Those who attack the status quo are always welcomed to the speaker's platform and the printer's shop, no matter how intemperate or outlandish their attacks on present institutions and practices might be. Those who take the more temperate course, counseling moderation and support for traditional patterns, can expect only lukewarm response from their audiences at best. Later on in his life, he expressed this painful lesson in what were to become the oft-quoted opening lines from Book I of his magnum opus.

> He that goes about to persuade a multitude that they are not so well governed as they ought to be, shall never lack attentive and favorable hearers, because they know the manifold defects whereunto every kind of regiment is subject. . .And because such as openly reprove supposed disorders of state are taken for principal friends to the common benefit of all. . .whatsoever they utter passes for good. . .whereas, on the other side, if we maintain things that are established, we have not only to strive with a number of heavy prejudices deeply rooted in the hearts of men, who think that herein we. . .speak in favor of the present state because we either hold or seek preferment, but also to bear such exceptions as minds so averted beforehand usually take against that which they are loath should be poured into them.

Hooker was discovering, possibly to his pain, that, by nature, humans resent authority and suspect those who defend it, no matter how nobly. Humankind loves the rebel who breaks the law and threatens order in the name of freedom. Instinctively, most of us resist those who argue against the purity of revolutionary ideals. It is an uphill struggle to convince us of the wisdom of choosing to submit to the ordering established values of the commonwealth.

The Churchmans Of London

When Richard Hooker finally put his tired body to rest on that autumn night in 1584 following his sermon at Paul's Cross, he had no idea that this large half-timbered house on Watling Street would be his home for the next decade.

John Churchman was one of London's leading citizens, with friends in high places. At the time of Hooker's first overnight stay in his home, he was a man of about fifty years, nearing the height of his influence and considerable personal wealth. By trade, he was a merchant tailor, dealing primarily in large wholesale transactions for finished woolen cloth in London, throughout England and overseas, especially in Ireland. In addition to his imposing house on Watling Street, a frequent gathering place for many of the most prominent clerical and business supporters of the Queen's policies, John had a summer home in Enfield, a prosperous suburban town just twenty miles up the River Ware, north of the city.

Churchman and his wife, Alice, lived in this fine townhouse with their teenage children, Joan and Robert, and four younger children, John, Mary, Ann and Elizabeth. They were still grieving the loss of their son William, a student at Corpus Christi, Oxford, who had died just a year earlier during the summer break from college, and two young daughters, Sarah and Katherine, who had died shortly thereafter. Hooker gave them some consolation during his few days with them. He had known William as a student at Corpus Christi during his own final years as a senior fellow and professor there.

During these first few days with the Churchman family, Hooker had an opportunity to meet his future wife, Joan. She was about seventeen when she joined her parents in welcoming Richard to the house. She was often at family meals where he was present. As the oldest Churchman daughter, already of about marriageable age, Joan was interested in the young bachelors who frequented the Churchman house. Hers would be a handsome dowry, sufficient to assure a match with someone far more promising than this struggling cleric whom she watched as he talked with her parents. She would have thought him uncommonly quiet and polite--a bit nervous perhaps, and not so polished as other men she had observed, clearly not a sophisticated London man.

Richard's first impressions of Joan were no doubt a mixture of disinterest and fascination. He had had precious little experience with women and, at age thirty, had probably resigned himself to (or been comfortable with) bachelorhood. This meeting of an older man of intellectual bent and limited resources from the provinces who was on his way up in his profession, and a young city woman of privileged economic circumstance, assertive temperament, and urbane tastes, was fraught with possibilities.

London, Hooker learned, was a surprisingly compact place. It took less than an hour to walk, in a leisurely fashion, along the river from the Tower of London to the Temple Bar. Most residents lived in an area of only about a square mile that held all of the city's twenty-six wards and more than one hundred parishes. Dominating this section of London was St. Paul's Cathedral in whose close he had just preached. When Hooker had the leisure to explore the Cathedral and its immediate precincts he could not help being impressed by the lively and colorful activity that dominated. Within the Cathedral itself, as well as in its external environs were to be found the chief employment centers and the major spots for hawking cheap (often stolen) merchandise. Here was everything from feathers, pins, dog collars, and earrings to furniture and window glass. The center aisle of the Cathedral was one of London's chief meeting places for business and social gossip. This was also a place to beware of conmen and pickpockets. Beggars abounded inside and outside of St. Paul's, as did poets singing their odes, painters adorning and selling their canvasses and musicians performing.

What may have particularly attracted Hooker in this part of the city were the dozens of booksellers in the churchyard area. The bookshops opened at 7 a.m. each morning. In front of each hung a colorful painted sign that was the bookseller's trademark and that might give some clue as to the type of book he specialized in. Hence, the signs of the Bible, the Holy Ghost, The Keys and Crowns, The Mermaid, The White Horses, The Roses, The Gun, and so on. Richard could not know that, within a few years, he would be looking in this very neighborhood for a book publisher for his own work.

As he strolled down Fleet Street toward the Inns of Court, he entered the area where lawyers, courtiers, politicians, bureaucrats and merchants did their shopping. The street was lined with stores where many of the fopperies of the age were made and sold. Here were purveyors of the finest silk fabrics, jewelers, hat trimmers, collar and ruff makers and other providers of the conspicuous consumption of this gaudy age.

Entering this border region between London and Westminster, between the world of commerce and the world of politics, Hooker could sense at once that he was in an altogether distinctive part of the city. Here more than a thousand law students lived, worked, and mingled with the attorneys, barristers, judges and other important elements of London's political and intellectual elite. The meeting ground of commerce, politics, law and intellectual creativity--all the elements of power and money were here. The pace seemed fast, stimulating, somehow urgent. Self-confident men, who clearly had arrived at a place of some consequence in their careers, elegantly attired in quilted doublets of Italian silk velvet and breeches thickly lined with wool against the coming winter chill, moved about their business with style and an aura of self-importance. They sported elaborate collars and cuffs edged with Italian lace, Flemish lace-fringed handkerchiefs tucked in their sleeves and elegant feather-plumed hats in a variety of colors and fabrics. Most of the younger men, still in summer livery, were dressed no less elegantly, turned out either in the finest quality linen shirts or brightly dyed and patterned doublets which, in either case, fell scarcely below the waist to be met by no breeches at all--just a pair of elegant tights.

Thousands of students lived in this area within the fourteen Inns on Fleet street, Chancery Lane, up on Holborne, all self-supporting and in daily contact with the barristers, judges and politicians who practiced their several professions in the offices, courts and halls within or immediately outside the Inns. Although far more practical and focused in educational goals than Oxford or Cambridge, these Inns were nevertheless, in their own way, major learning centers that informed and shaped the life of the nation.

9. Archbishop John Whitgift

10. The Temple Church

Chapter 6

Introduction To
Church Politics

── Cousin Walter ──

1584 was a landmark year in Hooker's life. There had been other important years, as we have seen: 1562, when, as an eight-year old boy, he had moved from the shelter of his mother's protection in rural Heavitree into the busy life of his uncle's Exeter and begun his formal schooling; 1569, when the fifteen-year old had entered Corpus Christi, Oxford as an under-prepared, under-funded undergraduate; 1574, when he had entered into the life of an Oxford tutor with the auspicious charge to his care of Edwin Sandys, son of the Bishop of London; 1579, when his career as a twenty-five year old Oxford don blossomed with important appointments and challenges.

What marks 1584 is that it signals Hooker's entry into national religious politics and so into the mainstream of the later stage of the Protestant Reformation in England. Hooker's baptism in the national political arena came at a time of rising hysteria over threats of foreign invasion and reinstitution of the Catholic religion. Memories of Catholic Mary Tudor were still vivid, and fears of Catholic Mary Stewart, the current catalyst for foreign and domestic plots against Queen Elizabeth and her brand of Protestantism, were in the forefront of political discourse.

Just as important as the real and imagined threats from Catholics to the Queen's safety and to her style of reformed religion were challenges to the established church from the radical Calvinists, many of whom sought not only further reform in theology and liturgy, but fundamental changes in church polity as well. It was, in fact, these alterations in the governance of the church, especially the threatened replacement of Queen and bishops by a largely decentralized structure with significant lay control, that most concerned the Queen and her chief ministers in these later years of the century. And, of course, once the decision was taken to execute Mary Stewart, and the Spanish invasion had failed and the Catholic threat was significantly diminished, the chief remaining enemies to established authority were perceived to be the radical Calvinists and church separatists, although these groups were, in fact, also much weakened by this time.

The political battles between the Queen's emergent Anglican church and its Catholic and radical Protestant enemies were waged in various locales throughout the later years of the sixteenth century: parliament, the royal court, the church hierarchy, the pulpits of the land, the universities, the streets of London, the printing presses.

Hooker's first entry into the political cauldron was his sermon at Paul's Cross and his meeting, at about that time, with Walter Travers, who was Hooker's cousin by marriage to one of Uncle John's daughters. Travers was one of the two or three leading exponents of radical Calvinism in England. He set forth his explosive doctrines in writings that were already being seen as basic documents of emergent English Presbyterianism, as well as through provocative sermons that he preached regularly at the Temple Church where he held the position of reader--a kind of assistant minister.

The first meeting of these two men, soon to become principal protagonists in the English Reformation, took place at about the time of Hooker's Paul's Cross sermon. It may have been Edwin Sandys, Hooker's former student and good friend--now a beginning law student at the Inns of Court and soon to be a member at Middle Temple Inn--who introduced the two men. Certainly, Edwin's stature as the son of the now archbishop of York and nephew of Miles Sandys, who was member of parliament, one of England's leading jurists and a prominent member of Middle Temple who was about to be elected its treasurer, gave Edwin social and political standing sufficient to make such an introduction.

Sandys no doubt considered his former tutor to be a promising gladiator to challenge Travers at the Temple. Hooker's Paul's Cross sermon and his lectures and talks at Oxford seemed to the moderate Sandys a welcome antidote to the threatening rhetoric of the Arch-Presbyterian, Travers. Edwin applauded Hooker's uncharacteristic voice of moderation and common sense, his preference for tradition and public order and his ability to organize and set forth convincing arguments drawn persuasively from first principles. Hooker represented a needed relief from the tedious line-by-line refutations that characterized so much of the church's apologetic writing. Far more urbane and sophisticated than his Oxford mentor, Sandys was able, even eager, to acquaint Hooker with the dangers inherent in Travers' sermons at the Temple Church, addressing week after week a captive audience of influential lawyers, barristers, judges and politicians in this, one of England's most important churches.

Sandys was among the first to congratulate Hooker on his Paul's Cross sermon and to mention to him the possibility, already under discussion by his father and others in the church leadership that he, Richard Hooker, might be chosen to replace Travers, who had been serving as *de facto* Master of the Temple during Master Alvey's long illness. For his part, Hooker was aware that success at the Cross would lead to more public attention than he had received to date. Part of him must have longed for such notice and the higher position in the church that might follow from it. Some of his genes, after all, came from those prominent and very public Hookers of Exeter; and he certainly could use the security of a higher standard of living than that afforded at Drayton Beauchamp parish. There was also much to be said for the opportunity to try out his ideas in the political arena.

Hooker knew that, as Reader at the Temple Church, Travers was an important part of the strategy of the radical Calvinists for taking control of the Church of England. The extremist ideas Richard had excoriated in his Paul's Cross sermon were openly expounded at the Temple and elsewhere in the city by Travers and dozens of other Puritan readers, or "lecturers" as they were sometimes called, at the most politically sensitive churches in London.

These Readers, in fact, occupied about a quarter of the pulpits in the city. When they preached they drew larger crowds than most of the sporting and cultural events in town. They were resident in many of the leading churches throughout the country, their number having doubled in recent years. Altogether, they represented as serious a threat to the established church from within as the Roman Catholics did from without.

It was undoubtedly the tolerant attitude toward "prophesyings" (informal out-of-church preaching and discussion sessions carried on by many of the Readers) that had allowed this Presbyterian movement to take hold so rapidly. With Archbishop John Whitgift now in charge, armed his *Articles of Subscription* and his episcopal visitations to individual parishes, these radical practices were slowly being exorcised. At about the time of Hooker's sermon at Paul's Cross, Archbishop Whitgift had removed one of the major Puritan ring leaders, John Field, from his post at St Mary Aldermary. Not long before, the Queen herself had said, with some exasperation, to then Archbishop Edmund Grindal that "it was good for the church to have few preachers. . .three or four might suffice for the country."

Hooker agreed that a little preaching went a long way. He usually preferred to emphasize common (corporate) prayers, the Sacraments, reading of scripture and delivery of prepared homilies. Too much preaching could breed trouble. Nowhere would the danger of undisciplined preaching be more apparent than at the Temple Church, where England's present and future political leaders attended services regularly. Despite efforts by archbishops and many bishops to deny most of the radical Calvinists decent clerical appointments and remove those who persisted in non-conformist practices, they could not easily prevent sympathetic gentry and merchants in London and elsewhere from endowing lectureships and readerships for Presbyterian troublemakers. Among the most prominent examples of this practice, as Hooker knew, were, in addition to Walter Travers and John Field, Robert Crowley at St. Giles Cripplegate, and William Charke at nearby Lincolns Inn.

Advocates of the Presbyterian discipline, like Walter Travers and Thomas Cartwright, claimed scriptural warrant for the use of lecturers and Readers. There were four "orders" of ministry as they saw it: pastor, doctor, elder and deacon. Of the two professional orders, pastor and doctor, the role of pastor was to exhort the flock, principally through his sermons, to follow Christ. The doctor's function was to interpret scripture and assure sound doctrine. His pronouncements should be communicated through his sermons, lectures, or readings, hence the terms "lecturer" and "reader".

Hooker quickly learned from his own experiences that bishops often had mixed motives about these readers. Since the dioceses usually lacked sufficient funds to staff churches, they might be glad to have this new source of manpower. Bishops may have disliked the theology of most of the Readers and abhorred their churchmanship, but they could admire their learning and the excellent preaching abilities that drew people into their churches. Puritan lecturers, including most prominently Walter Travers, were often among the best educated and most effective ministers in the church.

Hooker knew a good deal about Travers even before their first meeting in 1584. His cousin was, after all, one of the most famous radical Puritans in England, some would say second only in importance, among the emerging Presbyterians, to Archbishop Whitgift's other longtime nemesis, Thomas Cartwright. Although both Travers and Cartwright had sprung from the hotbed of extreme Calvinism at Cambridge, Hooker, as an Oxford man, was familiar with their writings and their general reputation. His own mentor, John Rainolds, a Calvinist who was sympathetic to both men, had made sure of that.

When apprised of the problem Travers was posing for church authorities by his presence at the Temple Church, Richard wondered why the Queen, who made all clerical appointments at this prestigious church, did not simply remove him. As he learned the answer to that question, he had his first real education in the subtleties of public policy formation in late Elizabethan England.

A major controlling factor in royal decision-making was that the Queen was largely dependent on her chief minister, the Lord Treasurer, William Cecil (Lord Burghley), to run the country for her and Burghley was a consistent sympathizer and protector of the more radical Calvinist leaders in the government and in the Church. More to the point, the Lord Treasurer was the very one who had arranged for Travers' appointment as Temple reader back in 1581 and was now urging the Queen to appoint him master of the Temple following Master Richard Alvey's recent death. During Alvey's illness, Travers had already begun living in the Master's house and serving as *de facto* rector. If the Queen were to follow her usual practice and accept Burghley's advice, there would be no hand left to restrain the radical activities of Travers and his allies. He would be free to turn the Temple into a national model for his Presbyterian polity.

Much as the Queen leaned upon Burghley, she disliked his support of the more extreme Calvinist practitioners in her realm. She was well aware that Presbyterianism struck at the very root of her episcopal church polity and ultimately threatened her own authority as ruler of both state and church. She turned to her new Archbishop, John Whitgift, to stamp out the dissident Puritan voices in the church. In so doing, she set up an antagonism between her chief advisors-- not for the first or last time, for this was a favorite ploy of this machiavellian monarch: divide and conquer or, at least, divide and survive.

Whitgift was a worthy opponent for the powerful Lord Treasurer. He offered his own candidate for the Temple post, Dr. Nicholas Bond, one of the Queen's own chaplains. Bond's theology and churchmanship were to the Queen's liking, but she judged her chaplain's health not sturdy enough to withstand the pressures of this tumultuous pulpit.

In pressing his case to the Queen against appointing Travers to the Temple post, the Archbishop had ample evidence to offer. Travers' own writing convicted him of disloyalty and disobedience to church regulations as promulgated by the Archbishop. His *Explicatio*, just released in a new edition at Cambridge, was so offensive to the church establishment that Whitgift had as many copies as he could find seized and burned immediately.

The Archbishop knew that to base his case against Travers primarily on the grounds of Walter's advocacy of a Presbyterian polity would produce the very sort of controversy at court and in the country that Elizabeth abhorred. Above all, this Queen prized policies that limited conflict and offered promise of as much public peace and tranquility as possible. The Archbishop needed a less divisive ground for his case against Lord Burghley's candidate. And it was readily at hand.

The very practical, non-ideological (and so, to Elizabeth, eminently acceptable) reason why Mr. Travers could not be master at the Temple, or the incumbent of any other church in the realm, was that he had never been properly ordained. He had, in fact, explicitly denied the efficacy of episcopal ordination as part of the heresy for which he had been expelled from Cambridge back in 1571. Then, while in exile in Antwerp, he had been ordained according to the Presbyterian manner, which required approval only by the congregation to be served. Now he was claiming that that spurious "ordination" qualified him to hold clerical office in the Church of England. Whitgift had a strong case against him on this point alone and could probably make it stick with the Queen, if not with Burghley.

Unbeknownst to Hooker or anyone else outside the Queen's inner circle, Whitgift had recently written Elizabeth a letter in which he condemned Travers in the strongest terms, describing him as one of the principal authors of dissension in the church, an open opponent of the *Book of Common Prayer*, an avowed foe of episcopacy, a person not properly ordained to serve in any English parish and a fomenter of religious discontent whose placement in a high post would do immeasurable damage to the peace and quiet of the realm. The Archbishop's blistering attack left no doubt that Travers was a menace whom the Queen could not possibly appoint to the Temple post, regardless of Lord Burghley's partiality toward him.

So as not to appear to be going around Burghley's back to the queen, Whitgift also wrote to the Lord Treasurer. In that letter, the Archbishop asserted his ecclesiastical authority and stated directly that Travers had never been properly ordained and had, in fact, resisted that process. The head of the Queen's church stated quite bluntly to the Queen's chief minister of state that he would never consent to Burghley's favorite Presbyterian (Travers) holding any position of any kind whatsoever in the Church of England.

The stage was now set for Hooker's entry into the fire-storm of church politics as it flared at the Temple Church in London.

——— An Important Proposal ———

Hooker's candidacy as master of the Temple Church was probably put forward by Archbishop Sandys. While there is no hard proof of this, the circumstantial evidence is compelling. A powerful advocate was necessary to secure Richard this high post since his own reputation was too slim to carry him forward on his own. Whitgift could have advanced Hooker's cause, without benefit of any recommendations. But, since the new Archbishop had stormy relations with Burghley, especially over this issue of the Temple Church appointment, an intermediary like Sandys was in the best position to offer a compromise candidate acceptable to each of the two men upon whom the Queen was relying for advice.

11. John Calvin

Sandys' credentials were more than acceptable to both Burghley and Whitgift. As Bishop of Worcester, London, and now Archbishop of York, he was a true brother in the episcopacy to Whitgift. The two had fought the hard fight together and had mutual respect for one another's arduous labors to establish a viable, reformed, episcopal church in England. Each, in his own way, had played an important role in building the emergent Anglican polity.

As for Burghley, he was far more likely to take advice from Sandys than from Whitgift. The Archbishop of York was, as we have seen, a purer Protestant, less pragmatic than the Archbishop of Canterbury. He was more in the camp of those advanced Calvinists admired by Burghley, men like Bishop Jewel and John Rainolds, than he was with those of a harsher political stamp, like Whitgift and Richard Bancroft. And we may assume that Sandys was pleased with Hooker's sermon at Paul's Cross, especially for its attacks on the more extreme Calvinist doctrines.

When Hooker learned that he was to be put forward as a candidate for Master of the Temple, he did not object. He was possessed of no more than the natural predisposition of any sensitive intellectual to doubt his suitability for such a high post. Despite what may have been a temperamental aversion to public life, born of long experience with happy productivity in the academic world, the honor, the prestige, the financial rewards, the opportunity to try out his ideas and himself in the arena of politics and power were all compelling. He was a Hooker, after all. He could hardly resist the thought that the Archbishop of Canterbury, the Lord Treasurer of England, and the Queen herself would all soon have his name on their lips as a man qualified for high office in the church.

Still, he must have wondered what Whitgift would think of him. Would he indeed be acceptable to the formidable archbishop? Had Whitgift even heard of him? In fact, we may be sure that Whitgift knew all about Richard Hooker. He had the best network of informers in the land (save only Burghley and Walsingham). His agents supplied him with information about who was doing and saying what in the church and the government. His right arm, Richard Bancroft, who would one day be the Bishop of London, had already briefed him on

Hooker's sermons at the Cross and elsewhere. The Archbishop had been pleased by Hooker's attacks on extremists.

Surely, the Archbishop had learned of one particular qualification that commended Hooker to his attention. That was the simple but crucial fact that he was not married. The Queen of England did not look with favor on married clerics and she rarely appointed them to high posts if she could avoid it. Some believed that Bishop Sandys had been denied the ultimate post at Canterbury in large part because, unlike Whitgift, he had not remained celibate.

Number twenty-nine of the Queen's *Injunctions* was reportedly her favorite. Roughly translated, it said: "You may marry an honest and sober wife if you must marry at all; but only if you feel you cannot resist the temptation and only then if your bishop approves of the lady." Shortly after Elizabeth became Queen, she ordered married men at the colleges to keep their wives at home. Richard knew that Dr. Cole had had to move his quarters out of Corpus Christi for just that reason.

As Hooker would soon learn, Whitgift was as smooth, shrewd, and politically astute as Burghley or any of his other Puritan foes in high places. The Archbishop had a reputation for listening sympathetically to the petitions of any highly placed lord or lady who might entreat him on behalf of a religious nonconformist. He could be all grace and charm, seeming to agree with them by his demeanor. He could please one and all with general reassurances, and rarely was known to deny any important person's specific desires to his or her face. Yet, by promising little that was specific in regard to the case at hand, he remained free to deliver virtually nothing at all and so to pursue his own preferred course of action. He made a very good friend and a very bad enemy. Richard was glad to be among those who might count the Archbishop of Canterbury as his supporter.

If Hooker could continue to avoid the marriage bed, he might look forward not only to the Temple post, but later on, to a deanship or even a bishopric. Whitgift and his Queen were always on the lookout for promising new talent to fill vacant sees. If Whitgift were impressed with Richard's performance at the Temple, he might at least have a chance for episcopal appointment. After all, his pedigree was not altogether unimpressive: good family connections in the west country; John Jewel as an early patron; Rainolds as a tutor; the archbishop of

York as a supporter. But he would need to perform well at the Temple, defend the establishment but not make political waves of his own, and remain celibate so that the virgin queen would not fault him for beating her to the altar.

The Temple Church

The Temple Church, which Hooker entered sometime in the spring of 1585 in order to observe a service conducted by Travers, was modeled on the Holy Sepulcher in Jerusalem. It had been built in the twelfth century, during the reign of Henry II, by the Knights Templar, hence the name Temple Church. The templars were legendary knights who had sworn that it was their sacred duty to protect pilgrims in the holy lands during the days of the crusades. Later, in the fourteenth century, when the templars had been disbanded, their church and other holdings passed to the Knights Hospitaller, known as the Knights of the Order of St. John of Jerusalem, and later Knights of Rhodes and Knights of Malta. This religious order subsequently lost the property to the crown during Henry VIII's dissolution program. The King then leased the buildings to lawyers who converted them into residences, halls and study areas--hence, the Inns of Court.

During the early history of the Temple Church and Inns of Court, the Master of the Temple had been one of the most powerful figures in England. In the reign of Henry II, the master, as the chief financier of the monarchy, held the crown's money in his hands. Important decisions of state were made at the Temple in those days.

The famous Round Church, now serving as the large narthex of the Temple, had been the first part of the church building erected and was one of a number of such structures built by the wealthy and powerful medieval templars in various parts of England. The one at Cambridge was still in use in Hooker's day. In 1185, none other than Heraclitus, the patriarch of Jerusalem, had been present to consecrate the Round Church. In the following century, the templars added the choir and thereby completed one of the most unique structures in England. The nave was awe-inspiring, some eighty feet long and forty feet high. The graceful fan vaulting rising from clusters of lovely purbeck marble columns, roofed a space of ethereal beauty into which light streamed from twelve lancet windows located in the south, east and north walls of the choir and fifteen windows to the rear in the round narthex.

Just as striking as the architecture and history of the place was the congregation, the barristers, lawyers, and law students now crowding into the Temple, chattering irreverently in noisy anticipation of Travers' appearance in the pulpit. These men were as different in dress and demeanor from his simple country flock at Drayton as they, in turn, had been from the usually polite students and faculty attending chapel services in their academic gowns at Corpus Christi. These lawyers and politicians were not coming to worship from the fields of husbandry or from the lecture halls and libraries of a university. Theirs was the world of power and money, of great affairs of state and commerce and smaller, but often contentious affairs of life, death and property claims.

The chambers and courtrooms from which this congregation came to church were venues where men were drawn to defend and advance their lives and properties, where fortunes were made and lost, lives and careers ruined or enhanced. These were the men who drafted, interpreted and applied the laws of the realm on behalf of clients who ranged from merchants and bankers to churches and colleges, from wealthy widows to poor orphans, from members of parliament to the queen's government itself. These were the lawyers--those lively, worldly, powerful advocates and adjudicators of the myriad rights and claims that were the marks of a society governed by laws.

We can imagine Hooker watching from one of the benches in the crowded church as Travers walked down the long nave toward the pulpit and then mounted it. It seemed that there would be no worship service this morning according to the prescribed form: no properly vested minister, no opening prayers, no common confession, no absolution, nothing except Travers' sermon. Was this the reason for his popularity with these secular lawyers? With him in charge, they could avoid prescribed religious services by attending a stimulating lecture by a fiery Puritan orator.

Hooker no doubt had anticipated that this exemplar of Puritan radicalism might be somewhat unconventional in his liturgical performance. But, since Travers had managed to survive as *de facto*

Master of the Queen's Temple Church for the past three years, Hooker expected a higher degree of orthodoxy than this! After all, just a year ago, under the late Archbishop Grindal's commission, Travers had written a respectable tract refuting the Jesuit Robert Persons' *Epistle of the Persecution of Catholics.*

It had been only a year since Whitgift had replaced Grindal and instituted a rigid policy of enforced conformity, including a rigorous censorship of religious publications. The new Archbishop was just beginning to remove preachers who refused to use the *Book of Common Prayer* and administer Holy Communion at least four times a year. Additionally, Whitgift was now requiring all ministers to subscribe to his *Three Articles* which affirmed that the Queen was the supreme governor of the church, that the *Book of Common Prayer* was consistent with Scripture and that the *Thirty-nine Articles* were the authoritative canon to be followed by all clergy in their preaching. Before long these policies would engender fierce opposition culminating in the infamous *Marprelate Tracts* of 1588-89 which attacked Whitgift and all bishops in a most personal and scurrilous manner, as the Puritan's rage against the Archbishop reached its fever point. By that time, Whitgift would be so bedeviled by enemies that he would turn to the best minds in the church to take up their pens to defend the established order and, indirectly, himself.

Travers began his sermon by saying: "Members of the two learned and honorable societies of this house, I bid you welcome to the House of God." These opening words, Hooker would soon learn, were the beginning of the bidding prayer that recognized the proprietary rights of the two Inns of Court affiliated with "this ancient church."

There is no surviving text of this sermon. Travers' writings of the time suggest that he may have taken as his text the seventh chapter of John's Gospel, verse 51. "Doth our law condemn any man before we have heard him, and know what he hath done?" He may have applied the words to his own case, pleading on his own behalf for no less justice from his accusers in the church hierarchy than that which was claimed for our Lord long ago by the "honorable counselor" who spoke the words in John's Gospel.

Travers had been serving as Reader at the Temple since 1581 when he returned from Antwerp and accepted Lord Burlegh's request to assist Master Alvey, who was too ill to carry on his duties. Until the death of Alvey earlier that year, Travers had been Master in all but name. Among the reforms that he had felt it imperative to initiate at the Temple was use of an "improved" version of holy scripture, *The Geneva Bible.* This version, he claimed, presented the New Testament in its purest and most accurate form.

Like others in the audience, Hooker would have been aware that the famous Calvinist looking down at them from the pulpit this morning faced the most serious threat to his ministry since he had returned to England as Lord Burghley's family chaplain in 1580. Whitgift had ordered total conformity to the established church discipline and already had begun removing Puritan ministers from their charges. He had recently seized and burned copies of the new edition of Travers' classic handbook for Presbyterian church organization, *The Explicato.* Above all, Whitgift had made it clear, as Travers and most everyone in his congregation today realized, that the increasing use of Presbyterian forms of church polity, which Travers had promoted nationally in his writings and sermons and which was now spreading rapidly in eastern England and the midlands, would no longer be tolerated. This still largely secret system of church governance involved creation of the so-called "classis" (later known as a presbytery or conference of ministers and elders) as a substitute for the diocesan form of regional church government.

Whitgift also forbade the practice of each congregation calling its own minister, voting on him and then (perhaps) sending his name to the bishop for approval. Hooker was among those who felt that this crude attempt to mix presbyterianism with episcopalianism fooled no one. What was really intended was the diminution (or elimination) of the role of bishops and an increasing role for lay leadership in the form of elders and deacons. This subversive movement, led primarily by Walter Travers, Thomas Cartwright, and John Field, was a carefully planned strategy to radically change, if not overthrow altogether, the polity of the established national church. The new Archbishop, the Queen and even Burghley could tolerate it no longer.

Hooker would soon learn that his radical cousin had already instituted most of the features of a Presbyterian system of church governance right here at the Temple Church, with the enthusiastic support of most of the lawyers and barristers in his congregation, especially those at the Middle Temple. Already, pastors, teachers (doctors)and unordained elders and deacons had begun to replace bishops, priests and deacons in the spirit and form of Temple governance. Arguing that lay elders and deacons could administer the Sacrament of Communion and oversee the faith and morals of the congregation because that was the practice in the primitive church of the Apostles, Puritans like Travers were openly flouting the polity of the church establishment.

Whitgift's new orders had not only reaffirmed that the church reorganization supported by Travers was illegal, but they also proscribed so-called "prophesyings" and "exercises." These were methods widely used by advanced Calvinists to affect some of their most cherished reforms by changing the names of key parts of the worship service and conducting them outside the regular places and hours of worship. They provided an easy way to avoid using the *Book of Common Prayer*, wearing vestments, kneeling at worship, obeying bishops! Henceforth, Whitgift ordered, all preaching and all public worship, by whatever name, would be done only inside church walls as a part of prescribed common worship; congregations would not vote on candidates for ordination before they were presented to bishops; and individual churches would have no legitimate standing except as part of the established national church that was governed by bishops in convocation under the headship of the Queen.

Hooker's cousin continued his sermon, asking perhaps whether Dr. Whitgift invoked the holy word as authority for his opinions about proper forms of worship and church discipline and concluded that he could not, because, for all his reputed scholarship, he would not find in holy scripture any mention of bishops, surplices, kneelings, altars, organs or established churches.

During the weeks and months following his first days in London, Hooker became increasingly familiar with the broader political scene, of which the brouhaha over the appointment of a new Master of the Temple was a part. He became aware of the flood of pamphlets, petitions, speeches, sermons and personal attacks being unleashed by

Travers and his compatriots. They had gone so far as to conduct a survey among ministers throughout the country that purported to show that if Whitgift's policies were enforced the church would lose many of its most talented clergy and influential laity. This public-relations campaign was aimed at the upcoming session of parliament, scheduled to meet late in 1584 or early in 1585. Hooker now saw clearly that the appointment of Travers at the Temple was one of the most important ingredients in a carefully conceived strategy to subvert the Church of England. With one stroke Calvinist extremists would gain the legitimacy that would come from controlling one of the most prestigious and influential pulpits in the country and, at the same time, they would have a base of political operations right in the heart of national politics.

In the midst of this turmoil, Archbishop Whitgift needed a man to fill the vital post at the Temple who was untainted by political controversy and known to be of learned, discreet and wise temperament, a man of sound religion and good morals who could bring stability and order to that important congregation and, by example, to the entire city. The living attached to the post was not great but adequate and the opportunity for further advancement was good. Whitgift offered the position to Hooker. Richard could expect to receive official letters patent for a life appointment from the Queen by about mid-March (1585), and should take over his official duties immediately thereafter. In the meantime, he was to keep his living at Drayton Beauchamp until next fall, but would have no further duties there once he began at the Temple.

Hooker accepted the offer with an altogether human mixture of pride and humility. He was a good man, but not without ambition.

———— The Encounter ————

Sometime shortly before his appointment to the Temple Church on 17 March 1585, Hooker left Drayton Beachamp and took up full-time residence in London. By the end of February, he had moved his few belongings out of the parish rectory at Drayton, settled into a room at the Churchman house on Watling Street, and begun to prepare his first sermons as master of the Temple. The invitation to stay as a more or less permanent boarder at the Churchmans, along with his friend Edwin Sandys and other long-term "guests," was a welcome relief for Richard. The Master's house at the Temple was in bad repair and was, at any event, still occupied by Walter Travers. By this time, Hooker had established a warm relationship with John Churchman and his family and felt quite at home with them.

News of Hooker's appointment at the Temple--and Travers' rejection--leaked out well before the assignment was official. Many, especially at Middle Temple, were not happy about it. They saw Hooker's coming as a repudiation of Travers and a victory for Whitgift. The choice of a Master had been an opportunity for the members at the Inns to be directly involved in an issue that touched one of the great religious debates of the day. They were lawyers and politicians, every one, and had taken this case very much to heart. The lines had been sharply drawn for and against Hooker, even before he was to begin his work. Most were not for him.

Richard was pleased to learn that Travers had apparently taken the news of his rejection as a candidate for master rather well. Once he learned that the Queen had made her final decision, he stopped his campaign against Hooker. In fact, he was meeting with members of the congregation informally, encouraging them to welcome and support his cousin as the new master.

Perhaps, Richard thought, Mr. Travers will be reasonable after all and respect the authority of the established church. Or, perhaps, on second thought, he had merely recognized the reality of his situation and shifted ground to a more defensible position. Certainly there was no indication thus far that Travers intended to leave his position as Reader and there had been no word as yet about removing him from that post. If he were to stay on, he would maintain full contact with residents at the Inns, preach regularly and be prepared to undermine anything Hooker said or did as master that was not to his liking.

Hooker's first recorded encounter with Travers was on an early evening in late March of 1585. The place may have been was a lighted corner in the ancient round narthex of the Church. The circumstance was a meeting Travers had requested in order to welcome Hooker informally and brief him on some important matters before the new master gave his first sermon. When Travers arrived at the historic church, he was not alone.

Travers began the interview by introducing the two men with him. They had been elected by the congregation to assist him in the management of the church, he explained. Hooker was shocked. Had Travers gone so far in the establishment of the forbidden Presbyterian polity as to institute the practice of elected lay deacons and elders? No wonder Whitgift wanted Travers out of here.

Hooker greeted the two men with Travers politely and inquired if they had been appointed to their posts by the Bishop. No, they had not. They had been chosen by the congregation to serve as "collectors" and "sidemen." Were these terms a subterfuge for the forbidden "elders" and "deacons" that Travers had advocated in his writings? Travers explained that the privy council had approved the use of "collectors," "sidemen," and "wardens" at the Temple long ago, ever since Alvey had been master. Their initial functions were to help with collecting alms and assuring attendance at services, but no doubt their role had expanded considerably to fill out Travers' Presbyterian expectations of lay leadership.

Hooker did not wish to begin his ministry at the Temple by disturbing a practice to which the congregation had been accustomed. But he informed Travers that they would need to seek the Archbishop's approval for such significant departures from the prescribed regulations concerning church governance. Travers objected that since these men had been duly elected by the congregation, no approval from any bishop would be necessary. Bishops, he said, had no authority here at the Temple. This church was responsible only to the Queen, through Lord Burghley and the privy council.

Master Hooker countered that it was precisely the question of whether the bishop or the congregation governed the church that was at issue between the Church of England and well-meaning persons like Travers who sought to replace the episcopal polity with the Presbyterian discipline. It was legally the case that the Queen governed here, Hooker said, but she did so through her bishops.

Travers could see at once that Hooker meant to be in charge at the Temple and that his own reforms were now in serious jeopardy. It was time for the Presbyterian tactician to shift his ground. His aim, after all, was not to subvert the episcopacy, he assured Hooker, but to affect a reform that would combine the best of the old ways with the more democratic congregational forms preferred by the men at the Inns and for that matter, by people throughout England.

Hooker's reputation for preferring tolerance and compromise to conflict and disorder had preceded him. But he was no fool. He knew that his cousin was not only a brilliant scholar and committed follower of Christ, but also a seasoned veteran of political wars. He took Travers' measure as quickly as that gentleman had taken his. He asked Travers if he intended to stay on as reader. When he had the unwelcome affirmative response, he assured his cousin that they could work amicably together so far as he was concerned and that he looked forward to a good relationship. Perhaps Walter would help him conduct his first service tomorrow morning. He wished to follow customary liturgical practice, insofar as possible, and would welcome Travers' assistance.

Travers' response was disturbing to Hooker. Walter did not expect Richard to do the morning service at all. In fact, he should take no services at the Temple until he had been properly "affirmed" by the congregation as its new master. Walter would be happy to put Richard's name before them officially tomorrow morning and recommend that they give their "allowance" for him to take charge of the church. This would serve to "confirm" his appointment and "seal" his calling to preach in the Temple.

Hooker was stunned. Travers' use of words like "affirm," "confirm," "allowance," and "seal" were code words signifying "election" by the congregation. His appointment had come from the Queen. He needed no approval from those to whom he would preach and minister. He said as much to Travers. When his cousin demurred, Hooker, ever the peace-maker, relented so far as to say that he had no wish to disturb local practice on such a procedural matter and would be happy if Walter would proceed to secure the congregation's affirmation of his appointment. If Richard thought this conciliatory gesture would assuage the Calvinist agitator, he was mistaken.

Following his meeting with Travers, Hooker was fully aware that the authorized liturgy he would employ at the Temple would be very different from what the congregation had grown used to under Alvey's and Travers' regimes. For those two, "preaching the word," not administering the sacraments, was the core event in worship. Richard knew that the Puritans despised the prepared homilies that were so often read out by unlearned men as a substitute for original sermons. In many respects, he agreed with them. He did not agree, however, with the Puritans' preference for extemporaneous ministerial prayers and sermons. Much better, he believed, to use the carefully prepared prayers of learned churchmen contained in the *Book of Common Prayer* than the supposedly inspired ministerial supplications of the moment. In any event, he was determined to affirm his leadership and to begin to establish a measure of orthodoxy at the Temple.

At the next Sunday service, which Hooker did not attend, Travers announced from the pulpit that he had had a most satisfactory meeting with Mr. Hooker and was happy to recommend that the congregation confirm him as the new master of their church. It was a painful deed for one who had so ardently coveted the position for himself. Certainly, it was a testimony to the sincerity of Travers' belief in the Presbyterian polity that he would recommend congregational election of a man who was his rival for advancement at the Temple and with whom he had such profound theological, liturgical and ecclesiastical differences.

But then, it was never the sincerity of either Travers or Hooker that was in doubt. What would be in question for centuries to come was the verity of their respective viewpoints, as these two gladiators, prophets respectively for the Presbyterian and the Anglican traditions, wrestled for the soul of the Church of England.

— Chapter 7 —
The Great Temple Debate

— The Maiden Service —

For seven years of his life, between the ages of thirty and thirty-seven, Richard Hooker was an important player in the politics of the Church of England, as Master of the Temple Church in London. That he never advanced beyond this position to achieve higher status and influence as a bishop, or at least dean of a cathedral, is owing to a number of conditions including his lack of a doctorate and the fact that he was not celibate. Of greater import was what he and others would learn about his opinions on important political issues and about his personality and character during these seven years of testing in the politically charged crucible of Elizabethan church leadership.

Even as history has obscured Richard Hooker, her muse has shrouded the "great debate" at the Temple between Hooker and Travers--surely one of the defining events in the story of emergent Anglicanism. As long ago as 1885, on the occasion of the gala celebration of the seven hundredth anniversary of the Temple Church, sermons by the archbishop of Canterbury and the master and reader of the Temple took not the slightest note of this event or of its protagonists, arguably the two most important occupants of the Temple pulpit throughout its long history. Nor was mention made at that time of Whitgift, Burghley, Aylmer, Leicester, De Corro, Raleigh, Coke, Sandys or the other Elizabethan figures whose formative religious and political struggles were often acted out in the Temple and her precincts. The speakers on that day in 1885 just droned on about the ancient founding of the church by the Knights Templar.

To redress the balance I have constructed a probable sermon and church service from early in Hooker's time at the Temple. The sermon is presented by direct quotation with some modernization of language and close paraphrase from Hooker's writings, especially *A Learned and Comfortable Sermon on the Certainty and Perpetuity of Faith in the Elect.*

He would use the 1559 *Prayer Book,* although he was aware of the Puritan's objections to that service, especially the removal in it of any condemnation of the pope and the compromise wording on the Eucharist. Later on he might be willing, in the name of church harmony, to use the service preferred in the Temple from the 1552 *Geneva Prayer Book,* edited by the Scotch Presbyterian John Knox and endorsed by Calvin himself. He was familiar with that book. President Cole at Corpus had helped to write it while he was in exile in Frankfort and it had been popular at Oxford.

Hooker, who loved music, may have decided to risk scandal at his maiden service as rector of this largely Puritan congregation by arranging for a modest choral presentation. He would make it clear in this and other ways that a new day was dawning here at the Temple. We will imagine four boy sopranos with the voices of angels would break into song at this point, just before his sermon, filling the sanctuary with the glories of a William Byrd motet. "Rejoyce, Rejoyce..." they sang forth in one of the finest compositions by this master of sixteenth-century English church music. Hooker was certain that Travers did not often, if ever, allow this sort of music. (Byrd was, after all, a Catholic!)

The motet concluded and the gospel read, Hooker opened the Book of Common Prayer and began the service that has been a familiar confort to Anglicans and Episcopalians for centuries.

> Almighty God, unto whom all hearts be open,
> all desires known, and from whom no secrets are hid:
> Cleanse the thoughts of our hearts by the inspiration
> of thy Holy Spirit, that we may perfectly love thee, and
> worthily magnify thy holy name, through Christ our
> Lord. Amen.

Richard continued his reading: "God spake these words and said, I am the Lord thy God, Thou shalt have none other gods but me." He was relieved when at least some in his congregation responded with enthusiasm: "Lord have mercy upon us and incline our hearts to keep this law." The reading of the Ten Commandments and the collect assigned for the day followed. Then Hooker read the prescribed collect for the Queen.

> Almighty and everlasting God, we be taught by thy holy word, that the hearts of kings are in thy rule and governance, and that thou dost dispose and turn them, as it seemeth best to thy godly wisdom: We humbly beseech thee, so to dispose and govern the heart of Elizabeth, thy servant, our Queen and governor, that in all her thoughts, words, and works, she may ever seek thy honor and glory, and study to preserve thy people committed to her charge, in wealth, and godliness. Grant this, O merciful Father, for thy dear Son's sake, Jesus Christ our Lord.

"Amen," the congregation responded.

The service proceeded through the readings of the epistle and gospel lessons and the recitation of the Nicene Creed. Then Hooker addressed the congregation with several announcements, reminding them of upcoming Saints' days, informing them that holy communion would be celebrated regularly on the first Sunday of every month and that it was their legal as well as their religious obligation to participate on a regular basis, no less than four times a year.

Now the new Master climbed up into the pulpit. A large six-sided sounding board hanging from the ceiling over the pulpit was positioned so that this hollow wooden structure could amplify and project Hooker's rather weak voice out into the church. After putting his text on the lectern, he looked out over the congregation and began his first sermon as Master of the Temple.

> That music was joyful praise to God. I am glad to begin my days with you on such notes. The Word of God read and preached out of His holy scriptures is surely an important foundation of our Christian life together. But ever since the earliest days of the ancient church, music has been a blessed part of our worship.

My own patron, the late Bishop Jewel of Salisbury, liked to say that people singing the psalms in church was one of the first signs that the Reformation here in England was succeeding.

Music is a thing which suits all ages and stages of life, as seasonable in grief as in joy. Music has the admirable facility both to express and represent better than any other sensible means, all of the risings and fallings and turns and varieties of passion to which the mind is subject. In future, we may add instrumental music to our worship here in the Temple.

I am aware that there are those who believe this is papist ornamentation. But the great prophet and psalmist David gave us not only the poetry of his songs but the precedent of instrumental music as well.

Speaking of David, remember how he exhorted us to 'worship the Lord in the beauty of holiness?' How fortunate we are to be able to worship in this magnificent ancient church, hallowed by the centuries of worshippers who have gone before us here. The majesty of this place provides us a special virtue, force and efficacy for prayer and worship because it helps to stir up in us devotion, holiness and actions of the best sort. Truly we are reminded that it is not only God's people who may be sanctified, but His Holy Temple as well.

There was a murmur of discontent in the audience at this point. For a moment Hooker had forgotten how opposed the Puritans were to the idea that a mere edifice might be a vehicle for God's Spirit.

My text is from one of my favorite Old Testament writers, the troubled prophet, Habakkuk. I have been preaching from this text frequently of late because I find this prophet's teachings rich in answers to questions that trouble us today, especially the issue of how we may distinguish between truth and error amidst so many conflicting religious opinions.

He read the text from Habakkuk 1:4.

> Devastation and violence confront me; strife breaks out, discord raises its head, and so law grows effete; justice does not come forth victorious for the wicked outwit the righteous and so justice comes out perverted.

"Does the prophet, in admitting the idea into his mind that God's law has failed, show himself to be an unbeliever?" Hooker asked rhetorically, and then went on:

> Because some have found it too easy purposely to distort and misconstrue what I have said in the past on this subject of faith and doubt, I will elaborate today on the question of why some people are able to keep their faith in the face of great threats to it, including their own doubts.
>
> None of us marvel that we neither recognize nor acknowledge the acts of God by reason alone, because we know that these acts can only be fully discerned spiritually. But those, like the prophet, in whose hearts the grace of God shines, who are taught by God Himself--why are they so weak in faith? Why is their assent to God's law so limited, so mingled with fear and wavering? It seems strange that they should ever think that God's law would fail them. But if we stop to think about it, such weakness of faith will not seem strange to us.

He paused here for effect before continuing.

> Some propositions are so evident to our minds that no one who hears them affirmed can doubt their truth--such as that a part of anything is less than the whole. But in matters of faith, we find the contrary situation.

Everyone does not agree to the truth of the same proposition. This is because, unlike angels and spirits in heaven who have certainty about things spiritual by the light of their divine glory, that which we here on earth see is only by the light of grace and hence not so certain as that which we see by the strong evidence of our senses or our reason.

Proofs are vain and frivolous unless they are more certain than the things they seek to prove. That is why we see everywhere in scripture the effort to prove matters of faith and confirm us in our beliefs by offering us evidence acceptable to our senses--our natural reason. I conclude therefore that we have less confidence about things taken on faith than about things perceived by the senses or grasped by our reason.

At this point, Hooker took a rather long pause as he moved his eyes slowly about the congregation before fixing his gaze on a different spot and then lowered his tone slightly.

And who among us does not have doubts about his faith at some time? I will not here recount the confessions of the most perfect of persons who ever lived on earth concerning their doubts. If I did so I would only belabor a matter well-known to every honest man of faith. The remedy for this doubt is what I just called the 'certainty of adherence.'

What I mean here is the certainty that comes when the heart simply adheres or sticks to what it believes. This happens because we know as Christians that God's promises are not only true, but they are also good. Therefore, even when the evidence of the truth of God's promises is so small that a man must grieve for the weakness of his faith in them, he still feels an adherence to them in his heart because he has once tasted the heavenly sweetness, or goodness, of those promises.

126

So it is that we will strive against all reason to hope against hope that God's promises are true. With Job, I may hold the immovable resolution that although God shall kill me, I will never stop trusting Him. Why? Not because God's law is **true** but because it is forever imprinted on my heart that it will be **good** for me, like Job, to believe in God.

To be sure, our minds are so darkened with the foggy damp of original corruption that none of us has a heart so enlightened in knowledge or so firm in love of God's promise of salvation that his faith is perfect, free of doubt. If there were any such persons, they would be justified by their own inherent righteousness. There would be no need for Christ. He would be superfluous.

Let him beware who claims a power he has not lest he lose the comfort of the weakness he does have!

Hooker continued his lecture for about thirty minutes, providing examples from Scripture to illustrate his main points. He was at special pains to demonstrate that the men of greatest faith, like Abraham, did in fact have doubts that were cured by appeals to their reason and senses. At length he reached a point in his text which he knew would be controversial.

As for the claim of some among us that the spirit of God within us gives certain and doubt-free evidence of His truth, this is not so. It would have been, had God chosen to reveal His power through visible effects as He has in nature, with fire and the sun which inflame and lighten the world. But in His incomprehensible wisdom, God has decided to limit the visible effects of His power to that degree which seems best to Him.

Richard lowered his voice once again for effect.

God provides us with certainty in all that we need to know for salvation in the life to come. But He does not give us certain knowledge to achieve perfection in this life.

"Even so, Oh God," he continued, raising his voice as if in prayer, "it has pleased You to have us feel our doubt and infirmity so that we can no more breathe than we must pray: 'Dear God, help our infirmity.'"

Hooker then continued on a different tack.

Now I turn to the question whether by the mere thought that God had failed him, the prophet Habakkuk killed God's spirit within him, lost his faith and showed himself to be an unbeliever. This question is momentous. The peace and tranquility of all souls depends on the answer.

In order to determine whether Habakkuk's doubt, and our own, marks us as unbelievers, we need first to examine the basic difference between one who believes in God and one who does not. The doctrine that forms the sure foundation for the believer is that the faith by which he is saved can never fail. It did not fail the prophet Habakkuk and it shall not fail you. This faith is a gift from God, what Saint John calls the 'seed of God' which is planted in the hearts of all who are incorporated into Christ.

But our faith does not mean that we will never sin, nor does it mean that we will never doubt God's promises. If we think that, we expect too much of ourselves. We deceive ourselves. What God's grace poured into His people does assure is that despite all sin and all doubt we will never be separated from His love or cut off from Christ Jesus. The seed of God abides forever in His children and shields them from receiving any irremediable wound.

Hooker turned his body slightly to face a different part of the nave, before continuing.

> I know that there are those who will not be convinced or comforted by my argument because, like Habakkuk, they are suffering such agonies of grief over their apparently lost faith that they cannot find their true selves within themselves. They search their hearts diligently and yet still lament for a thing that seems past finding. But in truth, joy is but a separable accident of faith and not the same thing. We would not even know delight if we did not also experience a healthy intercourse with the darkness of despair.
>
> Too much honey turns to gall and too much joy, even spiritual joy, will make us wantons (immoral, malicious, willful). Happier by far is that person whose soul is humbled by inner desolation than he whose heart is puffed up and exalted beyond all reason by an abundance of spiritual delight. Better sometimes to go down into the pit with one who is beholding darkness and bewailing the loss of inner joy and consolation and saying from the bottom of lowest hell, 'My God, my God, why hast Thou forsaken me?' than continually to walk arm in arm with angels; to sit, as it were, in the bosom of Abraham and to have no doubt and no thought except, 'I thank my God it is not with me as with other men.'
>
> No! Our God will have those who are to walk in His light feel from time to time what it is to sit in the shadow of death.

Hooker paused again before concluding.

> As we look at other people, we often compare them to ourselves and conclude that their tables are richly furnished every day whereas ashes and dirt are our daily bread; they sing happily before the beautiful music of

the lute and their children dance for them, whereas our hearts are as heavy as lead, our sighs are thick and our pulses too fast, our tears wash the beds in which we lie. The sun shines fair on them and we are hung up like bottles in the smoke, cast into corners like shards of a broken pot. Do not tell us about the promises of God! Tell those who reap the fruit of God's love. These belong not to us but to others. God forgive our weakness, but this is the way it is with us.

Well, let the frailty of our nature, the subtlety of Satan, the force of our own deceivable imaginations all be as we know them to be--ready at every moment to threaten the utter subversion of our faith. Yet faith is not really at risk.

If I remember that faith is never really at risk, who then can ever separate me and my God? I know in whom I have faith. I am not ignorant of Whose precious blood has been shed for me. I have a shepherd who is full of kindness, full of care and full of power. To Him I commit myself. His own finger has engraved this sentence on my heart: 'Satan has desired to winnow you as wheat, but I have prayed that Your faith in me shall not fail.' To the end of my days, therefore, I will labor to maintain the assurance of my faith like a jewel. By a combination of my efforts and by the gracious mediation of God's prayer, I shall keep my faith.

He had finished the sermon and felt it had been a good one and well received. Sound Calvinist theology, except for a reference or two to the possible efficacy of works. As this was one of his earliest services at the Temple, Hooker may have taken some time at this point to explain the changes that would continue to take place as he moved to reinstitute the authorized liturgy here at the Temple. He asked his congregation to notice that this morning he was wearing full vestments and had been using the authorized *Book of Common Prayer.* He may even have expressed his deep love for this beautiful book of Archbishop Crammer's and explained that since the time of the early church Christians had worshipped God in common prayer following a pattern not unlike what was prescribed in this wonderful book. In any event, here in the Temple Church, they were all under the Queen's ecclesiastical jurisdiction and would henceforth follow her rules for liturgical performance.

Hooker was aware that some in his congregation would agree with Thomas Cartwright that many of the forms of speech used in the *Book of Common Prayer,* such as saying at Communion: "eat thou" and "drink thou" to each particular person, rather than saying generally to everyone at once: "take, eat and drink," had been "picked out of the popish dunghill," to use Mr. Cartwright's colorful metaphor. But he urged them to abandon what he regarded as rigid, intemperate and exclusivist attitudes about the church and its services. Simply because a practice had been used for centuries in Rome and was not specifically mentioned in scripture was no reason to abandon it. Certain rituals are followed here in England because for us they are reasonable, familiar, comfortable, pious and not contrary to Scripture, he explained.

A further departure from ordinary practice that Hooker may have introduced at an early service was the celebration of holy communion, a service rarely used under the extreme Calvinist regime here. Once again, his intention was not to stir up trouble but to make plain at the outset his intent to have authorized liturgical practice installed under his leadership.

So that they would understand the spirit in which he was about to celebrate holy communion, Hooker explained that he stood squarely in the reformed spirit of Thomas Cranmer, as well as other great reformers like Bishop Jewel, Dr. Bucer and Archbishop Sandys. It was not so important, Hooker explained, to know whether the real presence of Christ's body and blood was to be found in the consecrated elements of bread and wine by means of transubstantiation, as the Romans would have it, or by consubstantiation, as many Lutherans held. Unfortunately, too many continued to be rent with contentions over this rather unimportant issue about exactly where Christ resides in the Eucharist when all agree that He does indeed enter the hearts of all believing participants.

Is the question of exactly how God works this miracle and exactly where Christ resides really so crucial? Hooker thought not. What was important was not how the elements were changed, if at all, but that those who receive them are, by faith, transformed through God's grace. The sacrament is an instrument for transforming men. Christ is to be found in consecrated persons, not consecrated elements. The real presence of Christ's most blessed body and blood is not therefore to be sought in the elements, but in the worthy receiver of the sacrament.

Hooker continued.

> Just a few final words before we begin the service. I want you to know that I regard the sacrament of communion as a means of God's grace and not merely a confirmation or seal of what He has promised in scripture. For me, this sacrament is as important, if not more so, than preaching. In fact, I would hold that reading of the holy word, religious education, study, prayer and common worship are all more edifying than preaching. You noticed, I am sure, that I placed no importance on memorizing my sermon this morning so that I might appear to be spontaneous, as many of our preachers, readers and lecturers do. I give you credit for the ability to follow my thoughts as I read them to you. In any event, God is not likely to reach you through my words so much as through the sacrament and your own response to reading and hearing His word.

Hooker continued.

> Brother Cartwright and his friends, by a too strict reading of First Corinthians, chapter five, would have us exclude from our company everyone who disagrees with our opinions on each detail of worship. Are we to brand such people as "papist" and exclude them from the Communion table as the "dogs, swine, beastes, foreigners, and strangers" that Mr. Cartwright says they are? I think not.
>
> God alone can know who belongs in His eternal, invisible church. He knows who among us are not as

we seem. But He does not ask us to dive into men's consciences but rather to take one another as we outwardly represent ourselves to be. In the eyes of God they are against Christ who are not truly and sincerely with Him; but in our eyes all must be received as with Christ who are not in any outward profession or action against Him.

"Therefore," Hooker finished, speaking each word slowly and clearly,

> henceforth all who have not separated themselves from Christ's visible church by their own acts of apostasy, heresy or schism will be welcome to participate in the holy communion services in this Temple Church. In future, you need only inform me before the service of your intent to receive Communion. Unless I have strong reason to think you unworthy, I will take you as repentant of your sins and welcome you to the Lord's Table. Because this is my first service with you, all who wish to participate will be welcome this morning.

Now Hooker came down from the pulpit and stood in front of the communion table. He was aware from the stirring and grumbling in the benches that there was some discontent with his open invitation. Puritans were used to a more restrictive interpretation of who was and who was not worthy to receive the sacrament. They did not approve the idea that each person could judge his own worthiness to do so.

After the almsmen had collected the offering, Hooker continued with words that have rung down the aisles and into the pews and benches of Anglican churches in every corner of the globe for over four hundred years: "Let us pray for the whole state of Christ's church," he said, turning to kneel before the table.

"Almighty and everlasting God," he read, "who by thy holy Apostle hast taught us to make prayers and supplications and to give thanks for all men: We humbly beseech thee most mercifully to accept our alms, and to receive these our prayers which we offer unto Thy Divine Majesty. . ."

Following strictly the rubric of the *Book of Common Prayer*, Hooker administered the two elements to himself before turning toward the congregation. The he bid them to come forward, kneel before the table and receive the communion.

First the bread. He said the words slowly and with notable conviction as he moved along the row of men, some kneeling and some standing, placing the wafer into outstretched hands or open mouths: "The body of our Lord Jesus Christ which was given for thee, preserve thy body and soul into everlasting life. . . . Take and eat this, in remembrance that Christ died for thee, and feed on Him in thy heart by faith, with thanksgiving."

Then the cup. Again slowly, with deep feeling, his voice conveyed the depth of his own faith: "The blood of our Lord Jesus Christ which was shed for thee, preserve thy body and soul into everlasting life. . . . Drink this in remembrance that Christ's body was shed for thee, and be thankful."

When all who wished to do so had received the sacrament and returned to their benches, Hooker looked out over his congregation and said in a loud voice, "Please all kneel now with me for the Lord's Prayer."

"Our Father. . ."

Finally, filled with the grace, peace and love of God, the new Master of the Temple finished the service with the familiar words of dismissal:

> The peace of God which passeth all understanding, keep your hearts and minds in the knowledge and love of God, and His Son Jesus Christ our Lord; And the blessing of God Almighty, the Father, the Son, and the Holy Ghost, be amongst you, and remain with you always. Amen.

Although he was not a fiery orator like Walter Travers, Hooker had no doubt impressed his congregation as a man of conviction and intelligence. As lawyers and students, they admired his keen mind and well-honed rhetorical abilities. He was persuasive. More than that, he seemed to be in touch with the great mysteries of the historic faith of the church and had a way of communicating the holiness and wonder of God and Christ that went beyond what they were used to experiencing at church services. Travers' messages tended to be moralistic, argumentative and worldly--full of dos and do nots, rights and wrongs, justification and renewal of the spirit. There was more peace, tolerance, forgiveness and love preached here today, mostly through a devout reading of the service. Withal, this was an experience many had not had in a long time, if at all--somehow more of a shared aesthetic transformation than a personal purification.

Most of them might still prefer Travers and wish he had been named master. But now, at least, they would be eager to witness and experience what was certain to be a lively debate between the famed Puritan reformer and this surprisingly able and engaging new champion of the established church.

——— Master And Reader ———

In the early spring of 1585, as Hooker took his first steps around the grounds of the Temple and Inns of Court during the days following his maiden sermon, he was probably struck by how public his new environment was. The Inner Temple's north entrance (a beautiful door built a decade earlier) faced on busy Fleet Street just a few paces from the Strand. Although set back a few hundred feet from the street, the church itself was a gathering place all day long for a nearly constant parade of people seeking a retreat or a place for either common social intercourse or serious economic and political deal-making.

As soon as early morning worship was over each weekday, the Temple became a public meeting place similar to nearby St Paul's. In fact, the choir of the Temple was sometimes used for committee meetings of the House of Commons, as was the great hall in the Middle Temple.

Hooker would have noticed at once that most of the students hurrying to and fro in the Temple grounds were attired in academic gowns not unlike those mandated at Oxford--plain dark frock coats and simple round caps. He had been informed of the Queen's strict dress code for law students here. No ruffles or velvet facing on the gowns and none of the much-favored white color for doublets or stockings were allowed. Even when walking outside on the city streets or in Westminster, students were forbidden from donning elaborate and colorful cloaks. Only "sad colored" gowns were permitted. For dress occasions, Spanish black was the sartorial order of the day. None of the fashionable long-curled hair (wigs or natural) was permitted. There were stiff penalties, Hooker knew, for disobeying these sumptuary rules, including fines and even expulsion. Only senior lawyers, barristers and benchers were allowed to be within the precincts sporting more elaborate livery and long hair.

The lovely Inner Temple gardens extending all the way from the south wall of that Inn, along the east side of Middle Temple Hall and down to the River Thames. The "great garden," so-called because of its impressive size and beauty, no doubt became a favorite retreat for the new Master of the Temple. He was aware of Shakespeare's dramatization of the legend immortalizing the red and white roses growing there. A century earlier Plantagenet and Somerset and their allies had left the noise of the Inns and halls and come outside into the garden to continue their epic quarrel. "Let him that is a true born gentleman . . .from off this briar pluck a red rose for me," Plantagenet had proclaimed. "Let him that is no coward or flatterer. . .pluck a white rose from off this thorn for me," came the bold rejoinder from Somerset. The War of the Roses! Was the story of the roses in the great garden only a poet's ploy? Perhaps.

Hooker would have enjoyed resting at the end of the garden along the riverside. A new set of stairs, financed in part by the Queen herself, descended from the gardens to the water where boats could be hired for journeys across or up and down the Thames. Richard could sit here on the wall and watch the busy river traffic coming and going along London's already ancient commercial highway. It provided a pleasant escape from the pressures of his duties as Master and a convenient place to clear his head.

Middle Temple Hall had been built about a decade earlier immediately adjacent to Essex House, the first in a row of great mansions lining the river embankment to the west of the Temple grounds all the way down to Whitehall. This hall had been financed and planned by Edmund Plowden, Middle Temple treasurer, and probably the most famous jurist of his age. In Hooker's time, the building was one of the architectural jewels of London--and remains so to this day. This grand hall served as dining room, lecture hall, classrooms and locus of grand receptions, some of national import.

Inside the vast one hundred foot-long hall, was a magnificently carved tall oak screen at one end of the room and beautiful stained glass windows arching high above toward the acclaimed double hammerbeam ceiling that rose nearly sixty feet from the floor, the finest roof in London. The twenty-nine foot bench-table, where senior lawyers sat, was the longest in the realm, a gift from the Queen. Hewn from a single tree, it had to be delivered by floating it down the Thames from the Queen's oak forest at Windsor to the Temple stairs. A smaller oak table ('cupboard'), served as a podium for the important law lectures given twice each year. It had been made from timbers taken from the hatch of Sir Francis Drake's *Pelican* (later, *Golden Hind*) after the great explorer's trip around the world. Such was the grandeur and import of Hooker's new bailiwick.

Unlike his predecessors, Hooker did not reside in the Master's house on the Temple grounds. As Alvey's *de facto* successor, Travers had been living there for some time after Richard's arrival. The Inns, which were required to pay the salary of the master, authorized income for both Travers and Hooker, even after the latter's appointment. Travers was reconfirmed as the rightful resident of the house as late as November of 1586, some eight months after he had been removed from his post at the Temple.

The rulers of the Inner Temple, always less enthusiastic about Travers than their Middle Temple brethren, showed more caution about continuing the reader's pay and benefits. Even before Hooker arrived on the scene, the word was abroad that Travers' days might be numbered. On 3 November 1584 the treasurer of Inner Temple, Nicholas Hare, ordered an audit to determine how much money might still be owing on Mr. Travers' pension, with an obvious intent to clear his accounts. In February of 1585, a full month before Hooker was officially confirmed as Master, the Inner Temple gave Travers official notification that he would no longer receive his 20s. annual fee. Henceforth, Mr. Hooker's work would be sufficient to meet the ministerial needs of the community. A reader would no longer be necessary. However, Travers' ever-faithful guardian, Lord Burghley, caused the privy council to intervene with the Inner Temple to reinstate Travers' stipend.

So it was that even before Richard arrived, Walter Travers had one more reason to feel resentment. Not only did his upstart cousin have decidedly wrongheaded theological views, not only had Richard usurped his own rightful succession to the mastership of the Temple, but now Mr. Hooker's presence was threatening his very livelihood.

For his part, Hooker was, to say the least, highly annoyed when, taking up his duties at the Temple, he found Travers still solidly entrenched there, living in the master's house and preaching regularly. Here was the disappointed aspirant for Richard's position watching his every move. Travers was obviously a popular minister who was being cheered on by a large and loyal following of Middle Temple men who liked him personally, had supported his bid for appointment as master and were not at all pleased with Hooker's presence among them. Furthermore, here, staring Hooker in the face, was stark evidence of the power of Lord Burghley and his Puritan allies to thwart Whitgift's efforts to rid the church of radicals like Travers.

Thomas Cartwright had recently returned from eleven years in exile to assume joint leadership with Travers and John Field of the English Presbyterian movement. Perhaps this had emboldened Travers, who by this time was already a leader of the London "classis," the hub of a national Presbyterian movement, within which he was a leading interpreter of doctrine and arbiter of disputes. Shortly after Hooker was installed at the Temple, there was a commotion surrounding Cartwright. He had no sooner set foot in London when Bishop Alymer had imprisoned him. Within days Cartwright was released by Burghley. Travers then joined Field and others in leading public prayers of thanksgiving for Cartwright's freedom. No doubt Travers felt the time was right for a frontal attack on Hooker at the Temple.

Not only did Travers have his ally Cartwright at his side, but his ardor was further fueled by the growing antagonism toward Hooker among Walter's followers at the Temple. The new Master's refusal to bend to Travers' suggestion and follow Genevan practice had understandably incensed those who had intended all along to deny

Hooker their allegiance. Hooker must have been surprised and hurt by how quickly the opposition had escalated. At first there was some public grumbling from the Middle Temple benches during services when he used the prescribed prayers, knelt at communion, prayed for bishops and preached anything but strict Calvinist doctrine. Such verbal opposition no doubt soon gave way to absenteeism from services. This was intolerable. Hooker warned the officers of the Middle Temple that if this were to continue he would have to inform the Archbishop. Severe sanctions would be brought to bear.

As the controversy over the form and style of worship services worsened, Hooker came to suspect that behind all his troubles was the subtle hand of his cousin, encouraging resistance in the name of an emerging Presbyterian movement that had no intention of losing control of this important church. Ever the charming and polite colleague in infrequent personal contacts with Hooker, Travers had been increasingly strident in his attacks on the Master's ideas during his regular Sunday afternoon sermons.

There was no doubt in Hooker's mind that Travers had intended all along either to convert him or unseat him. About a year later, in April of 1586, in his written response to Travers' formal complaints against him to Burghley and the privy council, Hooker wrote that his initial "offense" in not agreeing to Travers' advice on how to "seal my calling" had subsequently

> so displeased some that whatsoever was afterwards done or spoken by me it offended their taste. . .[to such an extent that] angry informations were daily sent out, intelligence given far and wide what a dangerous enemy had crept in; the worst that jealousy could imagine was spoken and written to so many that, at length, some knowing me well and perceiving how injurious the reports were which grew daily more and more unto my discredit, wrought means to bring Travers and me to a second conference.

Hooker met a number of times with Travers in mutual efforts to resolve their differences. He may also have consulted with his former mentor, John Rainolds, concerning his troubles with Travers. We know that the two were in contact about other matters at approximately this time.

Not surprisingly, Travers' account of meetings between himself and Richard differed significantly from Hooker's. In late spring of 1585, Travers painted a self-serving portrait of his attitude toward Hooker, claiming implausibly, that,

> I was glad the place [Master of the Temple] was given to him [Hooker], hoping to live in godly peace and comfort with him [but] contrary to my expectation, he inclined from the beginning but very smally thereunto, but joined rather with such as had always opposed themselves to any good order in this church. . .

For his part, Hooker asserted that many of the differences between himself and Travers were actually about "silly things" which "I would rather be as loth to recite as I was sorry to hear them objected, if the rehearsal thereof were not by him [Travers] wrested from me." It was Hooker's habit to describe as "silly" or "indifferent" matters which were, in fact, important enough for him to argue about. Silly they might be in God's ultimate scheme of things but not so unimportant that Hooker would fail to insist on having his way concerning them. What was at stake here was the polity, liturgy and theology of the Church of England. Hooker knew only too well that these were not, in common parlance, "indifferent" matters.

The Great Debate

Throughout the rest of 1585 and on into early 1586 the relationship between Hooker and Travers did not improve but took a different direction. Earlier attempts to reconcile differences and agree on a common integrated policy for managing the Temple and conducting services ceased. In their place a policy of separate but equal prevailed.

Each man had his own service to conduct as he wished, Hooker on Sunday mornings, Travers on Sunday afternoons. The morning rite was still the principal gathering for worship, receiving the sacrament and preaching. But at his simple afternoon service, where the sermon (lecture) was the major attraction, Travers proved himself more than Hooker's equal, drawing large, enthusiastic audiences to hear his ever-provocative anti-establishment lectures.

Before long, these morning and afternoon sermons became a running public debate between the policies and practices of a moderately reformed establishment church and the radical Calvinists who sought to replace that church with a new structure and a more reformed liturgy and theology. Students, lawyers, senior jurists, members of parliament and clergy of all stripes filled the Temple Sunday after Sunday to hear the great debate between the Master and the Reader. This was a better show than the monologue at Paul's Cross. Here at the Temple one could witness the great religious issues that divided the nation fought out in a public arena as two gladiators of equal strength did battle for the minds and hearts of an influential and sophisticated audience. As Thomas Fuller said in the next century, "the pulpit spake pure Canterbury in the morning and Geneva in the afternoon."

Many of those attending these Temple debates, including men like the fledgling member of parliament and future lord chancellor, Edward Coke, took notes throughout the sermons as carefully as they might have prepared briefs for their clients or bills for parliament. They were interested in capturing for their own use the arguments of Travers and Hooker. They also enjoyed keeping score for this was a contest, often an emotionally charged one. How effectively would Travers, in the afternoon, refute Hooker's morning arguments?

Travers had the advantage of being the second speaker. His informers rushed to his quarters after Hooker's sermon to give him a verbatim account, whenever he had not been present to hear it himself. He had several hours to fashion a convincing rebuttal. This opportunity, coupled with his considerable oratorical abilities and his personal popularity, made Travers a clear favorite to win the competition, especially since the judges were a predominantly Puritan crowd already disposed to agree with him.

According to the earliest and most widely adopted account of the debate, written by Thomas Fuller some eighty years after the event, Hooker was not an effective preacher. Fuller said of the Master that his "voice was low, stature little, gesture none at all, standing alone in the pulpit, as if the posture of his body were the emblem of his mind, unmovable in his opinions. Where his eye was left fixed at the beginning, it was found fixed at the end of his sermon." Furthermore, "His style was long and pithy, driving a whole flock of several clauses before he came to the close of a sentence. So that the copiousness of his style met not with proportional capacity in his audience. . .

On the other hand, Fuller's informants apparently assured him, "Mr. Travers's utterance was graceful, gesture plausible, matter profitable, method plain, and his style carried with it *indolem pitatis,* 'a genius of grace' flowing from the sanctified heart."

Here we have the pro-Calvinist bias of our only informant shining through brilliantly. Richard's supposed oratorical failings, even down to his "small" posture, are offered, no doubt, to suggest a "small" mind--one characterized by "unmovable opinions," no doubt as stubborn and unbending as the hated Whitgift himself. On the other hand, Fuller's favorite, the Calvinist hero, Travers, is given the "graceful," "plausible," and "profitable" voice to match his "sanctified heart." Once again, Hooker is the victim of a seventeenth-century chronicler whose sources were biased against him. In this case, a renowned church historian too readily accepted an oral tradition that projected Hooker as an ineffectual cleric dominated by the hated high-Anglican party of the day.

In his 1585 and early 1586 sermons, Hooker preached on a number of subjects, including the controversial issue of predestination. His idea that God's will for man is not absolute but conditional, because man has the freedom to disobey it and is therefore responsible for the evil he does, rankled Travers. Hooker's antagonist affirmed the predestination of man and yet exempted God from responsibility for the evil man does. Hooker found this inconsistent, while Travers, of course, cited Calvin in order to refute Hooker's position.

Hooker told Travers that he was tired of defending himself on this subject. He reminded his cousin that he had spoken and written often on predestination and that his ideas were well-known. He had preached on the topic openly at Paul's Cross in the presence of the Bishop of London and many other church and civic leaders and had never been reproached for his ideas. Consequently, it was ridiculous for Travers to suggest, as he had, that he, Hooker, stood alone in this matter and that both scripture and all the church was ranged against his ideas on the subject of predestination.

Furthermore, Hooker informed Travers, even if all the authorities in the world, including Calvin himself, were to disagree with him on this point--which they did not--Hooker's own rational faculty, which was his surest anchor in this sea of disagreement, told him that if God was not the author of the evil we do, then we must be free from His absolute predetermination to be the authors of evil ourselves.

Travers responded that it was presumptuous of Hooker to substitute his singular reason for the judgment of so many wise men in the church. He said that if Richard would only pray more earnestly about this matter he would discover the error of his thinking. Hooker responded that he would consider Travers' comments and preach on the matter again in the near future. Travers warned that if Richard did so, he would put the peace of the Temple in jeopardy because so many men would then feel obligated by conscience to speak out against the Master.

Another major area of disagreement in the morning/afternoon sermon debate was over whether faith in scripture or reliance on human reason and ordinary sense-perception provides the more certain assurance of the efficacy of God's promises of salvation. Hooker realized that his position on this vexing question was too subtle to avoid misinterpretation, or worse, misrepresentation. His thesis was that, although scripture contains all that man needs to know of God's revelation, God also gave man reason and sense perception so that he could have the further assurance that seems to be required by his weak and sinful nature. Hooker never questioned the supremacy of God's Word, only the weakness in fallen man for so often needing the assurance of his own God-given reason and sense to certify what was already sufficiently revealed in holy scripture.

Travers, who seemed to hanker for greater clarity than Hooker in this and most theological issues, took Hooker's words out of context to the effect that "the assurance of what we believe by the word is not so certain as what we perceive by sense." In Travers' view, "assurance of faith is sufficient beyond all human understanding." Not unreasonably, Hooker felt that his foes had oversimplified his own more subtle point in order to paint him as an opponent of the idea of the self-sufficiency of holy scripture.

Hooker thought it sad that everything needed to be so black and white for the Calvinist extremists. In heaven we might hope for such clarity but here on earth we must learn to live with ambiguity, tolerating one another's differences of opinion. Otherwise there will be no peace in the commonwealth.

The Roman Catholic Issue

On the first of March, 1586, Hooker stood in the Temple pulpit facing a full house. Word had got out that he would be preaching on matters involving Catholics. In early 1586, no subject touched a more sensitive nerve in Englishmen. Rumors abounded of Catholic plots at home and abroad to assassinate the Queen, invade England, put Mary the Scot, currently under house arrest, on the throne and restore the Roman religion. Nothing would inflame an audience more quickly than even a hint of pro-Catholic sympathy.

"This morning," Richard began his lecture, "I continue my discourse on the prophet Habakkuk who said, 'the wicked doth encompass about the righteous: therefore perverse judgment doth proceed.' But, who are the wicked? Who are the righteous? What is meant by perverse judgment?"

Hooker proceeded to answer the first question by citing St. Paul. The point he strove to make was that it is really none of our business first to identify and then judge and punish the wicked. Depending on what type of apparently bad persons we confront, we should either separate ourselves from them or leave them to the judgment of God.

Hooker knew, even as he spoke, how uncomfortable this idea was to the more advanced Calvinists who seemed to revel in judging those outside their community of the "elect," especially Catholics.

> As for the righteous there neither is nor ever was any mere mortal man who is absolutely righteous in himself, void of all sin, yet in every other aspect they agree with us that everyone has sinned, including infants, who, although they never actually offended, are defiled in the very nature of their human beings.

Indeed, there are many important areas of agreement between us and the Church of Rome. The Roman church teaches, as we do, that God alone justifies the soul of man without any coefficient cause of justification. They teach, as we do, that Christ's merit alone brings us salvation. They teach, as we do, that man is required to act in order to apply Christ's merits or else they would have no practical effect.

Hooker waited for quiet from the agitated congregation and went on.

In all that I have said thus far, we join hands with the Church of Rome. But now let me show you where we **disagree** with them. We disagree about more than we agree about. Most importantly we do not hold with them that God's grace may be increased by the merit of man's good works, decreased by man's bad works (sins), or lost altogether by commission of a so-called mortal sin.

This great error of the Roman Church leads to many others. For example, they hold wrongly that men may recover lost grace by such means as performing charitable works, applying holy water, saying *ave marias*, crossing themselves, receiving papal blessings, utilizing the so-called sacrament of penance, taking pilgrimages, enduring fasts and the like. This is the maze the Church of Rome lays out for her followers to tread when they ask her for the path to justification and salvation.

I cannot stand here this morning and uproot this corrupt Roman structure and sift and examine the rubble for you piece by piece. But I will set alongside it the true and solid foundation and framework which God has built for our justification.

In brief, God's foundation, as set forth in scripture, is Christ alone. Only He is righteous. There is no righteousness in me whatsoever except what may come to me by God's grace through my faith in Christ. All else, as Paul says, is dung. The Roman Church errs when it says or implies that there is some inherent righteousness in man. There is none.

Let it be counted folly, or frenzy, or fury, or whatever, it is nevertheless our wisdom and our comfort, and we care for no other knowledge in the world but this: man sinned; God suffered; God made Himself the sin of man. . .

Hooker continued.

You can see, therefore, that the Church of Rome perverts the very truth of Christ as we have it from the Apostle, when she teaches justification through some inherent grace in man.

Now these people of whom Habakkuk speaks, were they genuinely penitent and humble; did they strive earnestly to walk uprightly and keep God's laws? Not at all. These children of Israel were, as Isaiah tells us, a sinful and corrupt nation, laden with iniquity.

And yet, so wide are the bowels of God's compassion that even when we, like the children of Israel, are laden with iniquity and treat Him with disrespect He gives us the liberty to hope that whatever punishment we may deserve we will yet be treated no worse than unbelievers and be not overcome by pagans and infidels.

But the prophet Habakkuk not only complains that the righteous who call upon God have been treated badly whereas the heathen have been tolerated. He goes beyond mere complaint and breaks out from the extremities of his grief to infer that God's treatment of the righteous is perverse.

Hooker had everyone's attention now. Each person in his audience had felt the personal pressure of a Calvinist doctrine that assured a preordained salvation to the elect and yet seemed to require a disciplined schedule of good behavior by the saints in the midst of a thoroughly corrupt and hypocritical society that rewarded the infidels of the day. This did indeed seem a perverse judgment that God had placed on His chosen flock. How would Master Hooker resolve this dilemma for them this morning?

At this point, to everyone's shock and dismay, the preacher put down the papers from which he had been reading. He looked out at the congregation and said: "Clearly there is much more that you want to hear from me on this subject and more that I would like to say to you. But that will have to wait for another day."

There was a gasp from the congregation. Hooker had left them suspended at the denouement of his sermon and now took off in a completely different direction.

> Necessity, unfortunately draws me to another stake for the time I have remaining with you this morning. Like Paul and Barnabas when requested to preach again on a subject they thought they had covered, I feel obliged to comply and to return to a subject that I talked about the last time I preached on the text of Paul's letter to the Hebrews.

The congregation leaned forward expectantly in their benches. They knew what was coming. This was what they had hoped for--a further installment in the heated controversy between Hooker and Travers about the Church of Rome.

> In that recent sermon of mine, I concluded that because the Church of Rome was so corrupted and resistant to reform, we have rightly severed ourselves from her and that even the example of our fathers in that church cannot keep us in communion with her.
>
> Then I said something that has, as you well know, been called into question here in this Temple and elsewhere. I said: 'God, I doubt not, was merciful to save thousands of them although they lived in popish superstition inasmuch as they sinned ignorantly.' I ask

you to mark and sift this sentence carefully to see if it is worthy of all the attention given it. If, when I have finished, you find the notion to be made only of hay or straw, I will gladly set fire to it myself.

Two questions have been raised by this simple sentence of mine. First, whether our fathers, so infected with popish errors and superstitions could be saved; second, whether their ignorance is a reasonable inducement to make us think that they might be.

There is no question that the heresies of the Church of Rome are many and great, from claiming other written sources for God's revelation than the holy scriptures, to asserting that the bishop of Rome is head of the universal church, to presenting the bread in the Eucharist as being transubstantiated into Christ, to worshipping images, to calling on saints as intercessors and many other errors.

I have no doubt, nor have I ever claimed otherwise, that all those who persisted in these errors, after being admonished to abandon them, are condemned unless they specifically repented of their error. Nor have I ever said that all of our forebears in the Church of Rome were saved from damnation. I only said, and still say, that 'thousands' of them were saved by God's mercy.

It was an unfortunate error in judgment for our fathers [Roman Catholics] to follow their religious teachers and guides in the Church of Rome. But error is not heresy. And, in any event, what one man in ten thousand even understood what these doctrines meant? Surely there is a difference between those who followed and those who led. Shall we lap up all of our fathers in the Church of Rome in one condition and cast them all headlong into that infernal and ever flaming lake?

If we grant that some sinners among our fathers may escape God's judgment for popish heresy, how might that be accomplished? There was only one way for them. That was to appeal to God's saving mercy.

We know from scripture that this mercy is available only to those of faith. Thus, our question must be, were any of our forebears in the Church of Rome men of faith despite their errors. The answer is, yes.

The foundation of our faith, as revealed in scripture, is Christ the incarnate God and savior of the world. Even if weakly held and by a slender thread, this faith may save a man despite other errors of faith.

Richard changed the direction of his argument now, charting a course into more hazardous waters.

As I have said on other occasions, even the Church of Rome itself must be preferred to the synagogues of the Jews and Mosques of the Turks. For although Rome played the harlot worse than Israel ever did, yet she never, like the Jews, denied Christ; and so she is not quite excluded from God's new covenant in Christ.

We must think hard about this question of how many millions of our fathers, despite other grievous errors that they followed in the Church of Rome, ended their mortal lives uttering these words of faith with their final breath: 'Christ my savior; my redeemer.' Can we say that all such persons had failed to maintain their faith in Christ?

I do not think so. Even though it is true that the Church of Rome added works to faith as a condition of salvation, she did so only in relation to the application of Christ's merits. Never did she deny that redemption itself came from Christ alone and that He is the sole foundation of faith.

Even if I grant that the foundation of faith was overthrown when the Church of Rome added the pernicious requirements for salvation which I have already described, shall we imagine that the damage of such errors would so outweigh the benefit of their basic faith in Christ that even those who were never aware of these errors should be denied any hope of salvation?

Hooker now took the plunge into still deeper water. Speaking from the heart, he said:

> Is what we have here with the Church of Rome any different from the error of our Lutheran brethren who stiffly and fiercely maintain in their Wittenberg confession a similar doctrine concerning faith and works? Should we also condemn them?

Many in the congregation were amazed at what the preacher was saying. Was Hooker really comparing the followers of Luther with the hated papists? Hooker decided that he had come this far and might as well go all the way.

> I will go still further and state that the Church of Rome, however broken and misshapen by its heresies, is still part of the church. She has never directly denied the foundation of our faith. I do not intrude this idea upon you as some mere private opinion of mine. The best judgment of the learned men in the Church are of like opinion.
>
> I say to you: give me a man of whatever condition or estate, yea, even a cardinal or a pope, who at the extreme affliction of his life comes to know himself, and whose heart God has touched with true sorrow for his sins and filled with love toward Christ's Gospel and whose eyes are opened to see the truth and mouth open to renounce all heresy--am I still to think that because of this one error of adding works to faith such a one will never be permitted to touch even the hem of Christ's garment? And if he did so, might I never hope that Christ, in His mercy, might save him?

Hooker had now, although he may not have realized it at once, put his entire career in jeopardy.

> I tell you I would not be afraid to say unto a cardinal or a pope in such a case: 'Be of good comfort, ours is a merciful God.' Let me die if ever it be proved that simply an error would exclude a pope or a cardinal from all hope of eternal life.
>
> I confess to you that if it be an error to think God may be merciful to save men when they err, then my greatest comfort is my error. Were it not for the love I bear this error, I would neither wish to speak nor to live! Alas, was such a bloody matter really contained in this simple sentence in my recent sermon expressing hope for the salvation of some of our forefathers in the Church of Rome that so many had to come down so hard on me for it?

Hooker had just uttered the most dangerous words of his ministry. Fear of Catholic invasion ran high. To even hint at mercy for the pope was not only blasphemous but in the climate it was likely to be thought treasonable. He concluded his sermon:

> I trust that these ideas which I have been expounding are sound. Those who have attacked me because of them may well have injured my reputation. Despite that, I wish them every blessing in heaven for I have reaped much benefit from the labor they put me to in defending my position.
>
> I only regret that I had to spend so much of your time and mine in this endeavor. But because the love I bear the truth in Christ Jesus had been called into question, I dared not be silent. As for those who are the cause of all this controversy --and you well know who they are--I can only beseech them in the spirit of Christ's meekness to consider that a watchman sometimes cries 'enemy' when in fact a friend is coming. God knows

that my heart is free from any unfriendly intent or meaning.

And now, the God of Peace grant you peaceful minds and turn them to your everlasting comfort.

—— Attack And Response ——

In his afternoon response, Travers branded Hooker a near traitor for even hinting at the pope's salvation. Richard had crossed the line into forbidden territory.

In his rebuttal sermon, Travers argued against Hooker's ideas point by point, like a lawyer. He quoted from Richard's sermon as though he had a copy of it in front of him, enumerating what he called the serious errors in the sermon: that Hooker had said the Church of Rome was a true church, that he had said that thousands of our forefathers who lived and died in that faith were saved despite the error of joining works to faith and so forth.

Hooker had specifically forbidden Travers to refute his sermons in this public manner, at least until the reader had first discussed with him any disagreements he had with the Master's ideas. Richard was exceedingly angry upon hearing of Travers' disobedience. Before he could vent his ire by informing the Archbishop, or anyone else, of Travers' insubordination, Travers complained to the Lord Treasurer that it was Hooker and not he who had violated an agreement that the Master would not dispute with the Reader without prior private consultation.

Whoever, in fact, first violated any agreement to avoid disturbing the peace at the Temple by not publicly airing disagreements between "Geneva" and "Canterbury" does not much matter. There could be no keeping the lid on for long, such was the intensity of the issues involved. Still, we can appreciate Hooker's frustration over Travers' advantage in having his turn in the pulpit follow so hard on his own. Richard had to wait a full week to get back at Travers and when he did his opponent still accused him of breaking their peace pact!

Travers was meticulous in his ongoing refutation of Hooker's sermons. He took the Master to task for his interpretation of the Roman position on faith and works. The necessity of works is not merely additional or secondary for the Roman Church, as Hooker had claimed. Rather, works were an essential part of the papist's requirement for salvation. Travers simply ignored Hooker's subtle distinctions between types of justification.

The Reader also disputed Hooker's view of the Council of Trent, claiming that the Council had made works essential to salvation and that Hooker was in error when he said otherwise. Additionally, Travers disagreed with the Master's interpretation of Galatians, maintaining that the Galatians' requirement of circumcision did indeed amount to going beyond justification by faith in Christ alone, which is why Paul condemned them. Travers had not missed much.

Perhaps the worst of it was that Richard's cousin totally misrepresented his comment about Lutherans. He made it sound as though it were a major theme of Hooker's sermon to lump Lutherans and papists into one ball. Richard now wished that he had not put that short passage in his sermon. It had been a delicious but impetuous afterthought that he had been unable to resist. Lutherans, like Catholics, he knew, differed among themselves on theological questions. To be accurate he should have said that *some*, not *all*, Lutherans were as guilty as *most*, not *all*, papists of "overthrowing the foundation of faith" by addition of works.

Most damaging was Travers' response to Hooker's comments about the possible salvation of the pope and other Catholics. Travers said that he scarcely knew how to react to such an absurdity--that was his very word, "absurdity." Such favorable words as Hooker had spoken about the pope and the papists had not been heard in this realm since the days of Queen Mary, Travers charged. It would be up to the highest authorities in the realm to decide Hooker's fate if he failed publicly to recant these opinions about the Church of Rome.

Hooker flinched when he heard what Travers had said to Lord Burghley on this subject. The implication that he was a traitor was all too clear. Richard could see that Walter had cleverly tied their quarrel over faith and works with the national hysteria over the threat of invasion from Catholic Spain. And into the bargain he had attached to that same patriotic fervor his personal struggle with Richard for mastery of the Temple Church. To support Hooker was to support Rome and Spain. To support Travers was to support queen, country and church.

So far as we know, Hooker never publicly recanted his opinions on this dangerous subject. Regardless of the undoubted harm that his remarks and Travers' responses had done to his career, Hooker did not change his mind on the subject of the salvation of popes and other Catholics. Corrupt she may be, but the Church of Rome was the mother church still. Hooker would never renounce his faith in the promise of God's saving mercy for all who had faith in Him, regardless of their sins.

Hooker would pay dearly for these convictions. At the very least, these unrecanted sentiments about Rome made it unlikely, if not impossible, for Whitgift to promote Hooker in the church hierarchy. The Bishop of Rome may have appreciated Hooker's ideas on this and related subjects but the Queen of England and her closest advisors certainly did not.

Not only did Travers refute Hooker in sermons and in correspondence to Lord Burghley, but he also orchestrated a campaign against the Master throughout the church, even among members of parliament and the privy council. Travers' supporters saw to it that copies of their versions of Hooker's sermons and Travers' responses were circulated, sometimes even before Travers had delivered his remarks from the pulpit. An effort was underway to create a political frenzy at the Temple which would alarm the Queen, who hated such turmoil, and lead to Hooker's ouster.

Richard had some help in counteracting this considerable political challenge to his position. Powerful and savvy moderates within his circle included his host, John Churchman, and the famous Sandys brothers: his patron, Edwin the Archbishop of York, and Edwin's brother, Miles, leading barrister at Middle Temple Inn and prominent member of parliament. The Sandys brothers were visitors at the Churchmans, along with Richard's former student and friend, Edwin Sandys. These were the men who supplied the political savvy and clout that helped Richard retain his post amidst the firestorm raised by Travers and his allies over the Catholic issue. They probably advised Hooker that his best strategy was to ignore attacks for his supposed sympathy with the pope and concentrate instead on Travers' offense in disturbing the peace by openly disputing his superior on matters of doctrine. Such behavior was directly contrary to the Queen's injunction. Support for Hooker on this point could be had from all but the most rabid Presbyterians in privy council and parliament.

It was assumed that Travers would submit a formal complaint against Hooker to Burghley and the privy council. Hooker would need to respond with an answer as soon as Travers' objections were known. He should submit his document to Archbishop Whitgift, the proper channel for a response. In the meantime, Richard's important friends would apprise the Archbishop of the situation so that Whitgift would have time to prepare his position before Burghley got to the Queen.

By the time Hooker had set to work composing an outline of his charges against Travers and an explanation of some of his own statements on the issue of justification by faith and works and on the status of the Church of Rome, events overtook his pen. Travers was summarily dismissed from his post. Whitgift removed him on 23rd March 1586 before he could preach another sermon at the Temple. Within two weeks, news of his dismissal had spread by word of mouth and letter throughout the national presbyterian network.

One such letter from Yorkshire to "godly preachers" at Newcastle-on-Tyne carried the word from a "godly gentleman" in London that Satan himself, in the form of one "Master Hooker an Oxford man. . .teaching sundry points of doctrine savoring of a profane spirit" was "laboring to hinder the happy growth of the gospel. . ." Surely, it was a "matter of mourning that any bishop should command learned and faithful ministers [Travers] to be silent for speaking against" the ideas of Master Hooker.

The speed with which Whitgift moved against Travers and the discourteous manner in which he had him ejected from the Temple caused great consternation at the Temple. Even those who did not support Travers' views and were relieved to see him leave, deplored the Archbishop's methods. True to his reputation for arbitrary use of authority against his enemies--he could be most accommodating and even charming to his friends--Whitgift acted quickly and decisively against Travers. Almost as soon as he learned about what he perceived as Travers' insubordination to Hooker, he struck without warning to remove this man whom he had for so long regarded as one of the greatest threats to the peace and order of the Church of England.

The congregation had gathered at the Temple on that fateful Sunday afternoon in late March, eager as usual to hear Travers' refutation of Hooker's morning sermon. As the Reader mounted the steps of the pulpit, one of Whitgift's agents suddenly appeared and served him with a written injunction, signed by the Archbishop, ordering him to cease all preaching at the Temple. Though everyone present was terribly shocked, Travers took it well. Cautioning the congregation to be calm, he left the church and returned to his quarters.

The following Sunday, 30th March, Travers went to church in the morning and listened to Hooker's sermon, taking copious notes. Immediately thereafter he sent a letter to Burghley, no doubt at the Lord Treasurer's request, outlining fifteen specific charges against the Master of the Temple, focusing on his three sermons on Habakkuk dealing with justification, faith and works, reason and scripture and his dangerous comments on the pope and the Church of Rome. Also included was reference to Hooker's oft-cited critical ideas about the doctrine of predestination.

Hooker immediately wrote a response to Travers' charges and sent it to Archbishop Whitgift. The Archbishop's written reply to Hooker was somewhat ambiguous--less than completely supportive, Hooker thought. No doubt Whitgift found it difficult to deviate, as far as Hooker seemed to be doing, from strict Calvinist theology. Clearly, Whitgift was not pleased with any positive speech about the papists. Still, he was generally supportive of Hooker, his criticisms apparently intended only to soften Hooker's arguments, something Richard might have done himself had he had the same advantage of hindsight.

In the event, it became increasingly apparent that Whitgift was not really interested in the theological debate but was bent on removing Travers as reader at the Temple by any means available. He saw that his best weapon was one he had used earlier against Cartwright and more recently to prevent Walter's appointment as master at the Temple. Simply put, because Travers was not properly ordained, he had no right to serve in any English church, period. When Whitgift presented this argument to Burghley, that gentleman told Travers to send him a brief explanation about the validity of his ordination so he could use it with Whitgift. Travers did so, to no avail.

When two petitions to Whitgift, by way of the Lord Treasurer, had failed him, Travers decided to appeal directly to the privy council in the form of an official *Supplication*, defending his ordination, explaining his personal and professional relations with Hooker and attacking Hooker's major theological positions. This appeal was sent off in early April. Within a few days it was in the hands not only of members of the council but also of lawyers and students at the Temple Inns, the leading clerics of the church, members of parliament and, no doubt, the Queen herself.

As he prepared his *Answer* to Travers' *Supplication*, Hooker had in front of him a copy of that document, as well as copies of Travers' earlier petitions and his own notes on accounts by Sandys and others of Whitgift's reactions. He was especially distressed, in reviewing these papers, by the prejudiced accounts of his ideas spread abroad by Lawrence Tomson, member of parliament and long-time secretary to the powerful Puritan statesman, Sir Francis Walsingham. It is likely that Tomson had been attending Hooker's sermons regularly and reporting his take on them directly to Walsingham. Tomson was undoubtedly the principal informant on Hooker for the Puritan political oligarchy.

While Hooker was worried about Walsingham's ability to do him injury, he was angered by Tomson's interference. This spearhead for Puritan legislative activities was arguably the most radical of the more prominent and respectable Presbyterian scholars in the Commons.

Richard was familiar with Tomson's writings and found most of his work far too extreme for his taste. In fact, if there was a single author at this stage in his career with whom Hooker was more often in disagreement than Tomson, it would be hard to say whom that might be. Schooled at Magdalen, Oxford and thoroughly "reformed" at Geneva and Heidelberg, Tomson had published, in 1576, an annotated version of the *Geneva Bible* that was preferred by most Puritans over the authorized *Bishop's Bible*. His version was far more disciplinarian in outlook than the original 1560 edition.

Tomson was an exponent of the most extreme form of the doctrine of predestination, called supralapsarianism. He was also a translator of several of Calvin's sermons. Hooker wondered, when he perused copies of Tomson's reports on his own recent sermons, if this radical activist had been as inaccurate in translating Calvin as he was in representing his ideas. It was not so much that the reporting itself was inaccurate as that Hooker's ideas had been ripped out of their subtle context and made to stand alone as unequivocal propositions. In this form, he could scarcely have accepted them himself. As for Tomson's substantive refutation of his arguments, Hooker bristled at the man's arrogance and his *ad hominum* argumentation. It was no proof of one's own arguments to brand one's opponent as "ignorant," or a "dissembler," or a "mere beginning student [not] well-versed" in the great writers of the past and present.

When Hooker finished his *Answer* to Travers' *Supplication*, he realized that there was no point in sending it to Burghley or the privy council. There would be no favorable audience for him there. As a minister of the church, his superior was the Archbishop. It was inappropriate to go around the head of the church directly to the privy council, as Travers had done. A happy coincidence of propriety and politics dictated that Hooker address his appeal to his patron, Archbishop Whitgift.

Richard wrote his *Answer* quickly, in a day or two. He may have had some help from young Edwin Sandys who had moved into the Churchman house as a long-term house guest and whose fateful collaboration with Hooker on the editing and publication of his former mentor's important writings began at about this time, in the Spring of 1586.

——— Postscript ———

Walter Travers, even after his removal as Reader, remained in the Temple grounds. The Middle and Inner Temple Inns continued to pay his salary and to provide him with residence in the Master's house. Since he was now free from all duties at the church, he had ample time to write and work actively on behalf of the radical Presbyterian movement in London and around the country. At the same time, he could continue to stir up trouble for Hooker among the lawyers and students at the Inns.

An offer from the Earl of Huntingdon of a position in a church at Leicester, well outside London, no doubt approved by Whitgift, could not lure Travers from his command-post location at the Temple. He also used his private abode on Milk Street, just around the corner from Hooker's dwelling at the Churchmans', as a center for planning and orchestrating Presbyterian activities in London and around the country.

It is surprising that during these dangerous times Travers never suffered the fate of his colleague Thomas Cartwright, who was imprisoned for such activities as conducting forbidden synod meetings, writing illegal tracts, assisting others who did the same, and encouraging use of Presbyterian polity and liturgy wherever he could. Whitgift had planned to bring Travers, along with Cartwright, to trial before the church high commission. Richard Bancroft, Whitgift's chief agent for suppressing nonconformity, had secured evidence that Travers had plotted with others to encourage Cartwright to stand mute and not to cooperate with the commission's search for information about the Presbyterian movement. But Travers was never tried, undoubtedly saved once again by the waning but still significant influence of his patron, Lord Burghley.

Travers moved to Ireland in 1594. Here he embraced another great challenge--this time one that was likely to please rather than offend the Queen. In December of 1591, the Queen had authorized construction of the first and long-awaited English university in Ireland. A year later the new academic society, located in Dublin and named Trinity College, was ready to admit its first students. Roman Catholics in Ireland were dismayed at this development. It was obvious from the start that Queen Elizabeth would use the new college as a tool to stay the growth of political and religious resistance to her sway in this cantankerous and largely Catholic province. At last there would be an intellectual center congenial to Reformation theology, a training place for Protestant ministers, and a pro-English center for educating the future leaders of Ireland.

The founding provost of Trinity was Adam Loftus, the Cambridge-bred Archbishop of Dublin, an outspoken Puritan foe of Irish papalists. From the beginning, Trinity was a bastion of Puritanism with close ties to Emmanuel College, Cambridge. Lord Burghley had been a moving force behind Trinity College and was its first chancellor. When Loftus resigned in June of 1594, the Lord Treasurer used his influence to have his endangered and unemployed protégé, Walter Travers, named to the post.

Whitgift was delighted to have this nemesis out of the country, on assignment to fight Catholics rather than menacing the Church of England. Under Travers' leadership, Trinity might become a hot-bed of radical Calvinism but that was a penalty Whitgift was more than willing to pay in order to watch the formidable Travers do battle with rebellious Irish Catholics. Hooker, too, may have thought it far better that his cousin use his great talents to fight papalists rather than to make trouble for the established church at home.

Travers remained at Trinity until October of 1598 with most of his energy consumed in raising funds for the new college. He found some time to preach in the college chapel and to serve as lecturer in Latin. One of his students, James Ussher, would one day become Archbishop of Armagh, Primate of Ireland, and a leading figure in seventeenth-century Irish history.

Travers survived Hooker by thirty-five years, dying in 1635. The final decades of his life were times of intense frustration for the former leader of an important, but now dormant, movement. He lived in relatively obscure and modest circumstances, out of the public eye, too proud to receive aid from such important friends as his now famous former student at Trinity Archbishop Ussher of Armagh. Occasionally he found a pulpit where he could preach and have an opportunity to give aid and comfort to a fellow nonconformist.

Had Travers' talent, like Hooker's, run more to writing than preaching, he might have spent his final years composing a lasting refutation of Hooker's magnum opus, thereby having the last word in one of the most important debates of the English Reformation. The spoken word, at which he excelled, was compelling for the moment but soon forgotten, as Hooker often said. Written words, less exciting at the moment, could endure for centuries.

—— Chapter 8 ——

A Judicious Marriage

—— Master Of The Temple ——

With Travers gone from the Temple grounds after 1586, Hooker could spend more of his time tending to his pastoral and administrative duties as master. In addition to preaching and conducting services, he was expected to supervise the general religious life of the Middle and Inner Temple Inns, enforce church attendance rules and tend to the spiritual needs of this sophisticated and privileged congregation of lawyers.

As he settled into the routine of Temple activity, Richard appreciated how much it had in common with university life. Law students were engaged in tutor-directed studies throughout much of the day. Inns were like dormitories with impressive dining halls, much as he had known at Corpus Christi. The semi-pastoral setting of the campus, with its broad river frontage, lovely gardens and semi-cloistered atmosphere, was somewhat reminiscent of Oxford. His own weekly lecture/sermon stood, in some sense, for the required public lectures in theology at the university.

A less pleasant feature of life here at the Temple, also reminiscent of Oxford, was a student penchant for drunken and rowdy behavior. Discipline was, in fact, much harder to maintain. The students, most of whom were from privileged families, were older, more independent and uniformly wealthier than those at Oxford. They came here to acquire the important social graces of dancing, riding, singing and theater-going, as well as to study law, find entree into the commercial and political scene in London and, if possible, find a place for themselves in the Queen's government.

Away from the discipline of home or university, with the temptations of the fifth largest city in the world literally at their doorstep, many of these young men expressed their freedom in drunken brawling, whoring and other forms of serious mischief. The area around Temple Bar on Fleet Street was no place for the unwary when the students came out to "play" at night. Within the halls, bans against such practices as possessing swords and entertaining women were difficult to enforce, especially since some of the senior barristers, including such notables as Treasurer Popham himself, had, in their own younger days, been among the principal offenders.

Most of the 1,700 men who lived at the Inns in Hooker's day had come straight from Oxford and Cambridge, initially to one of the eight Inns of Chancery, each housing about one hundred men. They remained in a probationary status for about a year before moving to one of the four major Inns of Court: Middle Temple, Inner Temple, Lincoln's Inn, or Gray's Inn. As they entered the Inns, which, like the commercial guilds, were often called "societies" or "mysteries," these fledgling lawyers joined a fraternity within which they would learn and then practice the craft and art of the law. In much the same manner of John Churchman's merchant tailors and other commercial companies, the inns were social groups, complete with rituals, ceremonies and symbols that smacked of the medieval origins of the Temple itself--rich in religious and classical overtones. The lamb was the symbol of the Middle Temple, the pegasus of the Inner Temple. Each inn had its own special character. A little ditty went: "Grays Inn for walks, Lincolns Inn for a wall, the Inner Temple for a garden, and the Middle for a hall." As a member of an Inn, one was assured lifelong social contacts and economic support from his brothers. The Inns were a college, social fraternity, country club, civic club, professional organization and an extended family all in one.

Hooker quickly learned that the heart of each Inn was its great central hall. Often his duties as Master took him from the church into the halls to attend lectures, participate in public celebrations, visit the treasurers on Temple business or meet students for counseling sessions. Sometimes he just read or worked quietly on one of his sermons or other writings, at one of the long tables in the room.

Whenever Richard attended a formal lecture at Middle Temple hall and saw the speaker (usually a prominent national figure) standing at the grand "cupboard" in the center of the room to read his discourse, he would have felt an excitement he had not known at Oxford lectures. All around him were seated not academics and clerics but leading politicians, jurists, lawyers, members of parliament, sons of powerful English families, even peers of the realm. He may sometimes have felt out of place and ill at ease in such a politically sophisticated setting. Even so, he would be stimulated by this highly charged environment. His knowledge of current political affairs and the state of public discourse was honed to a fine edge during his years at the Temple.

Another early discovery for Hooker was that the meals here at the Inns were far superior to the fare he had endured for so many years at Corpus Christi College. Whenever he could, Richard took a free dinner with a bencher at the commons. He had a chair on the raised dais with the readers. From here he could survey the carefully stratified seating arrangements separating each level within the guild. Food and drink were plentiful, with mutton the usual main course. Even those who sat at tables farthest removed from the dais and paid more money for poorer meals dined better than they had when they were students up at Oxford or Cambridge.

As at Corpus Christi, however, table manners were far from elegant. Richard's dining experience at the Inns was far from elegant--certainly nothing like the charm and warmth he experienced when he ate dinner at "home" with the Churchmans. Reluctant clerks waited table here with the same lack of enthusiasm with which they changed the food-encursted coverings on the floor. There were pewter cups and plates but no table linen or forks were provided. As with other favored diners at the high table, Richard carried his own knife and fork with him and wiped his hands and mouth on the sleeves of his coat.

Hooker found dining and most other experiences more to his liking at Middle Temple than Inner Temple, probably because his closest personal attachments, with and through the Sandys family, were at Middle Temple. Nevertheless, his political and religious allies were predominantly at the other house, whose members were more frequently the favored first-born of the rich and famous. Not so bumptious as Middle Temple members, men of this society tended to dislike the radicalism of Travers and were glad to have Hooker's temperate influence in their midst, not that Middle Temple lacked a conservative tradition. After all, the moderate Sandys' clan found it a congenial home.

One consequence of the difference in social complexion between the two Inns was that, in Hooker's time and subsequently, more men of lasting fame passed through Middle Temple than Inner Temple. The rich, in those days of primogeniture, often rested on their wealth, contributing little of lasting historic value to society as compared with their younger siblings who had to stretch their wits and find their own paths to fame and fortune. Although many Inner Temple members in Hooker's day had noble titles, few had names that would be recognized beyond their own time.

On the other hand, Middle Temple members included such sixteenth century notables as the jurists Plowden, Popham, and Coke and serious students of law like John Meere of Sherborne. Many more, who would one day be famous, were not interested in the study of law so much as they were in exploiting the social and economic advantages of membership at the Middle Temple. These included the architect Inigo Jones, explorers John Hawkins, Walter Raleigh, Francis Drake and Martin Frobisher, statesman and scholar Thomas Smith, the poet George Sandys, and Raleigh's friend, also a poet and soldier of fortune, George Gascoigne. In subsequent centuries, the list of distinguished alumni would include the diarist John Evelyn, political philosophers James Harrington, Edmund Burke, the legal scholar William Blackstone and novelists Henry Fielding, Charles Dickens and William Makepeace Thackeray.

Of interest to Americans seeking some connection to Hooker is the fact that many famous colonial Americans were to claim membership in Hooker's favorite society. In fact, it is not too much to suggest that Middle Temple was a kind of nursery for political luminaries in the new world. No fewer than five signatories of the Declaration of Independence were members, including Thomas McKean of Delaware who became the first Chief Justice of the United States Supreme Court. The second Chief Justice was also a middle templar, John Rutledge of South Carolina, who had been one of the drafters of the United States Constitution. The honor role of Middle Templars who helped shape the American nation also included such men as Arthur Lee and Peyton Randolph of Virginia, John Dickinson of Pennsylvania and the colonial governor of New Jersey, William Patterson.

Before long, Hooker grew used to seeing many of the prominent figures of his day in his congregation and elsewhere in the halls and on the temple grounds. There was no reliable way that he could gauge the future importance of those at the Temple who were not yet fully established. Edward Coke of Inner Temple was, for instance, a frequent presence at the inns when court was in session although during Hooker's tenure his permanent residence was with his wife and children in Suffolk. Who could tell in 1586 that this promising new member of Commons, sitting in church and taking close notes on Hooker's sermons, would soon become one of the greatest figures in all English history: attorney general, chief justice, speaker of Commons, and author of the *Petition of Right, Bonham's Case, The Reports*, and *The Institutes of the Laws of England*--taken altogether probably four of the seven most important charters of modern constitutional government in England and America?

Hooker could not know what influence, if any, his lectures and sermons had on the minds of such prospective famous men as Edward Coke. Like all writers, teachers and preachers, he could only hope that his ideas would find fertile soil in some of his readers and listeners. He could not know, and neither can we, whether the great passion for the law that was to shine so critically for future centuries in the life and works of Sir Edward Coke was nurtured not only by what Coke learned from his legal studies at the Inns of Court but also from the inspiring lectures of the master of the Temple Church. What we do know is that Hooker's potential for influencing men like Coke was considerable. Hooker was a writer and speaker who, in that cynical, sophisticated, late Tudor world, had the ability to offer such powerful paeans to the majesty of law as this:

> Of Law can be no less acknowledged, than that her seat is the bosom of God, her voice the harmony of the world: all things in heaven and earth do her homage, the very least as feeling her care, and the greatest as not exempted from her power.

Much of the Master's time was spent responding to complaints and gossip about mundane affairs. As soon as Travers moved out,

Hooker gave himself some working space in the Master's house, where he could talk in private with templars and conduct the daily business that came his way. Usually there was nothing he could do but listen and sympathize. His days were filled with responding to such complaints as:

- Reductions in numbers of cook's assistants are delaying meals and making me miss religious services.
- Cutting back on gardeners and other servants is a foolish cost-cutting measure that we all regret.
- Both quantity and quality of food in commons are deteriorating badly.
- Penalties for missing lectures are unfairly administered.
- Attendance at religious services should not be required.
- My friend was higher on the waiting list for admission than so-and-so who was just admitted because of political influence.
- My family has come on hard times. Can you find me enough money to see me through the term? I will pay it all back. I promise.

Every chaplain in every age has heard these problems and will know what Hooker's life was like better than the rest of us.

A somewhat more unusual issue that Hooker was also unable to solve, but probably amused him more than most, involved the Earl of Leicester's garden. It seemed that some members of Middle Temple, whose chambers bordered on the Earl's adjoining gardens, cut doors through their rooms so they could walk out directly onto his otherwise very private property. That great man, or more likely his steward or head gardener, complained. As a result, in June of 1585, the Middle Temple parliament ordered the offending doorways to be walled up immediately. The outcries of righteous indignation, denial of responsibility and refusal to comply took a year to subside. Grumblings over this campus flap could still be heard in the summer of 1586.

For his part, the Earl of Leicester had more to think about than law students walking uninvited into his garden on the Thames. The gossip at the inns about Leicester, during those waning days of 1586, turned on a far more important issue. What was the role of their rich and powerful neighbor in the intrigues at court and in parliament on the question of the fate of Mary Queen of Scots? Everyone at the Temple, including Hooker, knew that the Earl was far away in the Netherlands as commander-in-chief of an English army aiding the Dutch in their rebellion against Philip II of Spain. It was a dangerous policy for Queen Elizabeth to pursue, tantamount to a declaration of war against Spain but the adventure was pursued eagerly, if not recklessly, by her erstwhile favorite, Leicester, who seemed never to tire of trying to impress his mistress with his daring-do.

Hooker may have gained inside information about this matter and other aspects of the high drama of politics at Westminster from his uncle, John Hooker. John, who would later write a description of the House of Commons and its procedures was in London to attend the session of Commons as a member from Exeter. While in town, the famous Exeter chamberlain and historian would have been eager to spend time with his now famous nephew. The meeting would have meant even more to Richard, who had had so little contact with his family and hometown.

If, as seems likely, the two men were together in late 1586 and early 1587, Richard would have acquired some fresh information about his father Roger's life and career in Ireland. He doubtless already knew of his father's death some years ago but would have yearned to hear more about his life. John probably told him about some of Roger's experiences managing the Carew estates in County Carlow and his exciting and dangerous life--fighting in the Butler Wars, being captured by those Kavanaugh ruffians. Richard would be especially intrigued to learn that his father had been appointed dean of the Carew parish church at Leighlin Bridge, where he had made his home. No doubt Roger had been appointed to that clerical post after Carew pushed the Kavanaugh tribe out of the Barrow Valley. Richard realized that this appointment in the church would not have required the sort of academic training and religious sensitivity that preceded his own selection as Master of the Temple. Roger's was a "battlefield" appointment made not by the church but by his patron, Peter Carew, who owned the church building and its properties. Roger's responsibility would have been mostly that of administrator and steward, not preacher and pastor. Still, how curious that his father had also labored in the church, a servant of the Lord.

——— The Second Joan ———

Much closer to home and heart than his dead father was Hooker's new wife, Joan. So far as we know, Joan was the most intimate and directly caring human being in his life.

Yet, for the nearly four centuries that Hooker has been part of the public domain, his marriage has been maligned. This misinformation and calumny started in the mid-seventeenth century when the Puritan historian, Thomas Fuller, told the world that Hooker had died a bachelor, without children. It continued with Izaak Walton's portrait of a henpecked husband cursed with a domineering mother-in-law, a homely, shrewish, incompetent, untrustworthy wife and spiteful children. At the end of the seventeenth century, Anthony Wood described Hooker's wife, Joan, as a "clownish, silly woman, and withal a mere Xantippe" (a reference to Socrates' mate who gave her name to the prototypical ill-tempered, scolding wife.)[5]

These gross misrepresentations persist into our own day. As we have noted earlier, at the base of Hooker's statue in Exeter, a tour guide intimated that Hooker was a simpleton in affairs of the heart who was seduced by a designing woman and her mother. It is far more likely that the "judicious" Hooker made a most fortunate marriage and was a devoted, much loved husband and son-in-law and a caring father.

When Richard and Joan first met, probably in 1584, he was an accomplished and confident thirty-year old Oxford don with a promising future. Although he had no wealth of his own, Richard was of respectable lineage. He already had excellent connections with several of the most powerful figures in the church and the universities.

---

[5] These false characterizations began after Hooker's death during Chancery Court trials in which his daughters sued the family of Joan's second husband, Edward Nethrsole, who had swindled them out of their inheritance. In order to discredit Joan, the Nethersoles spread false stories about her character. Hooker's first biographer, Izakk Walton, heard these stories in the seventeenth century from two of his Aunt's, who had been friends of the Nethersoles, and he recorded them uncritically in his wrting about Joan. Subsequent writers took these tales at face value until C. J. Sisson discovered the truth in the twentieth century. (See bibliography.).

And Joan, then aged about seventeen, was the oldest daughter of one of the most prominent business leaders in London. She lived with her parents, five siblings, and several servants in a grand house within sight of St. Paul's Cathedral and was accustomed to the constant comings and goings of wealthy and powerful men, with their incessant conversations about the great issues of the day——men who happily accepted the hospitality of her politically active father in his large house on Watling Street.

As a young woman growing up in Elizabethan England, Joan was schooled at home in the domestic arts and graces. By every means available, her parents raised her to become a dutiful wife, a producer of many children, a good manager of her future husband's domestic affairs and the spiritual core of her own future family. She learned by absorbing the atmosphere of the times that her major role in life would be as a devout Christian wife and mother. Because she was the daughter of prosperous London parents, Joan received at least a smattering of the education normally reserved for male children. She was among the estimated twenty-five percent of London girls of her day who could read and write. As such, she was exposed to some of the important religious and moral writings of the Reformation and at least a smattering of some of the Greek and Roman classics.

Joan's father, an enlightened and progressive man, was determined that his daughters make good matches and be a credit to him as successful wives and mothers so he may have employed a young cleric to tutor his girls. The clergy in London were eager to spread their religious ideology among young women. In fact, it was their intention to convert women to their points of view and, by all accounts, they had much success in this effort.

By the time Joan and Richard were married, on 13 February 1588, Richard, at thirty-three, was a promising cleric at one of the most important churches in London and had already achieved notoriety as the antagonist of the great Presbyterian scholar and preacher, Walter Travers. For her part, Joan was a mature young woman of about twenty, ready to assume her role as the mistress of an important clerical household. The "virgin queen" of England might not approve of her major clerics taking wives, and Richard might be somewhat older than most grooms of his generation, but in no significant respect was their marriage unusual. In fact, it was typical of their day (and ours) for a professionally rising but financially struggling man to marry a younger, wealthier woman. The bachelor's experience and promise matched the young woman's energy and dowry--two necessary ingredients for her to bear many children and manage a large household.

From their first days together in 1584, Joan was probably attracted to Richard. She was a mature young woman who knew she would make an attractive mate for one of the available men who frequented her father's house. Richard would have seemed different to her from the rest--older, quieter, more considerate of her feelings, more attentive--a good match for her own more assertive personality.

It is fair to deduce from Joan's recorded actions later in her life,[6] and from a discounted reliance on the aforementioned biased accounts of her relations with Richard, that she was a self-reliant, intelligent woman of high spirit. Although perhaps not a beauty, her assets were a good mind, a healthy body, a confident will. She was, no doubt, too aggressive and self-assured for some people. Her mother probably warned her about that. But Joan wondered how a woman was to survive in this man's world, unless she was sure of herself and what she wanted out of life.

The attraction was probably less instantaneous for Richard. During his first years at the Temple, he had more on his mind than love and marriage. He was fully occupied with the challenge of learning his new job, while at the same time dealing with Walter Travers and his obstructionist friends. Furthermore, he was aware that matrimony would only be an impediment to further advancement in the church.

Still, he could not help but notice the young woman who greeted him with a kiss many evenings when he arrived home at the Churchmans, a lovely custom reserved for house guests. Was he really still a guest? He caught himself watching Joan as she walked around the house with her long hair flowing freely in the manner of unmarried women of the day, blossoming before his eyes. It was a stimulating sight. Up to this point in his life, the only females Hooker had known were his mother,

---

[6] Shortly after Richard's death in 1600, Joan remarried, to Edward Nethersole, a leading citizen and former mayor of Canterbury. Nethersole turned out to be a scoundrel who cheated Joan out of her considerable inheritance. Joan resisted as best she could and after she died her three surviving daughters carried on for years in Chancery Court in London to reclaim their inheritance.

whom he could scarcely remember and while he boarded occasionally at uncle John's house in Exeter, his aunt Anastasia and baby cousins Anne, Grace, and Alice.

Their courtship lasted for about a year. Since they were already living together in the same house, it was a simple and convenient matter for them to experience the cohabitation that preceded many, if not most, marriages in Elizabethan England. After they were married, rather little changed in their domestic routine except that they shared the same bedroom on a regular basis and probably continued to enjoy the pleasures of a happy and vigorous sexual relationship.

In the summer of 1585 Richard and Joan decided to make a formal spousal announcement. John and Alice Churchman would have invited some friends for dinner to witness the proclamation and to assure that the espousal (engagement ceremony) was a festive occasion. Such an event was necessary to satisfy the legal and social requirements for marriage. However, Richard and his in-laws wanted a full church ceremony as well, following the traditional posting of wedding bans in church for three Sundays. Hooker believed in the sacramental nature of marriage and would be joined in that holy estate only by a minister of God using the rites of the Church of England.

As for John Churchman, he wanted a church wedding with a lavish reception to follow. His position as rising master of the Merchant Tailor's guild required nothing less. In fact, he would be disgraced socially if this were not a memorable affair. He would have invited his important friends and associates to the wedding of his oldest daughter. In addition to his colleagues at Merchant Tailors, the guest list would have included some of the most prominent people in London and in the church hierarchy, men like the lord mayor, the treasurers of Middle and Inner Temple Inns of Court, the Dean of St. Paul's, the Bishop of London.

The Sandys family was no doubt well represented by Miles, his sons, William and Miles and of course Edwin and his wife, who was ill at the time and would die within the year. Also invited would have been Edwin's older brother Samuel and his sister Margaret, who had married Francis Evington, a prominent merchant tailor, in this very church in 1575.[7]

---

[7] This was the same Evington who later served as trustee for the estate of Joan Hooker when her daughters were seeking to secure their inheritance from the family of Joan's second husband, Edward Nethersole.

George Cranmer was, no doubt, in attendance, along with members of his family, including younger brother William and sisters Susannah and Dorothy. These were the two women who, many years later, while living with Izaak Walton, would provide Hooker's famed biographer with bits of unflattering and inaccurate gossip about the young bride they watched so keenly on this happy day.

On February 13, 1588, John Churchman gave his daughter Joan in marriage to Richard Hooker in a service at St. Augustine's, the family parish next door to his home on Watling Street. The ceremony was all that Hooker could hope for. Alexander Nowell was probably present for the service. That spry octogenarian, whose grants had helped finance Richard's college education, was still Dean of St. Paul's, where he had presided since 1560. He would have been helped across Old Change Street to witness the ceremony and congratulate the Master of the Temple Church. John Aylmer, Bishop of London, may also have been in the sanctuary. And, Hooker's friend and colleague, the renowned Lancelot Andrewes, soon to be the new Dean of St. Paul's, may have helped officiate. Hooker's high standing in the Church would have required the presence and participation of such leading London clerics.

The service began with the beautiful opening words from the 1559 *Book of Common Prayer*:

> Dearly beloved friends, we are gathered here in the sight of God, and in the face of this congregation, to join together this man and this woman in holy matrimony, which is an honorable estate, instituted of God in paradise, in the time of man's innocence: signifying unto us the mystical union, that is between Christ and his church: which holy estate Christ adorned and beautified with his presence and first miracle that he wrought in Cana of Galilee. . .

Following the exchange of vows, the remainder of the service lasted about an hour. Richard and Joan may have held hands and heard the minister read the 127th Psalm, exhorting them to be fruitful and have children. They knelt together at the Lord's Table, recited the Lord's

Prayer, received communion, as required of all who are married in the Church of England. They sat in the choir and listened to a short homily on marriage by the rector. Finally, they heard the prescribed passage from Paul's Epistle to the Ephesians on the subject of the duties of husbands and wives to one another.

After the wedding, a lavish reception was undoubtedly held at the Churchman's house next door to the church, the house where Richard and Joan would make their permanent home. The guests making the short walk to the house would have been resplendently attired in the highest fashions suitable to their standings as leading merchants, jurists and clerics of the day: John and his colleagues in long silk brocaded robes over their finest doublets and slops (breeches), silk stockings and leather sandals; Alice and the other women, defying growing objections from Puritans to sartorial display, showing off elegant gowns of fine Italian silk, trimmed in Flemish lace, many in the latest French style with billowing sleeves and tiara-shaped black velvet hats. Inside the house, the guests would have been treated to an assortment of roasts, pies, cheeses, puddings—and malmsey, the strong sweet wine from Madeira so favored by the English of the day.

——— Married Life ———

There is no reason to doubt that Hooker found affection and emotional support, as well as some peace and joy in his marriage to Joan Churchman, as they settled into her father's house. It is fair to assume that Richard and Joan were part of the new trend toward a marriage based on mutual affection in which husband and wife chose each other as mates and then clung closely to one another for mutual support and nurture in a rapidly changing and often threatening social environment.

The sort of personal affection and intimacy that Richard now experienced with Joan he had not known since he was a very small boy living with his mother in Heavitree. No longer was he a lonely free-floating soul, solely dependent for his well-being on his own wits, the admiration and camaraderie of fellow intellectuals and clerics and the patronage of powerful benefactors. Now he could share his deepest hopes and fears, as well the normal events of his day, with a person who was a helpmate, lover, and friend--a woman who might occasionally offer some balm to his troubled spirit and help him to achieve deeper levels of self-confidence.

On a practical level, Hooker knew that he had achieved a good marriage. He had joined one of London's leading merchant families and thus acquired a social standing to match his high post at the Temple Church. Joan's undoubtedly handsome dowry, coupled with her father's broader financial resources and political influence, assured Richard a freedom from the monetary woes that had plagued his entire life. From this point on he would feel freer to make career choices not dictated solely by financial considerations.

During 1588 Richard was drawn into a plethora of small crises, most of them centering on the failure of younger members of the Inns of Court to attend worship services as required by the law of the land and the rules of the two Inns. Many of the lawyers and students living at the Inns found the prescribed services either too romanist or too evangelical for their taste. Some resented being required to attend any religious service at all. In late June, there was an order from the Inner Temple that any member who resided in chambers or ate in commons for as little as one week must attend services at the Temple Church weekly or pay a fine of twelve pence for each absence, unless he had been specifically granted permission to miss the service.

Hooker did not enjoy his inevitable role as enforcer of these attendance requirements and other rules he was expected to monitor. He especially disliked enforcing long-standing orders against women or "strangers" attending services at the Temple Church. He also found it stressful to hunt down the culprits who occasionally stole money from the Temple poor box, or to report students he saw wearing high boots, cloaks or hats in town. He knew that they could be dismissed on a second breach of this rule.

Richard Walter was one of a number of students expelled from Middle Temple for refusing to attend religious services. Since he and his friends had strong papist leanings, they may have thought Hooker would sympathize with them. When they refused to take Communion despite several warnings, Hooker had to report them to their bench and they were expelled.

Hooker may have felt some responsibility for the expulsions since his sermons seemed to support Catholics and might have prompted Walters and his fellow pro-Catholic students to think that the Master would champion their cause, or at least not report them for failing to practice their religion in the prescribed Calvinist manner. At all events, Hooker did not like being put in the position of judging and condemning the religious acts of others. He was learning, however painfully, that this was a price he had to pay for being Master of the Temple or holding any position of high responsibility. He began to think that this was too high a price to pay for fame and power.

Late in the spring of 1588, Joan told her husband that she was pregnant. The couple decided that if the baby were a boy they would name him Richard and if a girl, Alice, for Joan's mother. It is noteworthy that Richard's mother, Joan, was not chosen as a namesake, a further indication of her negligible role in Hooker's life.

As summer turned to autumn and the first hints of winter were borne on late October winds, Joan's pregnancy progressed apace with the Walter affair. That young gentleman continued to absent himself from required holy communion as a demonstration of his opposition to the prescribed services, while at the same time making regular entreaty for reinstatement at Middle Temple Inn. On 25 October, Middle Temple parliament ordered Walter to arrange conferences with Master Hooker. Richard was to examine Walter's religious opinions and ascertain whether his beliefs were heretical or even treasonous. Only if the Master certified that Walter was in conformity with established church doctrine and practice and that he was indeed attending services, would his petition for reinstatement be considered.

Hooker had already been meeting with Walter and other non-conformists--Catholics and advanced Calvinists alike. He wished to save them from persecution by the government as well as from further discipline by their inns. The entire process was not to his liking as it required him to make the very judgments he condemned in others. Yet he had no choice but to do his best to convince Walter and others to conform.

Walter explained to the Master that he believed he should be free to celebrate communion according to whatever rite suited his conscience. The Roman mass had been accepted here in England since time immemorial and had been the preference of Walter's family for centuries. He was a loyal subject of the Queen and rejoiced in the defeat of the Armada as surely as any Englishman. But how he worshipped should be his own affair.

Such an argument sorely tested Hooker's instinct for toleration. He told the student that what he believed was between himself and God but what he practiced in public must conform to the laws of England and the practice of the established church. England was a Christian commonwealth whose prince headed the church and whose bishops decided what kind of public religious practice would be followed by all citizens. Fortunately, the Queen had cut a wide swath for her people to follow. But it was a defined path nonetheless. To allow each of us to go his own way would produce anarchy and a godless society. Surely, Mr. Walter could understand that.

After several conferences, Hooker made enough progress in moderating Walter's passion for the mass that he felt comfortable making the necessary certification to Middle Ttemple to secure his restoration to that society. But that august body was not satisfied with the Master's recommendation. Carried away with the national hysteria over the Spanish invasion, they required that Walter put in writing for the house treasurer, Miles Sandys, his "detestation of all popish religion." Walter did so and, in February of 1589, was restored to his place at the Inn. By May, he was formally reinstated as "associate to the Bench" and allowed to "sit with them at their table."

Hooker undoubtedly hated the entire ordeal. It put into sharp focus a major dilemma of the English Reformation: how to assure freedom of conscience without weakening the authority of the church and disrupting the social order. This was a problem much easier to solve intellectually than in real cases involving real people. The Walter episode, combined with countless similar events, taught Richard a hard lesson about himself, one that he had begun to learn in his distasteful pulpit debate with Travers. He was discovering that he lacked the stomach for public leadership. Rainolds, Sandys, Aylmer, Whitgift, even Travers, were able to do what had to be done to other people in order to achieve religious goals which he often shared. He was able to make such painful decisions but only at great cost to his sense of well-being. It hurt him too much to judge and condemn others. He was in the process of learning that his true calling was elsewhere. He would analyze, write, preach, instruct, console, perhaps even inspire but, as soon as possible, he would remove himself from the political arena.

.   .   .   .   .

Like other Londoners in the late 1580's, Richard and Joan lived with the normal vicissitudes of private life--in their case, a first pregnancy for Joan and daily mounting pressures at the Temple Church and Inns of Court for Richard, in the midst of the great public events of the day: first, traumatic fear of impending Spanish invasion, then the patriotic catharsis over national victory. The fear of, and then the salvation from, conquest by the forces of Catholic Spain formed the dramatic backdrop for the Hookers' personal lives throughout most of this period.

Philip of Spain was on a holy crusade for the pope. His aim was to reestablish the Catholic religion in England. Jesuits and other papists were being arrested and imprisoned daily. Public executions for treason were common. An army was forming at Tilbury, commanded by Leicester. Men were arriving from all over England to join the fight. Large chains and cables had been linked and stretched across the Thames between Gravesend and Tilbury to keep out the Spanish fleet. Food in the city was scarce. Livestock had been driven inland so the Spaniards could not get it when they landed. Fresh meat was not on the menu at the Churchman's these days.

The Spanish fleet(armada) had been sighted in the channel off Plymouth! The alarm had gone out. Beacon lights were burning all along the coast from Cornwall to Dunkirk and inland as far north as the Scottish border. The Churchmans, like other prosperous Londoners with domiciles outside the city, made arrangements to leave London ahead of Admiral Sidonia's feared appearance off Margate and the Duke of Parma's invading army. It was much too dangerous for them in the city, especially with Joan's baby on the way. They were prepared, on short notice, to travel north to the safety of their country home at Enfield.

There was some fighting at sea but Parma was unable to land his troops. There would be neither an invasion nor a major sea battle. Some said the Armada had been scuttled by storms and the remaining ships were heading back to Spain. Spanish corpses lined English shores. The Queen's favorite, Lord Cecil, received a letter from Ireland reporting that over a thousand of those poor Spanish souls were washed up along just five miles of coastline in Sligo Bay in the far northwest of Ireland, just south of Donegal.

The important fact was that the Armada was defeated. Only half the Spanish ships made it home. The smaller English navy, with the help of God, had whipped them and saved England from Spain, the pope, and Roman Catholicism. God save the Queen!

Tiny Richard Hooker was born in mid-February, 1589 and was christened almost immediately at St Augustine's. Richard sensed, as he held his infant son during the baptismal service that the baby would not live long. The ceremony had more the aura of a funeral than a christening. Joan's confinement and delivery had not gone well. The family had feared for her life. John and Alice even considered having the fetus cut out in hopes of saving their daughter's life. Fortunately for Joan, this dangerous procedure was not performed.

When the baby arrived, he unhealthy, a scrawny bluish little tike who cried incessantly and pitifully for several hours and then only intermittently. Joan's milk came but the baby had trouble nursing. After a few days, little Richard stopped crying but slept fitfully, his tiny body twitching occasionally in small involuntary convulsions. From time to time, he would awaken and whimper softly.

Like other couples of their day, Joan and Richard were conditioned to expect the death of children, especially infants. Poor health of mothers, primitive birthing methods, rampant disease, especially in the city, were facts of life for them, facts that made infant mortality a common experience. Still, the realization of impending loss caused deep pain, especially for Joan. They decided to go to Enfield immediately in hopes that the better air there would revive the baby, but they knew that this was a desperate remedy, especially in the dead of winter. They probably hired a carrier's wagon for Joan and the baby, as neither of them was well enough to travel by horse and litter.

12. St. Andrew's Enfield

They had traveled along the road north out of the city before. It was often crowded with elaborate carriages carrying nobility and wealthy merchants to and from their country estates in the rich farmlands, pastures, and game forests stretching along the west bank of the River Lea all the way from Tottenham to Ware. The way led through Edmondton, then a small town not nearly so large or important a place as Enfield.

From time to time, Richard and Joan spied black-frocked clerics riding by on fast horses, either alone or in pairs. On a few occasions these men rode together with a well-dressed man or woman, obviously of high breeding. These were fleeing Catholic priests with their rich protectors. There was a tradition that this stretch along the river from Tottenham to Enfield was a safe haven for Catholic recusants, many of whom kept illegal priests more or less hidden in their homes. The principal focus of this activity was the Arundell family which maintained a large estate at Tottenham, as well as their famed palace on the Strand.

During the early years of Elizabeth's reign, Catholics such as Sir John Arundell and his friends were fined heavily for not attending the prescribed Protestant services.

Less cultivated travelers sharing the roadway with the Hookers on this February day were the Enfield maltmen bouncing along the deeply rutted road in their wagons, heavy-laden with great wooden vats of liquid malt called wort that had been purchased in Enfield. During the coldest months of winter, when the Lea was frozen over, these entrepreneurs hauled their valuable cargo along this road to the brewers and bakers of London. They were a rowdy lot, although usually no direct threat to respectable travelers except for their rough manners and a tendency to hog the road, forcing other riders into the ditches.

When Richard and his little family finally arrived in Enfield town, they probably stopped at the lovely parish church of St. Andrew to rest before proceeding on to the Churchman home. The Hookers were frequent worshipers here in Enfield, and the vicar, Leonard Chambers, and Richard were probably friends. Although St. Andrew's and the school attached to it faced onto the busy town marketplace, they were surrounded on three sides by woods and pleasant fields. This was a far cry from the sprawling, argumentative public arena of Hooker's Temple Church in London. Surely it would be so much easier to pray, think, study, write and raise a family in such a place as this, away from the broiling turmoil of London.

Baby Richard died and was buried in the cemetery at St. Andrew's after a short service for the family and a few friends conducted by Mr. Chambers. Joan Hooker would have more children, for a while at the rate of one per year, but the pain of the loss of her first child was obviously hard to bear.

By the time Joan returned to the Watling Street house in late spring, her spirits were much revived. She had the demanding daily routine of a prosperous young London housewife to distract her. There was much for her and her mother to do to manage this busy household. In addition to the needs of her younger siblings, there was Edwin Sandys, who had moved in with his second wife and three servants as more or less permanent house guests. Sandys' friends, including one of her husband's favorites, George Cranmer, were also frequent visitors. And of course her father had a steady stream of personal friends and business associates staying in the house. The convenient location of their domicile and John's position in the city made their home a magnet for guests.

Alice Churchman was glad to have her daughter at home to help with the many chores of running such a household. With servants to do most of heavy labor, the two women were responsible for tending the garden and harvesting its yields, fetching water from the well, shopping daily for food, yard goods and other necessaries. Indoors there was a host of chores that filled their day from before dawn until bedtime at nine or ten in the evening: planning and sometimes cooking and serving meals, cleaning, sewing, weaving, brewing, caring for the children, supervising the servants, entertaining their husbands' friends and guests.

When Joan, like other Elizabethan women, finally climbed into bed at the end of her long day and snuffed out her last candle, she was expected to respond to her husband's needs before she could go to sleep, or she might decide to arouse him to satisfy her desires. This might be a routine performance or a joyful romp, depending of the compatibility of the couple. With the exception of the emerging Puritans who were to dominate the next century, Elizabethans were not prudish in such matters. Women were sufficiently liberated to enjoy themselves in bed, even to the point of being the initiators of the fun. The church smiled on marital sex. The lively secular culture abounded with encouragements to sexual frolicking.

We may confidently assume that Joan and Richard were a compatible Elizabethan couple who loved each other and entered as fully and joyfully into all aspects of their marriage as any of their contemporaries in that lusty and uninhibited age. When they were in reasonably good health and Joan was not nearing childbirth, they ended many of their days in one another's arms.

— Chapter 9 —

Penman For The Church

— The Call —

What motivated Hooker to take up his pen and write a book that would become the definitive *apologia* for the Anglican Church? The answer to this question has long been a subject of speculation. Some have said, although no surviving documentation survives to prove it, that he was commissioned, formally or informally, by Archbishop Whitgift to write a defense of the church. Others have claimed that Hooker was so enraged by Travers' treatment of him in their debate at the Temple that he was psychologically driven to continue the argument in print. Another view is that he wrote the *Laws* primarily for his own intellectual satisfaction. A prevailing opinion is that Hooker was drafted by Edwin Sandys, George Cranmer and perhaps others, to write a polemical tract to assist them in efforts to crush the Puritans through legislative action in the Parliament of 1593.

To these explanations, each of which holds part of the answer to Hooker's motivation, we need to add that he was an introspective scholar who by dint of training and habit preferred to engage the issues of the day with his pen rather than with his voice. He learned from his tenure in the pulpit at the Temple that a public debating forum was not a congenial environment for him. He also learned that he cared deeply about the issues of the day and wanted to address them on behalf of the church in a more coherent and lasting manner than had been done thus far.

The primary motivation for Hooker to write his great work came from within himself. It is quite unnecessary to postulate a direct commission, either from the primatial See or from Edwin Sandys and other political figures, in order to explain Hooker's decision to write *Of the Laws of Ecclesiastical Polity*. His love for the church, which had nurtured him emotionally and intellectually for most of his life, his scholarly instinct to look beneath the surface of immediate arguments of convenience for important truths, his natural desire to best the famous Walter Travers and his presbyterian friends by shifting the venue for their debate from political polemic (oral or written) to a more serious intellectual ground and his simple human ambition to make a name for himself in the church in an arena where his talents excelled, were all drives within him conspiring and leading him to take up his pen on behalf of his beloved church and country and of his own inner needs for self-justification and recognition.

But was it necessary for Hooker to leave his secure post as Master of the Temple in order to write? Surely he could find time to write, along with his other duties. Other clerics of the day did so. His wife must have raised just this question when Richard told her that he asked the Archbishop, some time in 1589, to find him another position. She was not keen about an unnecessary career change which would cost her, in one stroke, the prestige of being married to the Master of the Temple Church and her desirable and convenient home at a good address in London. Why should her husband want to leave a position which assured him access to the libraries, printers and political connections that were so important to a writer? Surely London, then as now, was the place to be for an aspiring writer--or an aspiring anything, for that matter. Joan no doubt urged her husband to be sensible, remain at the Temple, endure some of the administrative annoyances there, delegate more of the clerical duties and settle in to write his tracts-- especially since she was pregnant again.

Perhaps another reason Hooker wished to leave the Temple was that he no longer felt challenged now that Travers was gone. Life had settled into something of an annoying routine. Perhaps he was bored. While some might find challenge in administrative detail, a man with an expansive imagination could be stifled by such tedium. Much as he had been stressed by the controversy with Travers and its aftermath, he may have missed the challenge to use his talents and energies to meet the Puritan threat and to secure his own credibility as Master of the Temple. Those had been difficult years, even dangerous, but nevertheless invigorating. By early 1589, the Armada was gone, the papist conspiracies crushed and the Puritans, with notable exceptions, in retreat. Most of the challenges in his career had waned. Now his days may often have seemed filled with routine activity.

Some of this he did not mind. He enjoyed the informal intellectual discussions at the Inns on theological and legal issues. He was happy to give advice and direction to some of the younger lawyers who came to him for counsel on a variety of matters, personal and professional. He relished the opportunity to use his influence from time to time to help a gifted student gain admission to one of the societies. However, much of his daily routine involved such unpleasant administrative tasks as enforcing church attendance, listening to constant carping from die-hard Puritans at the Inns about his use of established liturgical forms, and mediating disputes on matters that did not interest him.

For example, he was asked by Miles Sandys, treasurer at Middle Temple, to help resolve a dispute between the two Inns, at about the time of the Queen's procession in 1589. It was a petty issue, but important to the residents at each house. For a year or more there had been ongoing discussions about the need to repave the path from Middle Temple gate on Fleet Street down to the river. The two societies were unable to agree on how to finance the project, so Middle Temple just went ahead on its own, had the work done and sent a bill to Inner Temple for its half of the cost. Not surprisingly, that society refused to pay since they had never agreed to the terms. They insisted that Miles Sandys meet with a delegation from their house to explain why they should share in the cost of a job they had never approved. Was this to be the stuff of Hooker's career?

In addition to his desire for a more challenging but less contentious assignment, Hooker had another reason to believe that it was time to leave the Temple. He feared that his performance here might have been found wanting by the Archbishop and others in authority. He worried that his perceived Catholic leanings had made him *persona non grata* at the Temple and that he would soon be pressured to leave. There may, in fact, have been a fortuitous coincidence of the Archbishop's desire to remove Hooker from the Temple and Hooker's own wish to repair to a quieter living where he could study and write in peace.

As it turned out, Hooker did stay on at the Temple long after Travers' departure in 1587. He did not leave until 1591 when he accepted largely absentee livings at Salisbury and Boscombe in Wiltshire, staying on at the Churchman house to pursue his research and writing. As we will shortly see, it was not until 1595 that he finally left London altogether to accept a full-time residential cure in Bishopsbourne, Kent. By early 1589 Hooker's attention was turning more and more to what he by now regarded as the unfinished business of his debate with Walter Travers.

It is not so difficult to read Hooker's mind at this point. The Church of England could be destroyed by these constant attacks from radical Calvinists if her potential genius as a broad, tolerant, inclusive, *via media* between extremes was not fully explicated. No one had adequately explained the special quality of this reformed English church or set forth fully how it was grounded in God's law and in the history of England. Hooker thought he knew what this church was but no one, including himself, had adequately held up that vision. The definitive *apologia* for his beloved Church of England had yet to be written. Certainly he had not succeeded in articulating a clear picture of it within the compass of occasional polemical sermons in his Temple debate with Travers. In fact, that whole experience had demeaned the importance of the enduring issues raised by the Reformation in England. Sermons were not the medium for this work, nor were polemical tracts that merely refuted the attacks of the church's opponents. What was required was a thoughtful written exposition that went back to the first principles of human experience.

This would be a monumental undertaking but one that would prove ultimately to be the calling of his life. He would write the apology for the Church of England to explain and defend the church he loved. By late spring of 1589 he was well into the writing of his immortal defense of the church and by autumn had settled into a daily routine of reading and composition.

The first unveiling of the outline and preface of the *Laws* was offered to Edwin Sandys and George Cranmer who were living at the Churchman's while in London. Hooker respected the opinion of his friends, both of whom were good scholars. More importantly, they were sophisticated and experienced in the politics of religious debate in England and could give him advice on that score. Richard also had given his father-in-law word of what he was up to. With characteristic generosity, Churchman found extra space in his large but crowded house for Hooker to work on his book.

Hooker's first explanation to his friends about his project concerned his title: *Of the Laws of Ecclesiastical Polity.* His intention in the title, he explained, was to suggest two important points. First, that the key issue dividing members of the Church of England was church structure and governance and that within that framework were contained most of th important theological and liturgical issues of the day. On other matters, most everyone who was not a Catholic was some kind of reformed Calvinist. The second point he wished to make in the title was that, whatever the correct form of church polity might be, it would be discovered only by examining the fundamental laws of God and man, some of which were to be found in the customary practices of Englishmen.

Hooker's general plan for the work was to address the issues raised by Calvinist extremists, not by rushing in and refuting them one at a time, but by first examining the nature of all truth and knowledge and then addressing the question of how we discover the right answers to any important question. Next, he would discuss in detail types of law and which kinds govern which parts of our lives. His purpose here would be to demonstrate that it is law and not personal whim that governs all life, human and divine.

Addressing the epistemological issue--how we know what we know-- Hooker planned to deal in Book II of his work with the issue of whether scripture is the only source of knowledge of God's law. In Book III he would explore which forms of church governance are lawful. Book IV would deal with specific objections that had been made by Puritans and others against the laws of the English church polity.

He would use law as the organizing principle of his treatise. This was the best way he knew to shift the argument from the Puritan ground of self-authenticating scripture as the source of all knowledge. With this approach he had at least a hope of reaching some lawyers and intellectuals among moderates, men with good minds who already suspected the emotional appeals of extreme Calvinists. Grounding his argument in law and reason, rather than personal opinion, might give his ideas a wider appeal among influential people.

As for the more vexing practical issues of whether bishops or elders should govern the church, the role of the crown in church governance and whether church and state should be separated Hooker would deal with these matters in Books VI, VII and VIII. In Book V he would set forth and explain the virtues of the Church of England, especially its liturgy. He would refute specific complaints, notably those of Thomas Cartwright, but would also seek to rise above current conflicts to talk in positive ways about the glory and majesty of the liturgy and theology of the English church. He intended to demonstrate that this church had its own distinctive character among the Christian churches of the world and to show what its special spirit was.

As we know from their comments on Hooker's work, Sandys and Cranmer were generally pleased with the outline, except for what they saw as insufficient attention given to immediate political threats to the church and government from parliamentary Puritans. They had more interest in the Preface than in other parts of the work. Parliament would be reconvening within a year or so and they wanted Hooker to speak in his Preface directly to the issues of the day by attacking the political agenda of the Puritans, ridiculing their leaders and generally displaying his considerable rhetorical flair for political polemic.

In the event, Sandys and Cranmer, were never to be completely satisfied that Hooker was partisan enough in his Preface or other parts of the work to suit their more narrow political agenda. They eventually applied enough pressure on their mentor to induce him to add a final section to the Preface in which he displayed his rhetorical skills to the fullest in the cause of refuting the extreme Calvinism of the presbyterians and separatists.

In the Preface, Hooker displayed his gift for satire when he demonstrated the way in which, in his opinion, radical Calvinists manipulated Scripture to suit their purposes and then preyed on the gullible and weak-minded with simplistic appeals to people's natural suspicions and fears of authority. He laid bare Puritan tactics, exposing their uses of the Bible--how they induced people to find whatever suited their fancy in the Bible. "They fashion," he wrote, "the very notions and conceits of men's understanding in such sort, that when they read scripture, they may think that everything soundeth towards the advancement of that [Calvinist] discipline and to the utter disgrace of the contrary."

Hooker compared the method of Calvinist extremists like Cartwright with that of Pythagoras, thereby making his point very clear to anyone with a university education. In one place, he wrote words which have become a timeless attack on unsophisticated uses of Holy Scripture:

> When they and their Bibles are alone together, what strange fantastical opinion so-ever at any time entered into their heads, their use was to think the Spirit taught it them.

In another passage, which no doubt pleased Cranmer and Sandys, Hooker chastised Calvinist extremists for encouraging emotion, simplicity, self-righteousness and resistance to established authority-- and for disparaging education and higher learning as aids to discovering God.

> [Let] any man of contrary opinion open his mouth to persuade them, they close up their ears; his reasons they weigh not. All is answered with rehearsal of the words of John: 'We are of God; He that knoweth God heareth us; as for the rest, ye are of the world, for this world's pomp and vanity it is that you speak, and the world whose you are hears you. . .' Show these eagerly-affected men their inability to judge of such matters, their answer is: 'God has chosen the simple.' Convince them of [their] folly, and that so plainly that children upbraid them with it, and they say. . .'Christ's own apostle was counted mad. . .'

Hooker did not base all truth on formal scholarship. His appeal in the Preface to common sense as a basis for knowledge of God's will was a way of saying that truth is available to all thinking people, not just to professors and legal scholars. He made this point directly.

> The first means whereby nature teaches men to judge good from evil. . .is the force of our own discretion. . .[so that] whatsoever we do, if our own secret judgment consents not to it as fit and good to be done, the doing of it is to us a sin. . . . Some things are so familiar and

plain that truth from falsehood and good from evil are most easily discerned in them, even by men of no deep capacity. And in the same way, for the most part, are things absolutely necessary to all men's salvation either to be held or denied, either to be done or avoided.

Now that he had his outline in hand and a draft of the Preface completed and reviewed by a few friends, Hooker proceeded to work on the rest of his opus. Even with his duties at the Temple and family responsibilities as distractions, he calculated that he could have the entire work done by sometime in late 1592 or early '93. In the meantime, there remained the vexing business of securing Archbishop Whitgift's approval for the project and along with that, a new appointment somewhere outside the Temple.

———— The Commission To Write ————

In early May of 1590, Joan Hooker gave birth to a healthy baby girl who was christened on 10 May at St Augustine's Church, next door--the Church where Joan and Richard had been married two years earlier. The baby was named Alice, after Joan's mother, who by this time no doubt was a surrogate mother to Richard as well. Of the six children who would grace their marriage, Alice was the only one destined to have a long life.

At about this time Hooker probably had a meeting with Archbishop Whitgift, either on his own initiative or Whitgift's' to discuss his future. Any hope Hooker had for receiving a specific commission to write a defense of the church, much less receive financial backing for such a project, was disappointed. The Archbishop had already asked two other church leaders to undertake this work: Richard Bancroft, Bishop of London, and Thomas Cooper, Bishop of Winchester.

Coincident with Whitgift's failure to provide official sanction for Hooker's writings, was his failure to offer the Master of the Temple Church further advancement. There would be no deanship, much less a bishopric. Hooker's expressed views on Catholics were apparently too radical for the Archbishop; or, he may just have been annoyed at Hooker's desire to leave the Temple post. In any event, Whitgift extended an informal blessing upon Hooker's project, wished him well on its completion, and asked to be kept apprised of progress. He also promised to relieve Richard of his duties as Master of the Temple Church as soon as he could find a suitable living for him elsewhere, an appointment that would leave him more time for research and writing.

Throughout the remainder of 1590 and for most of the following year, Richard spent most of his spare time working on his book. Whitgift had made available his modest library at Lambeth Palace where Richard could find the resources he needed, the religious and pagan works of his favorites: Aristotle, Cicero, St Augustine, St Thomas Aquinas, Peter Lombard and others, as well as more recent works by Bodin, Machiavelli, Luther, Erasmus, Calvin, Beza and Jewel, right on up to the contemporary writings of Whitgift, Bancroft, Cartwright, Travers, Penry, Throckmorton, Udall and others. How much more pleasant were the hours spent reading and note-taking at Lambeth library or writing up at Enfield or at the Churchman house, than enduring the constant hassles of his job at the Temple.

A most important support for Richard, as he intensified his work on the book during 1590 and 1591, came not from the church hierarchy but from his father-in-law, who provided not only a retreat from his cares at the Temple, but also the invaluable services of his own secretary and amanuensis, the capable Benjamin Pullen. It was Pullen who, with painstaking diligence, translated Richard's hurried and often careless handwriting into a nearly perfect, printer-ready manuscript. When Hooker finally presented Pullen's copy of his book to the printer in early 1593, it was so beautifully and accurately done that the printer, John Windet, was able to complete the printing with unusual dispatch.

Edwin Sandys was a constant source of help and criticism throughout the long writing process. Living under the same roof allowed for efficient collaboration. Sandys was available to obtain materials from Lambeth, read and correct drafts, discuss ideas, seek out prospective printers and provide ready cash for buying paper, books and other supplies. Although Richard was not always happy with his friend's criticisms, he was grateful for his support and companionship.

George Cranmer also helped by reading drafts and making critical suggestions. Like Sandys, his offerings were substantive, usually urging a more focused attack on radical Puritan opponents of the church. Cranmer was especially keen about assuring accuracy in citations and a high level of scholarly polish. Together, Cranmer and Sandys urged Hooker to a more timely and polemical posture than he was inclined by temperament to assume. Richard's natural disposition was to explain, defend and extol, rather than attack. In time, he learned to take some pleasure in tweaking the advanced Calvinists with his satirical wit--a facility that improved with practice.

One person whose opinions he especially valued during these years of writing was his former tutor and sometime friend, John Rainolds. Despite their many differences on religious questions, Richard respected Rainolds' breadth of knowledge and his talent as a writer. He also coveted the reactions of a churchman and scholar whose views were more radically Calvinist than his own. Edwin Sandys did not share Hooker's high regard for Rainolds. The arch-Calvinist Rainolds was one of the extremists Sandys and his friends were battling in the political arena. Rainolds had recently been advocating at Oxford that all absentee livings in the church end immediately and that from now on there should be an emphasis on preaching over sacramental liturgies and a greater allowance of lay elders in congregational governance. He had even argued against excommunication as a punishment for heresy. On top of all that, a witness in Star Chamber had recently cited Rainolds for being a member of the illegal presbyterian classis at Oxford back in the 80s. Clearly this man was no friend of either the episcopacy or the *Book of Common Prayer*--the two hallmarks of Hooker's ecclesiology.

Nevertheless, Hooker persisted in his desire to have his former mentor's reactions to his drafts and, he hoped, Rainolds' approval of his work. He also wished to be as fair and balanced as possible in his attacks on some of Rainolds' positions and to stay in contact with one of England's most respected theologians.

During the early stages of writing, Hooker also sought the opinions of two other intellectual luminaries of the day. One was John Rainolds' successor as president of Corpus Christi, Dr. John Spenser. On a number of occasions, he sent portions of his manuscript to Spenser and received critical editorial suggestions. Spenser's views were more congenial with his own than Rainolds were, so much so that Hooker, later in life, felt comfortable naming Spenser literary executor of his estate. (The day would come when Spenser would be one of the principal editors of Hooker's writings and the author of a famous introductory epistle to the first posthumous edition of the *Laws* in 1604. Some would later go so far as to claim, mistakenly, I believe, that Spenser had actually authored sections of Hooker's book.)

The other scholar consulted by Hooker in these early years was Dr. Robert Some, master of Peterhouse, Cambridge. Some was an outspoken Puritan, who nevertheless had broken with the extremists during the separatist controversy and had engaged in public debate with both Penry and Throckmorton. Some's *First Godly Treatise*, was among the works Hooker read that had stimulated him to take up his own pen in earnest. From Some, as from Rainolds, Richard sought the view of an advanced Calvinist to give him prior notice of likely objections to his more moderate stance on controversial issues.

.   .   .   .   .

In April, 1591, Joan Hooker gave birth to another daughter. She was christened at St. Augustine's on the 21st of the month. The infant was named Cicely for Edwin Sandy's mother, wife of the redoubtable Archbishop of York. This name choice was further expression of the closeness of these three families: the Churchmans, the Sandys and the Hookers. Cicely Sandys was, by all accounts and by evidence of a surviving portrait, a beautiful woman. She was also a woman of remarkable spirit and intelligence, not unusual in this age of Elizabeth I. Little did the happy parents know on this April day, that, by the time their new daughter was in her teens, they would both be dead and their Cicely would be living with her namesake.

By the end of May, Joan was once again in Enfield, this time with two baby girls, well in advance of the oppressive heat and dangerous pestilence of London.

—— Appointment To Salisbury ——

Richard continued to commute back and forth to London, keeping up a presence at the Temple and spending as much time as possible reading at

Lambeth library and writing in his workroom at the Churchman house. Sometime in the middle of June he received official word from Lambeth that he was to be made a sub-dean and canon at Salisbury Cathedral. The income would be modest but he would be out of the Temple at last and have more time to devote to his book and to his growing family.

Joan would be disappointed by the news. She had hoped for something better from Whitgift. Her husband assured her that they would not have to move to Wiltshire since it was largely an absentee sinecure. Their lives would continue here in London much as they had, except that he would no longer go to the Temple each day and his income would be lower. He was not, after all, to be the dean at Salisbury. A sub-dean could only expect some small rural livings in the surrounding area. The money was not of primary importance, however. John Churchman would continue to provide home and hearth.

There was a living at Netheravon that went with the appointment at the Cathedral and Hooker was also to be rector at the well-endowed parish of Boscombe, just a few kilometers north of the Cathedral. A curate was available, or could be found, to manage the parish on a regular basis and to visit Netherhaven occasionally. Hooker's understanding was that the Archbishop intended these appointments as a way to free him for virtually full-time work on his book.

Hooker's new post at Salisbury was within the Queen's gift because there was no bishop in residence there at the time. Whitgift had taken the first decent opening the Queen had available, knowing how important it was for Hooker to leave the Temple and complete his defense of the church in a timely manner. He wanted to give Hooker an appointment that would allow him to stay in London with his family. The appointment as a minor non-residentiary canon was only to be temporary, until Whitgift could find him a permanent cure. Hooker would not be expected to spend much time at Salisbury or Boscombe.

In July Hooker went to Salisbury for his official installation at the Cathedral. As he rode across the Salisbury plain, down toward the city, past the great neolithic artifacts at Stonehenge, he would surely have recalled his visit to this area many years ago when he was just a raw youth on his way up to Oxford. How young and innocent he was then, filled with untempered awe at his first sight of the tall spire and even more overwhelmed by the towering reputation of his patron, the brilliant John Jewel. Now, nearly a quarter century later, he was returning to Salisbury, a seasoned church leader in his own right, no less in awe of this fabled place, but much better informed about how important Sarum (Salisbury) was to the history of the church.

While at Salisbury, Hooker made his formal subscription to the *Thirty-nine Articles,* signed the chapter register and attended the meeting at which he was installed as canon and member of the Cathedral Chapter. At his first meeting of the Chapter, he met and spent time with Nicholas Fuller of St. John's, Allington, a parish near his own new charge at Boscombe. Fuller was also new to the Bourne Valley, having been at the Cathedral for less than a year. Hooker had known him at Oxford where Fuller had been a leading Hebrew philologist and M.A. at Hart Hall.

Hooker certainly visited his new cure at Bosombe during his stay in Salisbury. St. Andrews, nearly two-hundred years old at the time, was a small Norman church. The exterior stone and flint construction and the interior nave, chancel and north transept are substantially as they were when Hooker first saw them more than four hundred years ago. He may have been somewhat disappointed with the church. The edifice was not so grand as his friend Laurence Chambers' church in Enfield, which he may have coveted, nor so picturesque and pastoral as his own charge at Drayton Beauchamp a decade earlier. He had expected a grander building from the fact that the living at Boscombe had a long and distinguished history and commanded a substantial endowment. Perhaps some day, he may have thought, Whitgift would find him something better than this, a living like his earlier retreat at Drayton Beachamp, but a place close to some great cathedral and library.

—— Of The Laws Of Ecclesiastical Polity ——

It is impossible to know with certainty exactly when the eight books of the *Laws of Ecclesiastical Polity* were completed. It is most likely that by the autumn of 1591, shortly after his return from his installation at Salisbury, Hooker had finished a first draft of the work. As he reviewed the manuscript over the next year or so, he had input from a number of friends and associates, most notably, Edwin Sandys, who was often resident with Hooker at the Churchmans house during those years.

—— Book I ——

Sandys, like most others who have ever read Book I, would have been impressed by Hooker's treatment of the origins and types of law and by his grounding of all human institutions, divine and human, in the reasonableness (lawfulness) of heavenly and divine ordinances. Clearly Hooker's writing in Book I ranks with the finest theoretical treatments of law and civil society. His exposition of the reasonableness of law, and his demonstration of how obedience to it is connected to God's rational purposes, is probably unparalleled in English writing. Not only did Book I serve as a superb introduction to the rest of the *Laws*, but it was, in its own right, a complete treatise. If Hooker had written nothing more, his place as a premier political philosopher would have been assured by this treatise.

Hooker defined law in such a broad way as to identify it with the order, harmony and reasonableness of all creation and not merely what could be enforced by a powerful ruler. He sought to provide a basis for distinguishing lawful from unlawful acts of rulers and subjects alike. The distinguishing characteristic of a law was not the sanctions behind it but the reasonableness of its commands. He asserted that the purpose (object) of a law, properly named, is virtue, goodness, the well-being of those upon whom it acts. Law is whatever reason defines as goodness and requires that we pursue. If a precept has been assented to in a commonwealth for a long time, there is a presumption that it is reasonable and hence a true law. We might say that law is reason embodied in custom. If an ordinance promotes virtue, conforms to custom and appeals to the common sense of our reason, it is probably a law.

The contrary claim of some followers of Calvin that all law comes from God and that He revealed His law only in scripture is an error, according to Hooker, because this opinion fails to account for the fact that so many of our laws, rightly defined, are not to be found in scripture. The Puritans err on several other points as well. For one thing, they oversimplify God's law for man by identifying it solely with His will. One of Hooker's most brilliant strokes in Book I was to affirm that God's very nature may be seen as the **reason** (law) which defines His own working, not merely His **will**.

13. Sir Edwin Sandys

Insofar as we will ever know Him, God **is**, the reasonableness of all things including Himself. God, for Hooker, is not an arbitrary and willful creator and judge, but a reasonable and so, lawful, creator. We know Him because He has given us the faculty of reason to be able to see His nature, i.e., His goodness--which is to say, His reasonableness.

In a broader sense, God's full nature, for Hooker, is ultimately mysterious because He often acts in ways that human reason cannot fathom. Still, insofar as God acts in the world, and especially toward man, He usually does so in a manner that is lawful, in that it conforms to the reasons for which He created man and the universe in the first place.

Another important part of Hooker's theory of law in Book I is his distinction between changeable and unchangeable laws. That distinction helps to explain why laws governing civil society may differ according to time and place but laws affecting our salvation and the working of nature and the universe are immutable. For Hooker, the Cavinist extremists were wrong in insisting upon one universal form of church government and practice for all Christians--which would be, of course, whatever polity they happened to prefer, most likely the presbyterian form. By casting this debate on the higher ground of the nature of law, Hooker illumined what for him was the answer to the vexing issue of what was correct church polity, namely, that while some matters are eternally fixed by God's immutable wisdom, others are left for humans to determine according to wider and more varying standards of reasonableness. Church governance and practice fall into this latter category.

Both in its broadest reach and in each small aspect, Hooker's grasp of law in Book I is the genius of the entire work. For him, law was the creative force of the universe. He tried to show how all existence: divine, angelic, natural, supernatural, human, national, international, religious and secular, is related in one vast, ordered, reasonable, system of law. Law is the origin, the explanation and the creative force for good in life. Law is the end toward which all things tend. It is the wisdom of God, the foundation of human society, the dictate of reason, the instrument of virtue. Hooker's famous summary cannot be improved upon.

[O]f law there can be no less acknowledged, than that her seat is the bosom of God, her voice the harmony of the world: all things in heaven and earth do her homage, the very least as feeling her care, and the greatest as not exempted from her power; Angels and men and creatures of what condition soever, though each in different sort and manner, yet all with uniform consent, admiring her as the mother of their peace and joy.

—— Books II, III, IV ——

The central theme of Book II is that the more advanced Calvinists err when they view scripture as the only law for man and that this insistence reveals their cramped and unphilosophical view of life, not to mention a serious epistemological dilemma. It was Hooker's intent in this Book to refute Thomas Cartwright's negative argument from scripture that, because the English church polity was not found there, it must be discontinued. The disciplinarians were far too extreme in their use of scripture, Hooker said. They would insist upon its approval for every minuscule part of life, even as to whether people should use rush or straw to cover their floors. As the Apostle Paul taught us, God's great wisdom is revealed in many ways, including His glorious work in nature, our human experiences with Him, the exercise of our reason, by personal inspiration and through His holy word.

Hooker agreed that scripture was the final authority regarding the purpose for which it was intended, namely, our salvation. In other areas, unless scripture specifically forbids it, we may act according to standards of truth as revealed to us by God in other ways. In any event, the meaning of Scripture is rarely self-evident. Hooker seems to be infuriated by the popular idea that any ordinary man's opinion was valid as to the meaning of God's Word. He wrote, in Book II, that such an idea being "once inserted into the minds of the vulgar sort, what it may grow unto God only knows. Thus much we see, it has already made thousands so headstrong even in gross and palpable errors, that a man whose capacity will suffice scarcely to serve him to utter five words in sensible manner blushes not in any doubt concerning matters of scripture to think his own bare YEA as good as the Nay of all the wise, grave, and learned judgments that are in the whole world: which insolency must be repressed, or it will be the bane of Christian religion."

Hooker thought that it was rare when the meaning of scripture was self-evident. The authority of the church and her scholars was necessary to interpret the holy word. If we must choose between the biblical interpretations of that time-honored authority, the church, and the opinion of some rebellious ministers dressed up as so-called "Disciples of God," the choice for Hooker was obvious.

Hooker tried in Book III to expand the definition of church polity beyond matters of governance and orders of ministry to include common prayer, ceremonial practices, baptismal and Eucharistic rites. There was more at stake in the conflict with Calvinist extremists than the choice between bishops and elders. To explain his ideas, Hooker appropriated and enlarged a concept that quickly became a hallmark of his *apologia* for the church. This was the distinction been matters essential to salvation and those things, such as forms of church governance, that were "indifferent" to salvation. The former were prescribed in scripture and universally applicable. The latter were important, but not essential, and might appropriately differ from time to time and place to place according to the varying traditions of nations.

Humans are to use their God-given reasoning power to understand and evaluate these "indifferent" matters of church polity and liturgy, even as they use their minds to interpret scripture in order to understand what is necessary to salvation. In each case, reason is the key! We never escape the need to use this incredible faculty. Hooker said that he marveled at the ingenuity of those biblical literalists who used their reason so willingly when disparaging reason's authority to understand the Word of God and yet denied its efficacy in discovering His will.

In one of the most important and memorable parts of Book III, Hooker made his plea for tolerance. Nothing better characterizes this premier Anglican than his insistence that men have no business judging one another as to who is and who is not a true Christian. He affirmed that all, including Roman Catholics, who profess one Lord, one faith, one baptism are members of the church, no matter how much they sin, so long as they continue in that profession of their faith. This was a powerful, if largely unheeded, message of reconciliation to a church torn by internal dissension.

In Book IV, Hooker made his case for the church's right to use or discard Romanist or reformed ceremonies and practices as it saw fit. It was only natural (reasonable) for English people to prefer Catholic practices since their fathers had been raised in that church. In any event, as he had shown in Book III, these were matters "indifferent," to be determined by reference to the customs of each country's own national church.

Throughout Book IV, Hooker used scripture to prove his points as he refuted Thomas Cartwright's criticisms of the established church, one at a time. Hooker found this sort of writing tedious. But it was characteristic of religious debate of the day and he knew it would please Sandys and Cranmer because it lent itself to isolating particular political issues.

Hooker's anguish over the religious intemperance of his day emerges with special eloquence in Book IV. He despairs over an age in which "zeal has drowned charity" and skill in argument has "quenched meekness" of spirit. He bemoans the fact, as he sees it, that Calvinist extremists cannot find more important things to occupy their time than quibbles and quarrels over church ceremonies. He opines that what really bothers these Puritans and disciplinarians is that church authorities do not seem to hate Catholics enough. Surely, the burden of proof is not on the Church of England to defend its traditional polity and ceremonies but upon those who would have the church change. Their mere "methinketh," he said, should have no credence before the established wisdom and authority of the Church of England.

——— Pressure From Friends ———

Throughout the remainder of 1591 and all of 1592, as Hooker continued the task of completing and revising the *Laws*, he reviewed suggestions from his readers, including, in addition to Sandys and Cranmer, John Spenser, John Rainolds, Lancelot Andrewes and Robert Some.

George Cranmer proofed many pages of the manuscript, notably Book VI, which dealt with the jurisdiction of church courts. George was a stickler for detail, often finding places where Hooker had been careless in citing sources or criticizing particular word choices and pointing out grammatical errors. He was, in many respects, Hooker's severest critic. For example, he did not like the phrase "obligatory declaration" in Book VI because he thought it failed to communicate Hooker's meaning that if someone disobeyed the law they would be punished. Why didn't Hooker just say what he meant? In another place, Cranmer pointed to the need for a parenthesis around a phrase and, in another, a sentence that began 'Towards thyself' he thought was poorly written.

Hooker's ego was probably bruised by these criticisms but he knew that he needed some help with his grammar and composition. He was also aware of his tendency to be a bit lazy about citations. He was so familiar with his authorities that it was a great bother to check them all for accuracy. At some of their sessions, Cranmer went so far as to correct Hooker's Greek. He even suggested that his mentor insert long sections of historical material that he had researched and written himself. Hooker may have taken offense, especially at some of George's substantive suggestions, and told him so. He would not soften his views on the jurisdiction of church courts, nor would he eliminate the controversial section on penance. It was not necessary to remind him that Dr. Some had said he wished for more perspicuity in his style, or that John Rainolds would be able to verify some of his citations. He could remember those painful items quite well by himself, thank you!

Edwin Sandys tended to be gentler than Cranmer with his complaints and suggestions, perhaps mellowing as he grew older. Edwin usually began his objections with friendly phrases like, "Probably" or "It seems to me that" or "I think." His recommendations for change, although fewer and often more gently proffered than Cranmer's, were no less substantive. He continued to press the issue of church versus civil court jurisdiction, and specifically challenged Hooker to show why cases involving marriage, bastardy and estate settlement should be decided in religious courts. He also worried about what he regarded as Hooker's carelessness in citing sources. He urged Richard to quote directly from Travers, Cartwright and other opponents more frequently and more directly throughout the work. Unless Hooker set forth the exact references he was refuting, his work would lack integrity. Edwin went so far as to tell his former tutor that, for his own good, he should be more careful about "bare narrations" that were neither quoted nor credited. He knew that Hooker had a great storehouse of knowledge in his head but urged his friend to be more precise about his sources.

.   .   .   .   .

In the spring of the year, Joan had good news for her husband. They would be parents again before winter and there was no reason not to expect another healthy baby. They would all go up to Enfield to escape the heat and pestilence of London. Richard could write there as well in London. If the newborn were a girl, they would name her Jane (Joan), for her mother. If a boy, it would be John, for John Churchman. (The supposition that the namesakes chosen were Richard's mother and uncle is unlikely.) In the event, Jane Hooker was baptized at Enfield on 1st October 1592. Hooker was thirty-eight years old. This was his third daughter in as many years.

.   .   .   .   .

Meanwhile, pressure was mounting on Hooker to ready his book for publication by the end of the year. The treatise was needed, as Sandys and Cranmer repeatedly reminded him, to serve as a reputable tract to counter anticipated Puritan attacks on the church in the upcoming parliament. Calvinist radicals were already gearing up for the session, scheduled for early 1593. It was clear that James Morice, Edward Coke, Walter Raleigh and others would press for legislation to overturn or at least restrict Whitgift's regulations on clerical conformity. Even the Queen's cousin, Sir Francis Knollys, who had been senior privy counselor in attendance at every session of Commons since the Queen's ascension, was rumored to be leaning toward supporting Morice's well-known antipathy to episcopal abuses.

The atmosphere would have been especially charged around the table at Churchmans' these days because Edwin Sandys was a member of Commons in this session and he had a keen interest in assuring that

Hooker's book speak directly to the issues likely to be debated there. Even more importantly, Edwin's Uncle Miles, now treasurer at Middle Temple and one of the country's most prominent jurists, had been sitting in every session of Commons since 1563 and was bound to have a major role in this one as a defender of the church from the radicals.

Hooker's colleagues wanted his book to be in Lord Burghley's hands before the parliamentary session began. If Burghley could be moved to at least a neutral position by Hooker's eloquence that would be a help. No doubt the Archbishop would also appreciate Hooker's assistance in this enterprise. To be useful in the upcoming parliamentary debate, Hooker's book would need to address the relationship of such radical groups as the Barrowists and Brownists to the mainline disciplinarian Puritans. If Hooker could make Burghley see that the natural consequence of continued leniency toward his Puritan friends and their Presbyterian discipline was to aid and abet the heresy and treason that almost everyone admitted was evident in Browne and Barrow, then legislation might be passed to curtail Presbyterianism, as well as Brownism and anabaptism.[8]

There was a real danger to be confronted here, Hooker's friends believed. If the Presbyterian polity which stressed lay supremacy and weak central authority in the church were to take hold, it was all but inevitable that the next step would be congregationalism with its elimination of all establishment in religion. Next to go would be royal headship, the episcopacy and, finally, the entire ideal of England as a Christian commonwealth. What remained would be a complete separation of church from state, with the church consisting of nothing more than a collection of individual congregations run largely by an uneducated laity.

No doubt, logic was stretched in this effort to demonstrate the necessary connection between the emergent Presbyterians and such sects as the Brownists and Barrowists. Nevertheless, Hooker probably would agree that a relationship did exist, even if it was not an inevitable one. All logic aside, in the world of real politics the connection was

---

[8] Robert Browne and Henry Barrow led radical movements to disestablish the church and make each congergation a separate governing unit. They also opposed infant baptism and were forerunners of the Congregational and Baptist denominations.

highly probable, if not inevitable. Therefore legislation was necessary to curtail, even outlaw, the Presbyterian discipline.

The part of Hooker's book that was most likely to be read right away by Burghley and others in parliament was the Preface. Since they would be too busy to bother with the rest, their attention would have to be captured in the early pages of the book. The Preface already had a polemical tone, as Hooker had no doubt intended from the outset. To make a specific case that the acts of the Barrowists and Brownists were directly attributable to the activities of the Calvinist extremists had probably not been part of his original purpose. But now there was the prospect of including a ban on activities by Presbyterians and separatists as part of a bill outlawing Catholic recusancy, a law which was sure to be popular.

Would Hooker be willing to make the necessary changes in his preface to help in this effort? Yes, he would try to do so, but he would not compromise his principles. Nor would he compromise the integrity of his book, which was, in his view, a single piece, argued from general principles to particular cases, from the first part to the last. He had made his purpose clear in the outline and Preface, vowing not to destroy the unity and symmetry of the work by inserting narrow polemical attacks where they did not fit into the overall design.

At the end of the day, however, an exasperated Hooker finally succumbed to pressure and added the desired polemic, a short piece, quite out of keeping with the tone and content of the rest, as a kind of addendum. At the very end of the Preface, he felt that this bit of political arguing would do the least damage to his intentions for the book as a whole.

Help From Friends

The Preface and first four Books of the Laws were completed and ready for the printer before the end of 1592, shortly before the opening of the 1593 session of parliament. Now its author faced the daunting task of finding a publisher. This would not have been a problem had his work enjoyed the imprimatur and financial backing of the Archbishop. But Hooker had no such backing. His work had never been officially commissioned, although, as we have seen, Whitgift had approved the project and found Hooker the livings necessary to support himself while writing.

The Archbishop had many claims on his increasingly limited resources and thought that, if Hooker's work were worthy, a printer would run the risk of absorbing costs of production against expected income from sales. In any event, Whitgift was not relying on Richard's book. He had recently encouraged a number of more prominent figures to defend the church. The Dutch theologian, Adrian Saravia, had just come out with his defense of the episcopacy. Thomas Bilson, soon to be Bishop of Winchester and Richard Bancroft, the formidable Bishop of London, would soon publish major defenses of the church as well.

For the next several weeks Hooker worked closely with John Churchman's able servant and secretary, Benjamin Pullen, as that able amanuensis transcribed the untidy manuscript into a beautifully written copy, ready for the eyes of the most exacting printer. With the many pages of his finished manuscript tucked securely in his cloak (fifty-three sheets when printed), Richard set out confidently into the crisp December air to find a printer. He knew many of them from his years of browsing through their bookstalls around St. Paul's and on Fleet Street. He visited several of them with his manuscript. He went, for example, to John Bill's shop in Paul's Churchyard. Bill had a good location and sales of his books usually went well. From Bill, as from others, he received a polite but negative response.

Seeking a fuller hearing, he went to his best hope--his cousin, John Windet, whose Cross Keyes press was down near Paul's wharf. He had never met Windet, but knew that he was the son of his Aunt Anne, one his father's five sisters. Windet told him that it would not take long to print the manuscript because it was written in one of the finest hands he had seen. Unfortunately, there was little market for theological works these days. A few years ago interest in religious conflict was high and he could expect to sell almost anything like this in short order. Even now, a work attacking the church might do quite well, but not one that defended the establishment. Hooker's book was just too great a financial risk, cousin or no.

Hooker may have protested that with parliament meeting again in a few months and prisons filling up with separatists, surely interest in religious books would quickly return. Windet was not moved by this argument. The fact was that this was a long book, with eight separate parts projected. Windet advised his cousin to sell his book to a printer who would do the entire work in installments. That way, if all copies of the first printing were not sold, they could be used in future printings that would include later parts of the work as they were completed. Yes, Windet would be glad to enter into such a contract, but could not risk his own money because he could not see a market for the book sufficient to return a profit in a reasonable period of time.

Richard was undoubtedly shaken by this response. Like all writers who have labored for years to complete a major work, he had become so immersed in his subject that he came to believe instinctively and uncritically in its merit. To learn now, near the end of his long travail, that very few would be interested in reading what he had written was almost too much to bear. He realized now that he would need to find a patron to underwrite the costs of publication.

He turned to his friend, Edmund Sandys for help. Sandys would have several motivations for assisting Hooker, among them were friendship for his former tutor, sympathy with most of Hooker's moderate religious views, a desire to influence Burghley and others in Commons and the financial wherewithal either to await a long-term return on his investment or to absorb a loss, if necessary. So it was that Sandys stepped forward at a critical moment in Hooker's life and became a friend indeed. Without his timely assistance, the *Laws of Ecclesiastical Polity* would probably never have seen the light of day.

Sandys proposed that Hooker entrust him with Pullen's copy of the manuscript and he would see what terms he could obtain out on the street. Then he would calculate a fair return for himself on his investment and a reasonable payment to Hooker as author. When he had done all this, the two men would reach a final agreement and proceed with the publication.

Hooker was so overjoyed that his book would soon be published that he did not concentrate much on the details. His over-riding desire was to see that as many people as possible read the book. He urged Edwin to make his calculations so as to assure a low selling price so that the work would be affordable, even if this meant that he made little or nothing out of it himself.

14. St. Andrew's, Boscombe

Early in the new year, Sandys explained to Hooker the details of a tentative arrangement he had worked out with John Windet for printing the book. Windet would produce an initial run of 1,200 copies at a cost for printing and design of £52 which Sandys would pay. The printer would guarantee the same cost per page for Book Five when that was ready. The total should run to about £125. Edwin would save some money by supplying the paper himself. He could obtain about 150,000 sheets, enough for this and future editions, at something less than 8s. per ream. Sandys figured the total cost for the first four books at £100.4s and, for Book V, £136.16s., for a total investment of some £237.

Sandys viewed this financial outlay not only as an expression of support for Hooker but also as an investment. Most of the receipts from sales would come to him, since Windet would be paid his costs in advance. With luck and patience, Sandys believed he could make a decent return. He and Windet agreed on a sale price of 2s.6d. a copy. That may not have been as low as Hooker wanted but it was a moderate price.

Under the rules of the Stationer's Company, the book had to be registered as belonging to one of their members, in this case John Windet. Windet agreed informally (illegally?) that Sandys would be guaranteed most of the sales receipts for himself, while the printer would retain rights to only a small sum to cover his costs for selling the book and for an additional profit. All rights to the book's earnings, other than those reserved to Windet, belonged to Sandys, since it was he and not Hooker who had the contract with the printer.

As a gesture of good faith, Edwin paid Hooker £10, in advance, for the Preface and first four Books. As soon as the rest was in Windet's hands, which he assumed would be soon, he would pay Hooker another £40--£20 for Book V and £20 for the final three. The author's total payment was to be £50, more than twenty percent of the receipts from sales necessary for Sandys to break even on his investment. This arrangement seemed fair to Hooker. Edwin was putting up the money and assuming the risk, although he also stood to get most of the gain if the book were to be a commercial success. Hooker felt that the real gain was his. At last, his book would be published!

In the event, Sandys' total investment in the first five Books, including his payments to Hooker, was to reach about £278 (probably as much as £20,000 ($35,000) in today's currency, a tidy sum even for a large book of some 125 folio sheets. Sandys eventually received a return on his investment, although sales were slow. By 1597, when Book V was printed, Windet had more than enough copies left of the original sheets for a new printing of the enlarged work. By 1611, the original copies of Book V had been sold. After 1611, the work sold more briskly. But Sandys shared in none of those profits. When Windet died in 1610, his apprentice and successor, William Stansby, reneged on Windet's agreement with Sandys and made a healthy return on subsequent editions of the book, without repaying Sandys for his costs in producing some of them. We may safely estimate that Sandys made a profit on the first edition of about £90, which he lost on later editions due to Stansby's dishonesty. (Strictly speaking, Stansby was within his legal rights because Windet's original agreement with Sandys was in violation of rules of the Stationers Company, which stipulated that sole rights to the work should be vested in the printer.)

On 29 January 1593, John Windet entered into the official Register of the Company of Stationers in London his rights to "The lawes of ecclesiastical policie [sic] Eight bookes by Richard Hooker." Hooker had sent a fair copy to the Archbishop a few weeks earlier so that Whitgift would have time to review the work and approve its hurried publication. The stationers register, therefore, carries the necessary words: "Aucthorized [sic] by the lord archbishop of Canterbury his grace under his hand."

Richard Hooker now belonged to the ages. Almost.

Windet set about at once to produce the book. As he had little time before parliament convened, he hired two additional compositors to assist him and his apprentice, William Stansby. With Pullam's clear copy from which to work, and Hooker's help in proofing the pages, the task was done in about three weeks, just a few days after the opening session of Commons, but still in time to be used by Miles Sandys and his colleagues before serious legislative business began in early March.

On 13 March, Lord Burghley received one of Hooker's personal printed copies of the *Laws*, sent to him by the author with a letter attached. The letter was not a dedication. If there had been a dedication, it would have been to Whitgift. Rather, what Hooker sent to Burghley, who had never done any good thing for him but, to the contrary, had consistently championed Richard's foes, was merely an acknowledgment of Burghley's great influence in parliament, in the hope that he might read and be influenced by his book. The letter said, in part:

> My duty in most humble manner remembered. . .I must in reason condemn myself of over-great boldness for thus presuming to offer to your Lordship's view my poor and slender labours: yet, because that which moves me so to do, is a dutiful affection in some way to manifest itself [that]. . .I am in that regard not out of hope that your Lordship's wisdom will the easier pardon my fault, the rather because my self am persuaded that my faultiness had been greater, if these writings, concerning the nobler part of those laws under which we should live, should not have craved with the first your Lordship's favorable approbation, whose painful care to uphold all laws, and especially the ecclesiastical, has by the pace of so many years so apparently showed itself. . .Wherefore submitting both myself and my simple doings unto your Lordship's most wise judgment, I humbly take my leave. London, the xiiith of March 1592 [old style]. Your Lordships most willingly at commandment. Richard Hooker.

When parliament convened in February, plague was already beginning to spread in London. More than 10,000 people died in the city that year, including the lord mayor and three aldermen. This devastation was exacerbated in 1594 by the start of five years of alternating drought and fierce rain storms. The resulting poor harvests produced widespread poverty, food riots and rampant crime throughout the country. 1593 was the start of a difficult period of sickness, death and social unrest--all accompanied by run-away inflation-- that lasted until the end of the century.

As soon as a copy of his book had been sent off to Burghley, Hooker and his family left the infested city for Enfield. He had done his part in the great anti-Puritan crusade and now was content to let his politically astute friends chart the course of events in parliament. They would keep him informed via messengers travering the route to and from Enfield almost daily. He had more important matters on his mind now as he made his way north with Joan and the girls.

He was worried about his wife. She was pregnant again. This was the fifth time in as many years. Joan had barely recovered from having Jane when she had conceived again. These early months were the most risky. Richard knew he had been little comfort during the frantic effort to get his book published. Now he could relax and devote himself for a while to his family.

The Hookers probably stayed away from unhealthy London for much of the rest of the year. Margaret was born as autumn turned to winter. She was named for Edwin Sandys' sister, the wife of Francis Evington, a family friend who would one day be master of John Churchman's Merchant Tailor's Company and a trustee of Hooker's estate. Never had the ties between the Sandys, the Churchmans and the Hookers been so strong as on the day little Margaret was baptized.

During 1594, it is likely that the Hookers once again stayed out of London as much as possible, although by late 1593 the plague had spread as far north as Enfield. Joan no doubt remained in Enfield while Richard traveled more frequently to Salisbury and Boscombe than he had in the past few years, assuaging some of his guilt for having paid so little attention to his responsibilities there. He may have preached several times at St. Andrew's, visited with his friend Nicholas Fuller at nearby Allington and spent some time reading and revising Book V of the *Laws* in the library at Salisbury Cathedral.

Of course, the Hookers did spend some time in London. Joan liked to be in the city occasionally to visit her friends, show off her four little girls and be seen in polite company with her famous husband. Richard, too, had not lost all of his taste for being close to where great events of the day were taking place. The Archbishop had been well-pleased with Hooker's book and had expressed interest in seeing the rest of it as soon as it was ready. He told Hooker he might have a better appointment for him some time soon. It could not hurt his career to stay close to Lambeth Palace.

Toward the end of the year, a messenger brought a letter to the Churchman house summoning Richard to Lambeth. Shortly thereafter, Hooker gave the news to his wife. They would be moving to Kent. The word he had was that William Redman, rector at Bishopsbourne and Barham, had been named Bishop of Norwich, and his living, which was the Queen's to give, was vacant. Richard told Joan that the rectory at Bishopsbourne was large and comfortable. And it was only three miles from Canterbury Cathedral!

15. St. Mary's Bishopsbourne

—— Chapter 10 ——

Pastor Of Bishopsbourne

—— Life In The Country ——

In January of 1595, thanks to Archbishop Whitgift, Richard Hooker found his heart's desire, a peaceful living in the lovely countryside just south of Canterbury. Here he could live comfortably, raise his family away from the clamor of London, minister to a manageable parish of God's English people and pursue his scholarly interests. He had realized the dream of many a cleric with an intellectual bent: to preach and administer the sacraments, tend a portion of Christ's flock and have time to read and write.

What could be better? The great library at nearby Canterbury Cathedral--far superior to that at Lambeth or the Temple--was available for his continued work on his *apologia* for the church. Old friends and congenial colleagues could visit him here. Safely removed from the hectic pace and foul plagues of London or Oxford, he could enjoy some leisure and have time for the joys and pains of a more secure family life. Best of all, he could practice what mattered most to him--the daily life of priest, comforter, preacher and shepherd for his congregation of country people.

It would have been difficult to find a more idyllic place to settle in all of England. Bishopsbourne was (and is) a pretty little village nestled in the bosom of the Elham Valley which falls gently down from the old Roman road between Canterbury and Dover. This road--today's A2--just a quarter of a mile up the path from Hooker's new church, was old Watling Street which ran, in theory, all the way from Churchman's house in London to Hooker's home here at Bishopsbourne.

Fields, dotted with grazing sheep, brightened by patches of wild flowers and delineated by occasional stands of beech trees, presented the harried Londoner with a bucolic setting for his new life. Hooker's

Bishopsbourne came complete with the small Neilbourne Stream running intermittently southward through the town center and farm lands spotted with substantial red brick houses and great black barns poking their roofs up behind the church steeple--and all of this only a short five miles from Canterbury Cathedral.

Hooker's appointment here became effective on 7th January, 1595. The post was in the Queen's gift, as had been his other two major appointments, at the Temple and at Salisbury. No doubt Elizabeth acted on the recommendation of her Archbishop who was fulfilling his promise to find Hooker a suitable living where he might finish his writings.

For some years before and after Richard's tenure at Bishopsbourne, the living at St. Mary's was attached to the chapter at Canterbury. His immediate predecessor, Dr. William Redman, had been Archdeacon at the Cathedral when he was given the living here. Hooker's successor, Dr. Charles Fothersby, was also to be Archdeacon simultaneously with his appointment at Bishopsbourne, becoming dean of the chapter in 1615. No doubt Whitgift encountered some resistance at Canterbury when he gave Bishopsbourne to someone like Hooker who was not a chapter member. An added problem was that Richard would be a full-time resident rector. This meant that most, if not all, the income from the living would be consumed by his salary. To lose such a tidy sum from the coffers of the chapter would meet disapproval from the canons who would otherwise have had most of that money to distribute among themselves. For his part, Whitgift was pleased to add Hooker to his growing list of well-educated and devout clerics who truly resided in their cures and ministered regularly to the parishioners in their charge.

When Richard and Joan moved into the rectory, they were making their first real home together. And a large house it was, with twelve rooms and separate bake house, wash house, stables and barn. Joan had come into her own at last as mistress of a substantial household. Her father made certain that the furniture and household items loaded into carts for shipment from London were more than adequate to fill his daughter's new home. Surviving documents tell us that among the luxuries of this rather affluent London family were nine large carpets, several valuable "turkey cushions" (richly colored wool-piled imitation velvet pillows) intended to make seating more comfortable and at the same time offer a social statement to guests of the now famous new rector of Bishopsbourne and a beautiful cupboard covering, called a "darnix." More substantial items included a large table, eight good stools, a cupboard, a plate cabinet, a set of andirons and a large walnut chair--all for the parlor. The chair was one of Hooker's prized possessions. Walnut was still rare in England.

In the hall they placed another long table, a number of shorter stools, a settle and a smaller cupboard. Upstairs, Hooker's study and small adjoining parlor held a square table, several "presses" (armoires), two trestle beds and a number of hampers holding his books and manuscripts. By the time they had finished moving in, the six bed chambers on the upper floors were filled with beds, truckles, feather mattresses, rugs, curtains, cupboards and chairs. The largest chamber, above the parlor, held the biggest bedstead and a substantial wood-paneled chest containing Joan's treasured linens: some twenty tablecloths, dozens of napkins, towels and, a great luxury in those days, a pair of bed sheets. The windows in most of the bed chambers were draped with green sage curtains. Joan felt fortunate indeed to have so much of this fine cloth--a blend of wool and silk resembling serge--and enough rods to hang the curtains on. Many trunks and wainscoted boxes arranged along the walls and under the windows held the pillows, bolsters and blankets that made life comfortable for this prosperous clerical family.

Dr. Redman had left the kitchen, buttery, wet and dry larders, bake house, wash house, barn and stables well-furnished. These accouterments, including cheese presses, butterchurns, large kitchen utensils, andirons, scales, kettles, kneading troughs, pumps, a few saddles, bridles, and the like, went with the living and were passed on from one rector to the next. An ample supply of wheat, barley, oats, and podder (green vegetables), a few chickens, hogs, cows and two geldings were also on hand to get the new occupants through the rest of the winter. Still, Richard and Joan found it necessary to supply some tables, chairs, presses and cupboards of their own in order to complete the furnishing of these working parts of the homestead.

St. Mary's was an ancient church. The building had been erected about 250 years earlier to replace a smaller structure that had been on the spot since Saxon days. The tower had been last repaired over a hundred years ago. The first thing that caught Hooker's eyes as he stepped into St. Mary's was probably the floor--lovely small medieval tiles spreading out over the entire expanse of the church. The floor was even older than the tower. The pride of St. Mary's were the famous paintings of scenes depicting death and resurrection. One showed the martyrdom of St. Edmund, the East Anglican king who had been killed by the Danes, accurately depicted with arrows piercing his body. Another displayed the story of St. Nicholas resurrecting three boys who had been murdered by a butcher who used children as his meat supply. In this scene St. Nicholas was depicted as a tall figure in bishop's robes blessing the three naked boys in the pickling tub.

When Richard turned around and looked above the doorway, he saw an armed giant, nearly twice the size of any of the other painted figures on the walls. This huge man, clothed only in a knee-length cape, was in the act of striking his lance into the body of a smaller kneeling figure. In addition to the lance, the giant bore many other weapons, including three daggers coming out of his mouth and two large swords on each side of his head. The small kneeling figure had his palms extended toward the viewer.

There were still more wall paintings. At the west end of the nave was a startling depiction of the resurrection. At the top of this painting was the Angel of Death with a chain extending down into hell, with the souls of the saved and the damned strung out along the length of chain. These souls were of all sorts: kings, archbishops, common people--all contorted in horrible writhings. At the bottom stood a figure on a tomb flanked by two angels. Hell was portrayed as a wide-open jaw with sixteen molars and curved canine teeth.

Looking up at the wall in the south nave high above him, Hooker saw St. Michael weighing souls in a scale of good and evil. On one side of the scale was a small kneeling figure, hands clasped in prayer, on the other side were heads of several of the damned being pulled downward by a small demon. A little to the right of St. Michael was a lovely painting, more peaceful than the others, of four holy women at the tomb of Christ.

How different this was from the stark simplicity of the Temple Church in London or any other church Richard had seen. How had the marauding Puritans ever missed this place? Was there a church left in all England with such religious art on its walls? This was right out of the last century!

Hooker probably never quite got used to the wall paintings, with their emphasis on judgment, damnation, death and hell. Although he loved religious art and was certainly no Puritan when it came to church decorations, he was no papist either. These paintings were, for him, too reminiscent of the superstition and terror that sometimes had been used before the Reformation to frighten Christians into submission to the church. Still, they were remarkable!

Much as Hooker relished his new life as an obscure country parson, he could not escape his past. By this time in his career, he had obtained a national, even international, reputation from the publication of the early books of the *Laws* and from his highly visible tenure at the Temple as the cleric who had stood up to the formidable Walter Travers. Consequently, there were frequent visitors to Bishopsbourne, breaking the rural calm. Some were old friends from Oxford and London. Others came to discuss theology and politics and to take the measure of this unassuming defender of the Queen's Church who seemed to aspire to nothing more than a quiet country living--highly uncharacteristic in this aggressive, grasping age.

Although he was pleased by visits from such friends as Edwin Sandys, George Cranmer, Bishop Andrewes, and Adrian Saravia (the new canon at Canterbury who soon became a close friend), Hooker discovered that his real joy was ministering to the everyday needs of the people of the parish: visiting their homes when they were sick, hearing their confessions, being present at times of personal and family crisis, administering Communion or making uninvited house calls simply to offer friendship and support. The people of the parish soon came to respect, perhaps even to love, this gentle scholar in their midst.

There were special festival days in the life of the parish for Hooker to enjoy. For example, in the spring of 1596, he participated in his first annual Rogation Sunday procession. Joan would bundle herself and her three little girls warmly against the chill morning air as the Hookers set forth to lead the congregation on this traditional perambulation around the boundaries of the parish. The official reason for the procession was to reaffirm the church's dominion over this region by physically staking out the area claimed by the people of St. Mary's on behalf of their parish church. The more mundane purpose was to have an enjoyable outing as a church family, traversing the fields and walking past their homes as they welcomed in the fruitful spring after the cold winter season.

In addition to pastoral duties, Hooker almost certainly enjoyed his preaching at Bishopsbourne more than any he had done before. Here he was not trying to win debating points with sharp Puritan opponents or to defend his right to hold on to a post. His sole aim was to preach the saving gospel of Christ to country people whose lives were beset not so much by great issues of state as by the mundane fears, temptations and hardships of life. He soon became comfortable using homely rural examples to make the gospel understandable to farm families. One of his favorite sermon themes was the relationship between God's promises and man's responses.

One Sunday, when he wished to illustrate the lesson that God rewards those who first bring Him their treasures, he used the familiar words of Solomon in Proverbs, chapter 3: "Honor the Lord with your wealth as the first charge on all your earnings; then your barns will be filled with plenty and your presses [vats] break with the store of sweet wine." Was the lesson here that our bellies must first be filled before we serve God, Hooker asked his congregation from the pulpit?

> No. But it is true that the cares and needs we have in this world are the greatest obstacle which keeps our minds from aspiring to heavenly things. Therefore, this promise is made to assure us that the best way to satisfy our needs is to first honor God. God will not allow those who honor Him to be worse off because of their service to Him than they otherwise would have been.

Alert to the trap of suggesting that man's good works could earn him God's favor, Hooker quickly added:

> This does not mean that our service of good works earns us such generosity at God's hands. That He rewards His servants comes not from worthiness of our deeds but from His goodness.

The question of how to be assured of God's favor was central to the concerns of simple people whose lives were constantly beset by the hardships of disease, early death, uncertain harvests, the rampant inflation of the day that brought ever-rising prices for necessary goods, and the general uncertainty and stress of living in an era of rapid social and political change. Generally, Hooker's counsel to his troubled flock was for them to have a patient and peaceful spirit, use common sense, follow the advice of wise Christian leaders and trust that God in His own way and in His own time would reward those who were faithful to Him.

Lest his people think that God was interested only in their making donations to the church, Hooker preached often on the more important offering, prayer. One of his most beautiful sermons on any subject was an explanation of Matthew, Chapter 7: "Ask, and it shall be given to you; seek, and you shall find; knock, and it shall be opened unto you. For whosoever doth ask shall receive; whosoever doth seek shall find; the door unto everyone which knocks shall be opened."

He began this sermon with the scriptural reading, and then continued:

> In these words we are first commanded to 'ask,' 'seek,' and 'knock;' secondly, promised grace sufficient to each of these tasks. Of this asking, or praying, I shall not need to tell you either at whose hands we must seek aid or to remind you that our hearts are those golden censers from which the fume of this sacred incense of prayer must ascend.
>
> Against invocation of any other than God alone in our prayers of asking, if all other arguments should fail, yet this bar might suffice: that whereas God has in scripture delivered us so many patterns for imitation when we pray, yea framed ready to our hands all suits and supplications which our condition on earth may at any time need, there is not one, no not one to be found, directed unto such as angels, saints, or any, saving God alone.

Gazing upward toward those haunting wall paintings, Hooker knew he must do all he could to rid his congregation of their inclination to venerate idols, especially the Saints. He rarely lost a chance to warn them that God alone was to be the object of their prayers. He looked down at his congregation and continued:

> Fervency and humility are the proper attitudes to bring to our prayers of asking. Our fervency shows us to be sincerely affected towards what we crave; but that which must make us capable thereof, is a humble spirit. Asking is easy, if that were all God did require. But seeking requires labor on our part, a work of difficulty. If we seek the counsel of those who are wise in these matters we will learn that the labor involved in seeking God is the keeping of His commandments.
>
> You see now what it is to ask and seek. The next duty is to 'knock.'

Following his usual mode of developing an argument in logical fashion, Hooker continued:

> There is always in every good thing which we ask and which we seek, some main wall, some barred gate, some strong impediment or other objecting itself in the way between us and home; for removal whereof, the help of stronger hands than our own is necessary. So knocking is required in regard to hindrances, lets, or impediments, which are doors shut up against us, till such time as it please the goodness of Almighty God to set them open.
>
> We know that God opened the door for the people of Israel when Moses did his part by knocking. Soon, however, some of the sons of Jacob stopped seeking or knocking, preferring a life of ease even at the price of slavery. Issachar was one of these, chastised by his father as one who 'though bonny and strong enough for any labor, doth notwithstanding sit still like an ass under

all burdens; he shall think himself that rest is good, and the land pleasant; he shall in these considerations rather endure the burden and yoke of tribute, than cast himself into the hazard of war.'

Hooker paused before continuing, to be certain that he had not lost his audience on this tour through ancient Israel.

We are for the most part all of Issachar's disposition. We account ease cheap, howsoever we buy it. And although we can happily frame ourselves sometimes to ask, or endure for a while to seek; yet loath we are to follow a course of life, which shall too often hem us about with those perplexities of knocking, the dangers whereof are manifestly great.

He concluded his sermon:

We will never fathom the circuit or the steps of God's divine providence. We can only be astonished by His means of keeping His promises to us and exclaim with the Apostle Paul: 'O the depth of the riches of the wisdom of God! How unsearchable are His counsels, and His ways past finding out.'

Let it therefore content us always to have His word for an absolute warrant; we shall receive and find in the end; it shall at last be opened unto you: however, or by what means, leave it to God. Let there, on our part, be no stop to asking, seeking and knocking and the bounty of God we know is such that He grants over and above our desires. Saul sought an ass, and found a kingdom. Solomon named wisdom, and God gave Solomon wealth.

Let us sing with the psalmist who said of the Lord's servant: 'He asked for life, and thou givest him long life, even for ever and ever.' Our God is a giver. And He knows better than we the best times, and the best means, and the best things, wherein the good of our souls consist.

The longer Hooker ministered at Bishopsbourne, the more keenly he realized the need for God's saving love amidst the often difficult lives of ordinary people. Theological debate on issues of predestination, the precise nature of Christ's presence in the Eucharist, whether Catholics were irrevocably damned and the question of which was the proper church polity seemed remote, if not irrelevant, to the needs of a grieving mother who had lost another infant child, a farmer with a failed crop, a vagrant begging at the rectory door for food and shelter. These situations called for the church's saving message of hope, peace, mercy, love--not moralistic recrimination, proclamations of God's judgment on the wicked or some kind of insistence on separating the elect from the damned. It was not that Hooker lost interest in the great theological issues of the day, but only that he found them less relevant in his life as pastor to rural working people than they had seemed in the intellectually charged atmosphere at Oxford or the political cauldron at the Temple.

Preaching sermons of comfort and hope and caring directly for people's spiritual needs through counseling in church or visiting in their homes often took precedence in his daily routines over revising the last Books of the *Laws*. When he did write, his passion was for polishing Book V, where he turned his keen mind to questions of worship, prayer, preaching, music and the great ceremonies of the church that brought meaning, joy and comfort to ordinary people: holy communion, baptism, prayer, confession, marriage, funerals, the "churching" of women after childbirth, special festival days. These were the aspects of life in the church he relished exploring in his sermons and writing, not so much because they challenged him intellectually as because they intersected his everyday experience as a pastor.

On more than one Sunday he sought to comfort his congregation by explaining why and how it was that good things in life often are preceded by or even grow out of failure, disgrace, pain, suffering and death. He had discovered that few messages fell on more eager ears than those that saw hope in despair and good coming somehow from that constant dread companion of all their lives--death.

A favorite sermon theme for Hooker was Hebrews, chapter three, verses 14-15. One Sunday he began his sermon by reading the passage:

> The children of a family share the same flesh and blood; and so He too shared ours, so that through death He might break the power of him who hath death at his command, that is, the devil; and might liberate those, who through fear of death, had all their lifetime been in servitude.

Then he continued:

> The very center of Christian belief, the life and soul of Christ's Gospel, rests in this: that by ignominy, honor and glory is obtained; power is vanquished by imbecility; and by death salvation is purchased.

He went on to explain how the Jews, who had longed for and prophesied a messiah, failed to accept Christ as the anointed one because he came not as a king but as one who would die foolishly and in shame. Even the Apostles made this mistake at first, he explained.

> It was not until Christ was dead, raised, and ascended to his Father that the right understanding of the ancient prophecies came to light. Until then, they never imagined that death was the means by which such great things would be accomplished. It was in this sense that the Apostle referred to the Gospel as a mystery, hidden since the beginning of the world, concealed from all former ages, and never opened until when it was revealed to the saints of God.

Hooker paused before posing the great conundrum of Christian faith and the horrible dilemma of his people's lives:

But why did the Son of Man, who had the power to create and sustain the world, need to die to deliver man when He could have done so simply by commanding it? If we enter into the search for what God intends to reveal to us, we can find a thousand testimonies to show that the whole scope of Christ in the work of our deliverance was to display the treasures of His infinite love, goodness, grace and mercy. Our deliverance He could have accomplished without His death. But that was insufficient to express His love for us; and so, "Behold," He said, "I lay down my life for them."

Now Hooker proceeded to explain why the only bar to Christ's promise of salvation was a person's explicit rejection of or contempt for this freely offered divine gift of a life of eternal peace and joy. He was echoing and expanding upon his sermons at the Temple where he had come dangerously close to espousing the Arminian and Pelagian doctrines of universal tolerance, love, and salvation. In this setting the idea that all of his flock could be saved from their pain and suffering somehow seemed right, despite the reservations about this which still lingered from his early indoctrination in Calvinist doctrine, and, dare he think it, despite the authorized doctrine of predestination in the *Thirty-nine Articles*. He continued:

If anyone is deprived of deliverance, the fault is his own. Let no man therefore dig the clouds to look for secret impediments to his salvation. Let not the subtlety of Satan beguile you with fraudulent expectations and drive you into such labyrinths and images as the wit of man cannot enter without losing itself.

Hooker may have caught himself here before actually naming what labyrinth of Satan he had in mind: that tortured doctrine of double predestination so dear to John Rainolds and other advanced Calvinists. He saw clearly now just how injurious such an idea could be to the lives of ordinary people struggling for hope and meaning in their lives, threatening them with eternal separation from Christ's love through no apparent fault of their own. How false such a notion was to the spirit of Christ and to the words of scripture! Still, there was no need this morning to cause controversy by attacking a sophisticated doctrine that few in his congregation knew or cared about.

He went on:

> The only fatal bar which closes the door to God's saving mercy is man's willful contempt of the grace offered to him. Upon this sure foundation let us therefore build: Christ died to deliver us **All**. You have the plain expressed words of our Lord and Savior inviting **All** 'to come unto him who labor.' You have the blessed Apostle's express assertion that Christ has by His death defeated Satan, to the end that He might deliver **All** who are held in bondage.
>
> Urge this idea upon yourself, God cannot deny Himself. And He preaches deliverance by His death to **All**.

There! He had done it! He had expressed what he had probably come fully to believe, that all who openly professed Christ's name could be saved by His grace and find hope in His love and care for them. If this be heresy to some, then so much the worse for them. He had learned from experience here as a country pastor what he had suspected all along to be the truth about Christ and His Gospel of good news-- that all who called on His name might have hope of salvation from fear, suffering and death.

He continued, turning his attention now to a constant concern of his people, their fear of death.

> Death considered in itself is an enemy. Because death has as yet the upper hand against all, conflict with it is naturally feared. And they who speak of it from a merely natural sense can only decide that it is all terrible. But there are many factors which can abate the fear of death. For example, one who despairs of life or lacks patience with it or has had enough of its

troubles and tribulations may be content to have them ended in death. Or, with Aristotle, one may say that like birth, death is beneficial to the state of the world. Birth stops death and death eases the ways for new births. We should be content to give place to others by our death even as in birth we succeeded those who died before us.

But the truest weapons we have to strike back against the natural terrors of death are first the submission we owe to God's will, at Whose commandment our readiness to die shows that we are called as His sons, and not as servants.

As sons we may take possession of our inheritance with joy. Those who lived as sons are blessed. The pains they suffered here are now ended; the evil they did is buried with them and their good works follow them. Their souls are safe in the hands of God. Not even their bodies are lost, but laid up for them.

He had spoken from the heart of some of his deepest personal convictions and undoubtedly believed he had given hope to his people while reaffirming his own faith. More than once he would be asked by members of his parish to elaborate further on why it was that God would allow such terrible sufferings among the faithful who came to services each Sunday, prayed regularly and tried earnestly to believe that they would receive the gift of eternal life. The common sense of the matter seemed to be that God was breaking his promises and rejecting rather than loving His children.

Hooker taught that God never totally forsakes His own, even though, from time to time, He tests His children severely by turning His wrath upon them. He cited Isaiah as an example, where the prophet says: "For a moment in anger I hid my face from you for a little season; but with everlasting mercy I have compassion for you, says the Lord, your Redeemer;" and Jeremiah saying, "I shall make an everlasting covenant with them that I will never turn away from doing them good," and John saying, "He loved his own to the end."

Hooker also taught his people that, although God may seem to reject mankind, even His own son, Jesus Christ, He never abandons a person completely, only partially and only for a time. Even then, it is the body and those lower parts of a person's nature, wherein the passions and emotions reside, that are cut off. Our intellects, our souls, the parts of us where reason, wisdom, judgment and the light of God's truth reside are not extinguished.

We are to remember, Hooker taught, that God gave Job's body over to be tormented by Satan but his life, his soul, was spared. In the case of our Lord and Savior, Satan and his "imps" were permitted to use whatever malice they could invent to inflict Christ's body. "They wounded his eyes with the spectacle of scornful looks, his ears with the sound of heinous blasphemies, his taste with gall, the feeling throughout his body with such torture as blows, thorns, whips, nails and spear could breed, until his soul was finally chased out like a bird." So terrible was his suffering that there is no reason to wonder why he cried out to God with such despair, "My God! My God!" And who, Hooker asked, can hear this mournful cry of Christ today and not feel that his own soul has been "scorched without leaving a single drop of the moisture of joyful feeling?"

When Christ cried out, "My God, my God, why have you forsaken me," His words, the force and vigor of His speech showed clearly that He had already "clasped God with indissoluble arms" and that God was already "abiding in the fortress--the very pinnacle and turret of Christ's soul." And so it is with us, Hooker taught, if we call out to God with such fervor in the midst of our own despair.

As to why God went to so much trouble and allowed His creatures to cause themselves so much grief in order to love them fully, Hooker had no easy answer to offer. He thought the best response to questions about the workings of God's awful intelligence was an amazed silence.

Adrian Saravia

Shortly after Hooker's arrival at Bishopsbourne, he began to enjoy the company of Dr. Adrian Saravia, the renowned Dutch theologian who had recently been named a canon at Canterbury. The two men were kindred spirits and soon became friends. Saravia (1523-1613) was the most prominent Dutch theologian living in England during the Elizabethan and Stewart times. Although a leader in the Calvinist church in the Netherlands, Saravia gradually became convinced that the episcopal polity in England was preferable to the Presbyterian organization. He was highly favored and generally supported in England by Leister and others in Elizabeth's court as well as by Archbishop Whitgift.

Hooker was familiar with Saravia's most famous writing, *Of the Diverse Degrees of Ministers of the Gospel,* the strongest defense of the episcopacy he had ever read. Published in March of 1590, while Hooker was still at the Temple, the book was an immediate sensation for its claim that God Himself had established the rule of bishops in the Church and that therefore their authority was *ius divinum.* Hooker knew that this treatise was part of an ongoing debate between Saravia and Theodore Beza, Calvin's successor at Geneva. In 1592, Beza wrote a *Response* to Saravia on behalf of Calvinists everywhere who saw his ideas as a frontal attack on the Presbyterian discipline. Travers and Cartwright were particularly incensed by Saravia.

Whitgift did not commission Saravia to write *Diverse Degrees* although he encouraged the writing. The clever Archbishop used the Dutchman as he had Hooker, enjoying the benefit of his defense of the church without running any political or financial risk. Hooker and Saravia may well have found common ground not only in many of their shared views on religious issues but also in their respective opinions of the *modus operandi* of the machiavellian Archbishop of Canterbury.

As their friendship ripened, Hooker and Saravia found many areas of agreement. One was on the question of predestination. Back in 1590, Whitgift had asked Saravia to draft an assessment of a controversy over the doctrine of predestination. As a long-time Calvinist, Saravia could hardly dispute God's predestination of all acts of men. Yet he was troubled by the consequent idea that man is morally unaccountable for his actions. Hooker was wrestling with the same problem, and reaching much the same conclusion, in his forthcoming Book V of the *Laws.* In fact, discussions with his new friend may have helped Hooker clarify his opinions as the two scholars shared insights and authorities on this most troublesome issue of their day. Hooker would have described for

Saravia his Paul's Cross sermons and subsequent debate with Travers at the Temple. He would be reassured when Saravia confirmed his own opinion that while God knows all, He does not hinder man's freedom to choose good or evil. Hooker would be supported also by Saravia's opinion that a possible consequence of man's freedom is good works--an evidence of faith. None of these issues was a simple matter of black and white, the two men agreed. Above all, one must keep an open mind and adopt the broadest possible position on issues like these.

During their visits with one another, at Bishopsbourne and Canterbury, Hooker learned that his new friend was a master at collecting multiple church livings, usually paying scant attention to any that involved pastoral and preaching duties. Saravia had been rector at Tatenhill, north of Birmingham, for eight years while he was simultaneously a prebend at Gloucester. Apparently he had spent little time at either place. Now that he was a canon at Canterbury, he still retained the other posts and was also rector at Lewisham and at Great Chart in Kent. Sitting right here in his parlor, Hooker had a living example of the abuses of multiple livings and absentee clergy which the Puritans rightly attacked and the church labored to reform.

Did Adrian have a moral problem accepting positions that he never really filled? Would he be able to meet any of the rector's obligations at Great Chart and Lewisham, much less Tatenhill and Gloucester Cathedral, and still attend chapter meetings at Canterbury? No doubt the two men discussed the issue. Richard, after all, had taken largely absentee posts at Drayton Beauchamp, Salisbury Cathedral, Boscombe, and Netheravon. Both men knew they were part of a serious problem. They probably comforted one another that there was no other realistic way for the church to compensate its officials and scholars except to continue the regrettable practice of absentee livings. Guilt, like misery, loves company.

——— Book VII ———

In their frequent meetings during the final years of Hooker's life, the older scholar was especially helpful in the shaping of Book VII of the *Laws* that dealt with the episcopacy. Richard had this Book, along with Books V, VI and VIII, in draft form as early as the spring of 1593, before coming to Bishopsbourne. Publication had been delayed because Sandys and Cranmer wanted him to make changes--and Sandys, after all, was paying the costs of publication. Now Saravia helped him refine Book VII so that it became the most polished of the final three.

The Dutchman went so far in his support of the episcopacy as to say that if there were indeed a single best form of church governance, it would be rule by bishops. His reading of scripture taught him that there was a difference between the Apostles and other ministers. His reading of history made it clear to him that, in theory and practice, there had always been a gradation of ecclesiastical authority among clergy, with bishops, patterned on the twelve Apostles, at the top. Over many years, he eventually reached the conclusion that Christ Himself had probably chosen the episcopal form as best for His church. But he drew a distinction between the general matter of who governs the church and the narrower issue of how ministers are made. In theory one might hold that a call to the ministry comes from God and then is received and validated in many different ways, including election by a congregation, and yet, at the same time, maintain that supreme authority in the church belongs to bishops, not congregations with their elders and deacons. By this theory, Saravia's ordination in Holland was valid in the Church of England so long as he fully accepted the authority of English bishops over him.

Hooker may have pointed out to his friend that this was fine in theory but that as a practical matter, if bishops did not have the power to make ministers, then any other authority they had was greatly diminished. Saravia, in turn, may have insisted that he was talking only about foreigners ordained in their own countries and then coming, at the sufferance of English bishops, to serve as ministers in the Church of England. In no way would legitimacy of foreign ordination apply to Englishmen who were ordained abroad and then claimed admission to the English clergy solely on the strength of such ordination. A man like Hooker's nemesis Walter Travers, who openly defied episcopal authority in his own church by refusing to submit to its authority over him in the matter of ordination, had no legitimacy in the church and was, in the eyes of Whitgfift, little short of committing treason.

As the two men shared experiences and opinions on the subject of ordination, they agreed that how ordination occurs is not a matter of ultimate importance that touches salvation. The form might vary according to a country's traditions and customs, so long as it was done in a reverent manner, acknowledging that a call to ministry comes from God and that the church, by whatever means, merely confirms God's choice.

The two men did not agree, however, on Saravia's assertion of the divine authorization of the English episcopacy . The Dutchman went too far for Hooker when he claimed that Christ Himself had set bishops over His church. Hooker did not think it possible to know God's will so definitively on such a secondary issue as this, one clearly not essential to salvation. Also, he thought scripture to be not nearly so definitive on this question as his friend did. Hooker was willing to concede that the order of bishops might have been divinely established, but not that it was definitely so. In Book VII, he went so far as to say that it was due to "divine instinct" that the Apostles began this "sacred" regimen of bishops. He also claimed that the institution had the authority of tradition, having been with the church in some form or another for more than fifteen hundred years. He was aware, however, that congregational approval of new ministers was often a part of the process in the early church.

On balance, Hooker preferred a commonsense position affirming only that there was at least as good a case to be made out of scripture for episcopal polity as for the Presbyterian form and that the English preferred their system of bishops because it was reasonable and conformed nicely to their history and traditions. He would rather just let if go at that. He was not inclined to be pressured into saying more than he believed about the origins of bishops' powers merely because such a statement might be politically advantageous to the church establishment.

For his part, Saravia probably found Hooker's views on the episcopacy timid. Bishops of the day needed unequivocal support from scholars like Hooker and himself. Bishops were in a difficult position, caught between the crown, on whom they depended totally for appointment and support, and their clergy, who screamed constantly for more independence. The real intention of such troublemakers as Travers and Cartwright in their quibbling over the liturgy was to gain freedom from bishops and eventually to overturn the episcopacy altogether. One need only take a good look at the *Second Admonition* or at Cartwright's *Reply* to Whitgift's *Answer* to see that this was the case.

Hooker agreed with his friend that many Presbyterians had ulterior motives when they attacked church ceremonies. Their true aim was to topple bishops and, perhaps, kings as well. Richard had said as much in the opening lines of Book VII. In Book VIII, Hooker went still farther and warned that some of the Protestant extremists meant to strike against the monarchy itself. For the present, they deferred to the Queen for political advantage but their true intent was to ease her out as soon as possible.

Withal, there was ambivalence in Hooker's attitude about the episcopacy. His advocacy, in Book VII, of good livings, titles, retinues of attendants, handsome estates, special social and legal privileges and large financial endowments for prelates may be taken as indication that bishops, if not divinely ordained, were the next thing to it. Hooker justified such wealth as a practical aid to social cohesion in a commonwealth where bishops, like judges, scholars and ministers of state, required the financial independence and social status that would engender the public deference necessary to maintaining the general well-being of the community. Such outward signs and tokens of office signify to everyone the importance of a social hierarchy within which each person may find his own place, and so his own peace and safety.

Having said this much for the status of bishops, Hooker assured Saravia that, as he saw it, the true measure of good bishops was not that they be rich and titled. A bishop must be a wise and careful shepherd of Christ's flock. Hooker was dismayed by the abuses committed by too many bishops of the day and said so forthrightly. He enumerated the travesties of prelates who carelessly ordained their clergy, corruptly bestowed church livings and held parish visitations to see what extra income they might glean from them. Rather than instructing and supporting their ministers, some bishops continued to engage in the foul system of encouraging multiple livings beyond the legitimate needs of the recipients of them.

Defending bishops was always difficult for Hooker. On the one hand, he was aware that Calvinist extremists exaggerated episcopal abuses for their own gain as they "gaped after spoil" with their "gleeful attacks" on the supposed wealth of prelates. At the same time, he recognized that many objections were justified. A system so riddled with corruption and abuse was difficult to justify and the injury that issued from defects in the episcopal system of the day was exceedingly great. If bishops did not begin deporting themselves in a proper manner, they would never be respected. The church at large would be the loser, so it was imperative to get the episcopal house in order before it rotted from within.

Saravia may have warned Hooker, as the two reviewed drafts of Book VII, that his friend was coming dangerously close, at one place, to pointing an accusatory finger at the Queen as the one responsible for abuses in the church. This was where he wrote that, despite all the pressures upon "her royal majesty" to appropriate church wealth for her own use, "her sacred majesty" has given her word not to seek or allow "gain by pillage" of the church. Though not exactly saying the Queen was at fault, merely using the words "pillage" and "her royal majesty" in the same sentence could be misunderstood. Queen Elizabeth's propensity to acquire whatever she laid her hands on, in the church or anywhere else, was so well known that even to raise the issue could cause trouble for Hooker.

In the final analysis, Hooker was keen about the need to support bishops and their financial independence even if they were sometimes corrupt. In his view, it was a mistake to rob them of their wealth because that was the same as robbing Christ. He wrote in Book VII that "even if bishops were all unworthy, not only of [their] living, but even of life, yet what hath our Lord Jesus Christ deserved, for which men judge Him worthy to have the things that are His given away from Him unto others that have no right unto them? For at this mark it is that the head lay-reformers all aim."

Furthermore, it made no practical sense to plunder the church. The gain to the state would be much less than the loss because "no one order of subjects whatsoever within this land bears the seventh part of what the clergy bears in the burdens of the commonwealth." Each year, Hooker claimed, the government took some £26,000 from church revenues. All the world could see that the church had fallen to a low ebb as a result. It was deplorable! "To rob God, to ransack the church, to overthrow the whole order of Christian bishops. . .what man of common honesty can think it. . .lawful or just?" Hooker asked.

He was clearly overwrought by what he saw as a weakening of the church through the systematic despoiling of its wealth by the government and the consequent corrupting of bishops. But, Saravia saw another side of Hooker as well, perhaps a less practical, more spiritual, side, when Richard said, on the same subject: "After all, if in the end those of us who labor in the church are reduced to begging for alms, we will be no worse off than our ancestors who worked before us to guide people to salvation."

——— Book V ———

During his time at Bishopsbourne, Hooker published his most enduring contribution to the Anglican tradition: his explanation and defense, in Book V of the *Laws*, of the faith and practice of the Church of England. No other treatise has had a more profound influence on the spiritual life of Anglicans and Episcopalians. In Book V Hooker gave the church he loved her most complete and inspirational raison d'être. He completed in this Book the formulation of the basic spirit of Anglicanism, begun by Archbishop Cranmer fifty years earlier in the *Book of Common Prayer*. Hooker brought Cranmer's book to life, giving it meaning for clergy and lay people, as well as countless writers and scholars outside the church.

Because Hooker was a reluctant, if effective, political polemicist, his heart was always in Book V, the least political part of his treatise. Influences by outside persons, like Sandys and Cranmer, had little if any impact on this portion of his work. Archbishop Whitgift, to whom Book V is dedicated, may have helped shape some parts of the work, and trusted theologians whom Hooker respected, such as Adrian Saravia and Lancelot Andrewes, may have made suggestions. But, excepting some of his sermons and tracts, Book V is as pure and undiluted an expression of Hooker's thinking on the subjects he cared most deeply about as we shall ever see.

Book V reads, in parts, as though it were written for the ages. Nothing done by Jewel, Whitgift, Bancroft, or any other apologist for emergent Anglicanism, is comparable. Hooker went far beyond mere refutation of criticisms of the church by such Puritans as Thomas Cartwright. He offered a positive justification for the entire worship service: why Anglicans prefer prescribed common prayers to what they often regard as either the minister's personal catharsis, or worse yet, just so much quasi-spontaneous babble; how and why Anglicans use the psalms and litanies; their joy in church music, beautiful sanctuaries and appropriate clerical vestments; why sermons are so much less important to them than prayer and the sacraments. As long as there is a Church of England and a world-wide Anglican community, Hooker's Book V will endure as their most important *apologia*.

Hooker's reflections in Book V on prayer are especially noteworthy as examples of the enduring influence of this part of the *Laws* in shaping one of the main pillars of Anglican religious thought and practice. Prayer, he believed, was the very raison *d'etre* of the church. "Is not the name of prayer usual to signify. . .all the service we ever do unto God?" In one place, he wrote of how prayer can come in many forms: "Every good and holy desire, though it lack the form, has, notwithstanding, in itself the substance, and with Him, the voice of prayer, who regardeth the very moanings, groans, and sighs of the heart of man." In another place, he explained succinctly some of the conditions that must prevail for a prayer to be efficacious: "firstly, the lack of that which we pray for; secondly, a feeling of want; thirdly, an earnest willingness of mind to be eased therein; fourthly, a declaration of this our desire in the sight of God. . ."

He repeatedly made it clear that for prayer to work, the supplicant must first believe in God's mercy and acknowledge dependency on Him.

He always emphasized the primacy of faith and the sovereignty of God as keys to prayer.

When Cartwright objected to the "prayer for deliverance from all adversities," solely on the ground that he could find no warrant for this kind of prayer in holy scripture, Hooker did not spend much time "quibbling" with "T. C." but went right to the heart of why he thought it was beneficial to have such general prayers for deliverance from future calamities, as well as from those that presently afflicted people, whether or not these prayers were set forth in scripture:

> To think we may pray unto God for nothing but what He has promised in Holy Scripture we shall obtain is perhaps an error. . . . Prayers are unto God most acceptable sacrifices because they testify we desire nothing but what comes by His hands; and our desires we submit with contentment to be overruled by His will.

Hooker was making the point here that it is good to pray to God for that for which we have no foreknowledge because that is a way of demonstrating total reliance upon Him. Hooker elevated the argument with Cartwright and others from a bickering over what scripture does and does not mean to a rational discussion of the relationship between faith and prayer.

Common (corporate) prayer has always been a hallmark of Anglicanism. Hooker explained that it is often preferable to private prayers because, when God's people gather as a community to worship, they are the very Body of Christ and their single voice rises up to God with an assurance, a worthiness, a shared judgment and a public consensus which soars beyond the mere private petitions of individual believers.

When he defended the Church's common prayer "for the salvation of all believers," Hooker was treading on dangerous grounds. In that age of strident anti-Catholicism, a general prayer of this kind was easily construed as including the hated papists within the folds of its entreaty to God. But Hooker insisted on emphasizing God's love for all His children and His likely response to all who called upon Him in faithful prayer. This is a theme that shines throughout all Hooker's writing and marks his Anglican heirs with the sign of Christian tolerance and inclusiveness to this very day.

> Christian charity thirsteth after the good of the whole world. . .[because God's] **desire**, is to have all men saved, a work most suitable with His purpose who gave Himself to be the price of redemption of **all.** . .

Concerning the state of all men with whom we live,. . .we may till the world's end. . .always presume that. . . there is hope of everyman's forgiveness. . . . And therefore charity which hopeth all things prayeth also for all men.

Another of Hooker's lasting contributions in Book V is his treatment of the sacraments, especially the eucharist. His resolution of the argument about the presence of Christ in the elements has endured within the Anglican community over the centuries. In the midst of the terrible disputes between transubstantialists, consubstantialists and those who saw the sacrament as a mere symbol or token of some mysterious act of God, Hooker said simply that man will never know in what form Christ is manifest in the sacramental elements any more than he will know in exactly what way God is incarnate in Christ. But Christians do believe that Christ is incarnate in the sacrament just as God is incarnate in Christ, even though they cannot know how this works. The doctrine of incarnation has been a key to Anglican understanding of the eucharist and other miracles of God ever since Hooker made it so.

He also insisted that the eucharist is not, as the Puritans said, a mere symbol or naked sign intended to teach something about Christ. Rather, sacraments are "heavenly mysteries" and "visible signs of invisible grace," a grace so real and present that it actually "worketh salvation."

How are we to be certain that the sacrament "worketh salvation?" Not by debating the issue, said Hooker, but by experiencing God's grace through the act of **participating** in the eucharistic liturgy. When we "participate" in Christ's incarnation in the eucharist, as we are supposed to do on a regular basis, God makes His "glorious presence" known to us and "delivereth into our hands that grace available unto eternal life." As we are co-mingled in the eucharist with Christ, we participate in His resurrection. What happens within the renewed life and spirit of the believer as he participates in this act of communion with Christ is our evidence of Christ's real presence, not what does or what does not happen to the elements of bread and wine.

Consequently, Hooker says, we should not concern ourselves with the unanswerable question of exactly **what** or **who** is present in the elements of the eucharist. The elements "contain **in themselves** no vital force or efficacy, [and] they are not physical but **moral** instruments of salvation, duties of service and worship, which unless we perform as the Author of grace requireth, are unprofitable. . . ." It is our "performance" which makes the miracle work. If we do not faithfully receive the sacrament, if we do not participate with God and Christ as partners in this holy transaction, then there is no holy communion, no eucharist. Our participation in this liturgy is indispensable to the process of Christ's incarnation in us.

This "participation" is mutual. Man and Christ possess each other in the Eucharist.

> Participation is that mutual inward hold which Christ has of us and we of Him, in such sort that each possesses the other by ways of special interest, property and inherent copulation.
>
> For does any man doubt but that even from the flesh of Christ our very bodies do receive that life which shall make them glorious at the later day, and for which they are already accounted parts of His blessed body? Our corruptible bodies could never live the life they live, were it not that they are joined with His body, which is incorruptible, and that He is in ours as a cause of immortality.

Book V is a storehouse of what was to become Anglican/Episcopal doctrine. So much of it shows Hooker's commonsense approach to complex theological issues as well as his gift for soaring prose, the sort that loses precision as it gains altitude but endures at lofty heights. For example, on the always complicated issue of the Triune God--the Trinity--he wrote:

> The Father as goodness, the Son as wisdom, the Holy Ghost as power do all concur in every particular, outwardly issuing from that only glorious Deity which they all are. For that which moves God to work is goodness, and that which orders His work is wisdom, and that which perfects His work is power. All things

240

which God in their times and seasons has brought forth were eternally and before all times in God, as a work unbegun in the artificer, which afterward He brings into effect. Therefore whatsoever we do behold now in this present world, it was enwrapped within the bowels of divine Mercy, written in the book of eternal wisdom, and held in the hands of omnipotent power, the first foundations of the world being as yet unlaid.

Hooker wrote much in Book V about the nature of the church. Once again, the doctrine of incarnation was at the core of his thinking. Anglicans and Episcopalians since Hooker have uniformly defined their church as the Body of Christ in the world. For Hooker "body of Christ" was not a cold doctrine. This body was a community filled with love and mutual support for its members. It was a living body of loved and loving believers. The humanity of Hooker is never more evident than when he speaks of the church, his own true mother.

The church is to us that very mother of our new birth, in whose bowels we are bred, at whose breasts we receive nourishment.

We are. . .in God through Christ. . .from the time of our actual adoption into the body of His true church, into the fellowship of His children. For His church He knows and loves, so that they which are in the church are thereby known to be in Him. Our being in Christ by eternal foreknowledge saves us not without our actual incorporation into that society which has Him for their Head, and makes together with Him one Body. . .

God made Eve of the rib of Adam. And His church He framed out of the very flesh, the wounded and bleeding side of the Son of man.

Hooker completed his editing of Book V during his early years at Bishopsbourne. It was published in 1597. By then he had finished the final three Books as well, although Book VIII still needed more work. Sandys and Cranmer were still pressing him to include more specific refutations of the Barrowists and Brownists and an attack on atheists. Some of this political material he eventually agreed to include. Even Book V has a polemical cast at some points. But for the most part, in this timeless Book V he had written an apology for the church that rose above contemporary politics to a higher ground from which it would illumine the lives of literate Anglicans and Episcopalians down to the present day.

—— Chapter 11 ——

The Final Years

By all accounts, Hooker was never physically vigorous. His rather early death at age forty-seven may have been the consequence of unhealthy living conditions he endured at Oxford and the numerous plagues he survived at college and in London. The emotional stresses of his career at the Temple and continual harpings by Sandys and Cranmer to revise his magnum opus did nothing to improve his constitution. Although his spirits revived in Bishopsbourne, his body did not.

His frail physical nature was not helped by trips to unhealthy London to visit Joan's family, to discuss his book and other church business with friends and colleagues and to attend special family celebrations. One such special occasion at the family church of St. Augustine's was the christening of his and Joan's sixth child, her first live birth in four years. This happy event took place on 21 June 1596. Little Edwin Hooker was named either for Richard's former patron, the late Archbishop Sandys, or for the archbishop's son, Richard's patron and friend, Edwin--or both. Once again, there was the prospect of a male heir to carry Hooker's name into the next generation.

Edwin Sandys was probably present for the christening and may have used the occasion to suggest more revisions in the *Laws* and to bid Hooker and the Churchman's farewell as he prepared for an extended journey on the continent with George Cranmer. Close friends since their days together at Corpus Christi under Hooker's tutelage, these two men traveled in Europe together for more than two years, visiting political and religious leaders. The trip was to be formative for Sandys' reputation as a religious thinker in his own right, for it led him, unwittingly perhaps, to spread some of Hooker's ideas onto the international stage. As a result of his trip, he wrote an influential treatise, not published until 1605, entitled *A Relation to the State of Religion*, reissued in 1629 as *Europae Speculum*. In the spirit of his mentor, Sandys recommended in this work reconciliation among the reformed Christian churches of Europe. His debt to and extension onto a broader canvas of Hooker's ideas is clear in the book's opening words:

> Having now almost finished the course of travel, and coming to cast up (as it was) the short account of my labors, I shall here endeavor briefly to relate what I have observed in the matter of Religion. . . In those Western parts of the world, their divided factions and professions and differences in matters of faith, and their exercises of religion, in government ecclesiastical, and in life and conversation, what virtues in each kind emanate, what eminent defects. Moreover, in what terms of opposition or correspondence each bindeth with other, what probabilities, what policies, what hopes, what jealousies are found in each part for the advancing therof: and finally, what possibilities and good means for uniting, at least wise the several branches of reformed professions.[9]

Sandys and Hooker could not agree on revisions in Books VI, VII, and VIII before Sandys' departure for Europe in 1596. Therefore those Books were not included with Book V in the forthcoming 1597 edition of the *Laws*. Edwin was still balking at Hooker's treatment of the courts and religious penance in Book VI and found his support of the episcopacy in Book VII and royal headship of the church in Book VIII not sufficiently fervent. Hooker was disappointed by this reaction. The entire work was now completed to his satisfaction. Nevertheless, he continued to labor at revising parts of the work, although with decidedly less enthusiasm. With Sandys and Cranmer out of the country for an extended time and Joan safely delivered of his new son, Hooker worked

---

[9] Sandys had a distinguished career in the years following Hooker's death. He was knighted under James I and served as Treasurer of the Virginia (London) Company where he was instrumental in planting the first colony in Virgiinia and advocated representative government in the new world. He may actually have visited the colony. Geroge Cramner was killed fighting in Irleand in 1601 while serving as Secretary to Lord Governor , Baron Mountjoy.

to prepare Book V for publication. It was ready by early 1597 and printed later that year. Thereafter, he largely abandoned further work on the last three books.

Hooker hoped the words of his dedication of Book V to Whitgift would not seem to lack sufficient deference. Perhaps he should not have referred so pointedly to the need for reform in the church; but he was confident the Archbishop would approve his closing words referring to their common mother, the church--that great body they had both labored so hard to defend:

> That God which is able to make mortality immortal give her [the church] such future continuance as may be no less glorious to all posterity than the days of her past rule have been happy to ourselves. . . In which desire I will here rest, humbly beseeching your Grace to pardon my great boldness and God to multiply His blessing upon them that fear His name.

Hooker had little time to celebrate the appearance of Book V in print before terrible tragedy struck. In July of 1597, his son Edwin died, little more than a year old. Joan had taken the baby up to Enfield hoping the change in air would help. In mid-July Richard was summoned north to bury his second son in the Churchman family area of the St. Andrew's churchyard, next to his little brother Richard.

Returning to Bishopsbourne, Hooker sought comfort for his grief by ministering to his flock. He found it especially restorative to console a member of his congregation who had recently lost his wife. He told the widower and his children: "When the Apostles and disciples grieved at the death of our blessed Savior, He reassured them that He would never leave them, but be with them till the end of the world. 'Where I am, you shall be. My peace I give you. Let your hearts be not troubled.' No less has He promised you in your grief."

As to why one's beloved family members should be taken by God when so many who are less worthy are blessed not only with long life but also with great prosperity and good health, Hooker replied to the grieving husband, and all who had faced similar tragedy:

We can never fathom the ways of God. But do not imagine that those blessed in this life with riches and other good fortune are happy and contented. If they seem happy, theirs is a vainly imagined felicity. In fact, they are often anxious and without contentment, lacking any peace of mind and spirit.

We must be patient in our grief. Patience is the virtue that can sustain us until the worst of the pain is gone. In the meantime, take comfort in the chorus of praise we sing for your beloved, as we have for all the saints departed this life in the fear of God. Within the bosom of our Savior's Church you and I can both take our comfort.

As for the fear of death engendered by loss of loved ones:

There is no disgrace in being afraid. Let no one tell you that because Christ promised salvation it is a sin to be afraid of death. Fear is a natural feeling. But we are blessed, you and I, because we know where to take our fears. We run headlong into the church, the body of Christ, where we will surely find grace to overcome our terrors and then be comforted by the assurances of our Savior.

Hooker did not speak to the grieving parishioner in generalities only. From the pulpit, he assured him that his wife would be missed by all members of the little church family who admired and loved her.

Before I say too many words and bring more wounds than comfort to your spirit, allow me to say of your beloved wife that she was truly a virtuous gentlewoman in our parish who lived a dove and died a lamb. She was an example to all of us with her hearty devotion to God, tender compassion to those in need, motherly affection to servants, kindness to friends and a mild disposition toward all. To women she was a model of rectitude, with her quiet tongue, except when duty required her to speak out, and of patience, even in the midst of her own pain.

.   .   .   .   .

Adrian Saravia visited Bishopsbourne frequently during these final years of Hooker's life. As experienced men of the church whose careers had been defined by the religious controversies of the age, Hooker and Saravia spent many stimulating hours together during the closing years of the century in the relative peace and calm of Bishopsbourne discussing not only immediate political issues but also their respective ideas on broader theological and ecclesiological questions. Hooker's recently published Book V was grist for their mill. It was reassuring to Richard whenever a man of Saravia's experience and erudition spoke admiringly of his work, as the older man did now concerning the place in Book V where Hooker explored the relationship between the Book of Common Prayer and the civic virtue of citizens. Prayers spoken in common, within God's House, were not mere petitions to the Almighty, but the common voice of the whole people ascending in prayer to the Redeemer. When Hooker wrote that these prayers were the basis of the moral strength of the English as a people, he was doing much more than merely responding to Cartwright's pesterings about whether one should stand or kneel at prayer, how long the service should be and where the sermon should be placed in the order of the service.

Saravia approved of Hooker's claim for the Prayer Book that it played a central role in the relation between religion and civic virtue. Prayer Book usage was, for Hooker, the essential means whereby the commonwealth might achieve its intended end: a happy life, well-lived, protected against wickedness and malice and enlightened as to the nature of public duties, both religious and civic. No private extemporaneous prayers, such as the Puritans advocated against the Prayer Book, could ever hope to perform this great civic function of uniting a whole people of God in an act of public common worship.

Hooker proclaimed this general theme of the integral relationship between common religious worship and civic virtue in the opening words of Book V:

> True religion is the root of all true virtues, and
> the stay of well-ordered commonwealths. Let polity
> acknowledge itself indebted to religion; godliness being
> the chiefest top and wellspring of all true virtues. . . .So
> natural is the union of religion and justice, that we may
> boldly deem there is neither, where both are not.

This theme was made more even explicit in Book VIII where Hooker made the point that church and state together make a single society, a Christian commonwealth. This was the heart of Hooker's political philosophy and Saravia applauded it. Both men believed that there was no one in the Church of England who was not at the same time a citizen of the English commonwealth, or any member of the commonwealth who was not also a member of the Church of England. Citizens exercised their civic duties as members of the commonwealth and their religious duties as members of the church. But in all things they were members of the Christian commonwealth of England. For all their protestations to the contrary, what many of Calvin's disciples in England were trying to do was separate church and state, the Brownists and Barrowists being at least forthright in this error.

Hoping to tempt Hooker into a good debate, Saravia challenged his friend with the fact that there had been a single Christian commonwealth for centuries under the headship of the pope. Have we Protestants not fractured that unity with our reformation of religion? Hooker responded that, to the contrary, in those commonwealths where the bishop of Rome held sway, there are in fact two separate societies: a church, which he rules, and a civil society ruled by a secular prince. In this realm of England, however, there was but one society: a true Christian commonwealth headed by only one ruler, a sovereign queen.

This raised the dangerous question of what recourse there was if a monarch like Queen Elizabeth were sinful and corrupted the church with her decisions. A most perplexing issue! For his part, Hooker followed the lead of the influential thirteenth-century English jurist Henry Bracton who had said that the monarch in England had absolute powers only under the law--never above it. Hooker wrote rhapsodically on this subject:

> Happier are the people whose law is the king in the greatest things, than those whose king is himself their law. Where the king guides the state and the law the king, that commonwealth is like a harp or melodious instrument, the strings whereof are tuned and handled all by one. We are blessed by the wisdom of those who founded our commonwealth that, although matters may be subject to the king's power, yet that power is limited in all its proceedings by the rule of law.

Hooker was frankly ambivalent on the thorny issue of whether, when the prince abused his authority over them, the people had a right to reclaim their original power by overthrowing him. The answer was, yes and no. Yes, if the compact by which political power was originally transferred from a society to a monarch prescribed reasons and methods for removing him. Even then, there must be a tradition of acquiescence by the king in such provisions. No, if there is no prior constitutional method described in the compact that first created the government. After all, the people formed government in the first instance because their facility for disagreement prevented them from living peacefully together in a natural and ungoverned state. Thus, in theory there was a right to unseat an unjust king but in practice this was a highly circumscribed right, one not quite justified in Hooker's political philosophy.

In Book VIII on the matter of the king's headship of the church, another issue emerged-- that of the role of the clergy in limiting the monarch's authority. There was a long tradition in England of shared governance of the church. Although the king appointed bishops, for example, and had a voice in approving church law, these acts were rarely consummated without the initiative and approval of higher clergy or a church convocation. Certainly, the king ought never to act as a judge in a court, especially a church court. About the most Hooker was willing to say about such royal power was that no important ecclesiastical decision might be made without the king's consent. This was a far cry from the authority over the church soon to be claimed by the first

Stewart king of England. Saravia no doubt argued with Hooker that he was far too restrictive in his view of royal headship of the church.

Hooker was on especially difficult ground in Book VIII when he spoke of the prince as below the law and the parliament as the chief law-making body, He did not view the parliament as a simple legislature concerning itself with such matters as "the regulation and sale of leather and wool." It was much more than that. It was "the high court of parliament," empowered to pronounce and enforce through its various parts the many types of law--constitutional and statutory, civil and ecclesiastical--that rule the land. Supreme among the parts of the high court of parliament is the king. But he may never alter any law or statute of parliament nor dispense with any legal contract or title, because his power has derived from the ancient common law of the body politic. He is like "a watchman" or agent of the public welfare who always has at heart the best interests of his subjects. If he should act otherwise, he is not a king at all but a tyrant.

It is not surprising that it would be many years before these sentiments of Hooker's ever saw the light of day, and then only during a time when anti-royalist sentiments were in the ascendancy. As the politically savvy Saravia no doubt pointed out to him, his comments on royal authority were not likely to please the Queen. He was far too qualified in his support of the monarchy to suit Elizabeth, much less her probable successor, the King of Scotland. Perhaps Sandys had done him a favor after all in resisting publication of his last three books.

. . . . .

Whenever Hooker went into the sanctuary of St. Mary's to pray alone, but especially on Sundays at the services of common prayer, he gave thanks for this beautiful, hallowed church building, In the recently published Book V of the *Laws*, he had written:.

> Our Puritan brothers complain that we make too
> much of our church buildings and other outward signs
> of God's presence among us. But they are wrong. For
> it is vital that all we do in praise of God correspond to

the power and majesty of the God we worship. This correspondence between our inner spiritual lives in God's presence and the outer world in which we must make our way, we express in the beauty and majesty of our church buildings, rituals of worship, attire of clergy, and all the outward forms of our praise.

Taking still more material from his book, as author-preachers are inclined to do, Hooker went on in the same vein.

The so-called purifiers of our religion say we should keep our sanctuaries bare of all adornment so as to imitate what they call the "nakedness of Jesus" and the "simplicity of the gospel." But where, I ask you, my friends, has God anywhere said that He wishes to dwell in a beggarly fashion and takes pleasure in being worshipped nowhere save a poor cottage? Through all history, men of faith have praised God by making their temples of worship their most glorious buildings. It is true that God cares most for our inner spiritual affection toward Him. But surely He must also approve a cheerful affection in us, one which regards nothing too beautiful or dear to be expended in the furniture of our worship of Him. Our grand church buildings serve as a witness to the world of God's almightiness, Whom we seek to honor with our most lavish outward expressions of His power and glory.

"And the same goes for all of the outward signs of our worship," Hooker continued.

Our celebration of special Saint's days, the naming of churches for saints--like our own St. Mary the Virgin-- the wearing of the surplice, kneeling and standing and sitting at different parts of the service, using the sign of the cross, all of these we practice these by long tradition of the Church in England as seemly expressions of our praise for God and not out of desire to imitate the Roman Church.

What bothered Hooker most about these Puritan attacks on traditional forms of worship was the need to answer them at all. Yes, it was true, the church preferred to follow the "grey hairs" because they had more experience and sense than those who seemed to like change for its own sake. For us, he wrote in Book V,

> The authority of the established church in all such matters is sufficient warrant for our religious practices. And to those like Thomas Cartwright who ask why we hang our judgments on the church's sleeve, I say that. . . . the opinion of the historic church ought to be sufficient to shut the mouths of those who, with nothing but the authority of their own interpretation of holy scripture, bark against our traditional religious forms and practices.

Probably nothing irritated Hooker more than the Puritan opposition to music as a part of worship. He wrote:

> Withal, what offends me most among the many attacks upon our worship is the picking away at our music. Our very soul responds to music, finding there the harmony which defines its nature. In musical harmony, the image and character of both virtue and vice may be perceived, while the mind is being delighted. Music touches the divine within us. It is a thing which delights people of all ages and in all conditions of life. Music is as seasonable in grief as in joy.
> Music has that most admirable facility of expressing and representing to our minds more deeply than any other sensible means, the very standing, rising and falling, the very steps and inflections, the turns and varieties of all passions whereunto our minds are subject.

More than that, music can **initiate** these movements of our minds and souls.

Late in 1599, Hooker was jolted by one of the worst shocks of his life. An anonymous tract that specifically attacked his book appeared under the title, *A Christian Letter of certaine English Protestants, unfeigned favourers of the present State of Religion, authorized and professed in England; unto that Reverend and learned man, Mr R. Hook. Requiring resolution in certaine matters of doctrine (which seem to overthrow the foundation of Christian Religion, and of the church among us) expresle contained in his five books of Ecclesiastical Pollicie.*

Adrian Saravia may have been the first to bring Hooker a copy of this work and to try to soften its blow. By this time, Saravia was well-acquainted with his friend's sensitivity to criticism. He would have told Hooker that now that his work had been attacked in print, he had finally arrived as a great writer. He should now write his "defense," and later, a "reply" to the "answer," and so on.

The speculation was that this anonymous piece had been hatched at Cambridge. A group of fellows there was upset with what they saw as the threat of arminianism[10] in Hooker's writings. That old predestination issue continued to plague him. A prime candidate for actual authorship was Andrew Willet who was rapidly gaining a reputation as one of the most learned writers among the Puritans. He had a church just outside Cambridge where he kept in close touch with Puritan friends. Although he professed loyalty to the Church of England, Willet kept his senses alert for hints of papism, opposition to predestination, or any smell of arminianism. Some would count him as not the most extreme of Puritans, but perhaps somewhere in the middle of that group.

Why, Hooker wondered in anguish, would they accuse him of undermining the established church when it was these very Cambridge radicals from whom he was defending the church? The clear answer to that question, Saravia may have told him, was that Hooker had frightened his foes into action. They were worried about his attack

---

[10] Arminianism was promulgated by Jacobus Arminius (1560-1609), the founding theologian of the Dutch Reformed Church. The central tenet is that the strict Calvinist doctrine of predestination is too rigid. He taught that God's sovereign will and human freedom are not incompatible.

on them because it was so different from what they had endured until now from defenders of the established church. No one had ever so systematically torn apart their discipline and laid bare their true intentions as he had. Puritans and Presbyterians had to take him very seriously and so had chosen to say that it was he, and not they, who undermined the true church.

Hooker's initial responses to the *Letter* were visceral. He wrote out some of them passionately in the margins of his copy of the tract. The author, he felt, was attacking him "without eyes for he seems not to perceive the bare meaning of the church's most basic teachings and doctrines. I think his godparents have much to answer to God for not seeing that he was better trained in his catechism class." At a place where he was criticized for a ponderous writing style, Hooker wrote: "How this asse runs, kicking up his heels as if a summerfly had stung him." In another place, Hooker advised the author to go "read some good catechisms." In another, he wrote in anger, "You lie, sir."

Eventually Hooker came to see, perhaps with help from the older and, in this instance, more dispassionate Saravia, that there was substance to some of the points made in the *Letter* and that these deserved thoughtful replies. After all, there were twenty-one separate objections to some of Hooker's most cherished positions on virtually every subject, especially his views on free will, grace, predestination and the sacraments.

Still, the more Hooker read the tract the angrier he became. The author of the *Letter,* whoever he was, was far more personal in his attacks on Hooker than Walter Travers ever had been. He went so far as to accuse Richard of hypocrisy for trying, as he said, to reinstitute popish religion under the guise of attacking Puritan extremists. He accused Hooker of "hoodwinking" his readers, of "beguiling" and "bewitching" them with a "popish brew," of "lulling them to sleep" with his rhetoric while he undermined the church..

Despite his pique, Hooker had to admit, to himself at least, that the author of the *Letter* had hit upon a clever stroke in twisting to his own purpose Hooker's opening metaphor about dreams at the beginning of the *Laws*. Hooker had written that he would not "through silence permit things to pass away as in a dream." Like a distorted echo, the *Letter* mimicked and mocked Hooker with these words: "When men dream they are asleep, and while men sleep the enemie [Hooker] soweth tares, and tares take root and hinder the good corn of the church before it be aspied. Therefore wisemen [Willet and friends] through silence permit **nothing** to pass away as in a dream."

In time, Hooker cooled down and penned a tract which might serve as either part of a response to the *Letter* or as a preamble to the final three books of the *Laws*. He continued working on his reply until the time of his death. It was more important, he felt, to use his waning energy to complete this major defense of his *apologia* for his beloved church than to do any further editing of the last three books of the *Laws* which had been by now altered to his satisfaction, needing only a propitious time for publication.

In his study Hooker gathered up his earlier tracts and sermons written on predestination, grace, and the sacraments, as well as relevant parts of the fifth book of the *Laws*. Drawing on materials he had used long ago in his *Answer* to Travers' *Supplication*, he nearly completed his response to attacks against him on the predestination question. He also managed to put forth some of his answer to criticism of his positions on the sacraments and grace before his energy gave out. Unfortunately, his answer to the *Christian Letter* was still incomplete and in rough form when the end finally came.

In October of 1600, Joan Hooker urgently summoned Dr. Saravia to Bishopsbourne. Her husband was dying.

During the last months of his life, Hooker was too weak to continue his pastoral and priestly duties, much less to complete any revisions in Books VI through VIII. He could only hope that among his friends there would be someone who would see that his unpublished works were edited and published. His wish was fulfilled. Almost immediately on news of his death, Archbishop Whitgift commissioned Dr. William Covel, a fellow at Queens College, Cambridge, to answer the *Letter*. In 1595, Covel had written his own defense of the church entitled, *Polimanteia*, in which he called Hooker a "defender of true religion."

Covel's defense of Hooker's *Laws* appeared in 1603 under the title, *A Just and Temperate Defense of the Five Books*. Comparing this work with Hooker's notes toward his own response to the *Letter* makes clear that Covel's work fell short of what Hooker would have accomplished had he lived to write his own reply. In fact, Covel did little more than quote Hooker's own words from the *Laws* to defend him. Still, Covel did say in his *Defense* that Hooker's book was "incomparably the best that ever was written in our church."

As he prepared to die, Hooker took comfort that his prosperous father-in-law would see to the needs, comfort and long-term financial security of his wife and children. It was a reasonable surmise, but not to be. Within a year of Hooker's death, John Churchman was plunged into financial ruin as his investments in Ireland fell victim to the economic and political turmoil in that troubled land. His loses had disastrous consequences for Joan Hooker and her children.

Richard advised Joan to find another husband when he was gone. His girls would need the protection of a father. Joan was still young and Richard would leave her a dowry sufficient to make a good match for herself. He drafted a will and then reviewed it with Edwin Sandys and Adrian Saravia, and then with Joan, so that she would be clear about the provisions before the document was formally drawn up and proved (notarized). Under the terms of the will, Joan, as his "beloved wife," was to be his sole executor and principal remainder beneficiary. John Churchman and Edwin Sandys had agreed to be general overseers of the estate. Richard bequeathed £100 each to Alice, Cicely, Jane and Margaret as dowries to be paid at their marriages. In the event of the death or failure to marry of any of the girls, the others would share the forfeited amount.

His other bequests were few: £5 to the poor at Barham parish and 50s. for the poor at Bishopsbourne, £3 for a new pulpit at St. Mary's. (After Hooker died and Joan was preparing to remarry, an inventory of household goods, including Hooker's books was made. The estimated value came to over £500. This, coupled with payments from Sandys on Hooker's book, when completed, would make a good dowry for Joan.)

On 20th October 1600, Hooker's will was registered. From that time on he was confined to his bed. On the first day of November, Saravia was pleased to find Hooker sitting up and looking somewhat revived, after some period of watching silently by his friend's bedside while the dying man ate nothing and said nothing, apparently in a semiconscious state. Able to converse briefly, Hooker asked his friend to hear his final confession and give him the sacrament when his time came. He would like a simple funeral service following the rites in the *Book of Common Prayer*, with burial in the churchyard at St. Mary's. No, he did not want to be buried in London, nor did he want word of his death sent to London until after he was interred. Would Adrian see to these details?

The next day, Saravia found Hooker worse than he had left him and tried to awaken him before it was too late. Richard opened his eyes and whispered to his friend that it was time to administer last rites. Adrian heard his brief confession. Hooker said simply: "I commend and bequeath my immortal soul to God's merciful care."

Saravia could tell that Hooker was slipping away. He quickly withdrew the host from his case and forced it between his friend's lips. "This is my Body. . ."

About a week later, Philip Culme dismounted his hard-ridden horse in the Hooker stable, ran up to the rectory and banged hard on the front door. When Joan Hooker answered, Churchman's apprentice explained at once that her father and mother were on the way down from London and had sent him on ahead to see to her needs. Assured that Mrs. Hooker had everything under control, Culme then explained his other errand concerning the safekeeping of her late husband's manuscripts. Joan directed the messenger to Richard's study. Philip mounted the stairs and soon began to fill his cloak bag with a treasure.[11]

---

[11] This theological treasure would make Hooker arguably the most influential and formative thinker and writer in the long history of the Anglican/Episcopal world-wide religious community, now 7 million strong. In some branches of this denomination he has come close to sainthood. His book is still required reading in seminaries and in the America Episcopal Church he has been given his own day (November 3rd) in the official Church Calendar.of Fesats and Fasts.

Bibliography Of Works Consulted And Used

ADDISON, WILLIAM. Worthy Dr Fuller. New York: The Macmillan Company, 1951.

ALEXANDER, J. J. "Ancestors of John Hooker." Devon and Cornwall Notes and Queries, 1936-37. 19. 222.

ALYMER, JOHN. Letter to Whitgift. *23 November 1589. Lambeth Palace Library: Fairhurst Papers, MS 3470, fol. 129.*

(ANONYMOUS). A Christian Letter of a certain English Protestants, unfeigned favourers of the present state of Religion, authorised and professed in England: unto that Reverend and learned man, Mr. R. Hoo. Requiring resolution in certaine matters of doctrine (which seem to overthrow the foundation of Christian Religion, and of the church among us) expreslie contained in his five books of Ecclesiastical Pollicie. 1599. (British Library 3932639). Folger, IV, 6-79.

(ANONYMOUS). Consecration of the Temple Church: Sermons Preached at the Celebration of its Seven Hundredth Anniversary. London: Macmillan & Co., 1885.

ARBER, EDWARD, ed. A Transcript of the Company of Stationers from 1554-1640 AD, II. Privately printed for John Windet. London, 1875.

AUSTIN, PETER AND ORGAN, TOM. Report on the Conservation of the 14th Century Wall Paintings. Available as an unpublished research paper from St. Mary's Church, Bishopsbourne, Kent, 1995.

AVIS, PAUL. Anglicanism and the Christian Church. Minneapolis: Fortress Press, 1989.

AYRE, JOHN, ed. The Sermons of Edwin Sandys, D.D. Cambridge: The Parker Society, 1841.

----------, ed. The Works of John Whitgift. Cambridge: The Parker Society, 1853.

BAIKIE, JAMES. The English Bible and Its Story. Philadelphia: J. B. Lippincott Company, 1925.

BAILEY, HENRY. Salisbury Cathedral Library. Salisbury Cathedral, 1978.

BAUCHAM, RICHARD. "Hooker, Travers and the Church of Rome in the 1580's." Journal of Ecclesiastical History, 29: 37-50, 1978.

BAYLIS, T. HENRY. The Temple Church of St. Ann, An Historical Record and Guide. London: George Philip and Son, 1895.

BEDWELL, C. E. A. A Brief History of the Middle Temple. London: Butterworth & Co., 1909.

BEIR, A. L. AND FINLAY, ROGER. The Making of the Metropolis: London 1500-1700. London and New York: Longman, 1986.

BELLOT, HUGH H. L. The Inner and Middle Temple. London: Methuen & Co., 1902.

BESANT, WALTER. London in the Time of the Tudors. London: Adam & Charles Black, 1904.

BOGGIS, R. J. E. A History of the Diocese of Exeter. Exeter: William Pollard & Co., Ltd. 1922.

BOOTY, JOHN E.. "Introduction: Book V." Folger. VI.I, 183-231.

-------- Hooker and Anglicanism." In Studies in Richard Hooker: Essays Preliminary to an Edition of His Works. W. Speed Hill, ed. Cleveland and London: The Press of Case Western Reserve University, 1972.

-------- John Jewel as Apologist for the Church of England. London: SPCK, 1963.

-------- "Richard Hooker, Anglican Theologian." Sewanee Theological Review, 36:2, 186, 1993.

-------- "The Quest for the Historical Hooker." The Churchman, 80:185-193, 1966.

BORER, MARY CATHCART. The People of Tudor England. London: Max Parrish and Co., Ltd, 1966.

BOWEN, CATHERINE DRINKER. The Lion and the Throne. Boston: Little Brown and Company, 1956.

BRAUDEL, BERNARD. The Structures of Everyday Life, I. New York: Harper & Row, 1981.

BRAYLEY, W. AND H. HERBERT, A Concise Account Historical and Descriptive of Lambeth Palace. London, S. Gosnell, 1806.

BRIGDEN, SUSAN. London and the Reformation. Oxford: Clarendon Press, 1989.

BROOK, V. J. K. Whitgift and the English Church. London: The English University Press, 1957.

BRUCE, JOHN and THOMAS BROWNE, eds. *The Correspondence of Matthew Parker*: The Parker Society. 1853.

BULL, HENRY, ed. Christian Prayers and Holy Meditations, 1556. Cambridge: The Parker Society, 1842.

BURNBY, J., ed. Elizabethan Times in Tottenham, Edmondton and Enfield. Edmonton: Edmonton Historical Society, 1995.

BURNETT, DAVID. Salisbury, The History of an English Cathedral. London: The Compton Press, Ltd., 1953.

BYRNE, MURIEL ST. CLARE. Elizabethan Life in Town and Country. 1925. Gloucester: Alan Sutton, 1987.

CANNY, NICHOLAS. The Elizabethan Conquest of Ireland. New York: Harper & Row, 1976.

CARLISLE, NICHOLAS. A Concise Description of the Endowed Grammar Schools in England and Wales, I. London: Baldwin, Cradock & Joy, 1818.

CARLSON, LELAND H. Martin Marprelate Gentleman Master Job Throckmorton Laid Open in His Colors. San Marino: Huntington Library, 1981.

CARLTON, CHARLES. The Court of Orphans. Leicester: Leicester University Press, 1974.

CARTWRIGHT, THOMAS. A Reply to an Answere made of M. Doctor Whittgife Againste the Admonition to the Parliament By T.C. Lambeth Palace Library: 1574.03.

CHANDLERY, P. J. From Tower to Tyburn. London: Sands & Co., 1924.

CHARTIER, ROGER, ed. "Passions of the Renaissance." A History of Private Life, III. Cambridge: Harvard University Press, 1989.

CHURCH, R. W., ed. Hooker Of the Laws of Ecclesiastical Polity, Bk.1. Oxford: Clarendon Press, 1896.

CHUTE, MARCHETTE. Shakespeare of London. New York: E. P. Dutton and Company, Inc., 1964.

CLAY, WILLIAM KEATINGE. Liturgical Services Liturgies and Occasional Forms of Prayer Set Forth in the Reign of Queen Elizabeth. Cambridge: The Parker Society, 1847.

-------- <u>Private Prayers Put Forth by Authority During the Reign of Queen Elizabeth</u>. Cambridge: The Parker Society, 1851.

CLIFTON-TAYLOR, ALEC. <u>The Cathedrals of England</u>. Norwich: Thames and Hudson, 1967.

COLLINSON, PATRICK. <u>Elizabethan Essays</u>. London: Hambledon Press, 1994.

-------- <u>The Elizabethan Puritan Movement</u>. London: Methuen & Co., 1967.

-------- <u>The Religion of Protestants: The Church in English Society 1559-1625</u>. Oxford: Clarendon Press, 1982.

CORPUS CHRISTI ARCHIVES. <u>Liber Admis 1517-1646</u>; <u>Liber Magni</u> (Unnumbered folios).

COVEL, WILLIAM. <u>A Just and Temperate Defense of the Five Books</u>. London, 1603. Corpus Christi College Archives: Fulman Ms #1682, 215.E.1.15 a ff..

CRANMER, GEORGE. <u>Concerning the New Church Discipline, An Excellent Letter Written By Mr. G. Cranmer to Mr. R. H.</u> c.1592-93. <u>Works II</u>.

--------, <u>Notes Upon Mr. Hooker's Sixth Book</u>. Corpus Christi College, Oxford. MS 295, fol. 3.1.

CRESSEY, DAVID. <u>Birth, Marriage, and Death: Ritual, Religion, and the Life Cycle in Tudor and Stewart England</u>. Oxford: Oxford University Press, 1977.

CRUISE, CONOR AND O'BRIEN, MARIE. <u>The Story of Ireland</u>. Englewood Cliffs: The Viking Press, 1968.

CURTIS, EDMUND. <u>A History of Ireland</u>, 6th ed. New York: Barnes and Noble, 1950.

CURTIS, MARK. <u>Oxford and Cambridge in Transition 1558-1642</u>. Oxford: Clarendon Press, 1959.

DARLEY, GILLIAN AND SAINT, ANDREW. <u>The Chronicles of London</u>. London: Weidenfeld and Nicolson, Ltd., 1994.

DAVIES, HORTON. <u>Worship and Theology in England 1534-1603</u>. Princeton: Princeton University Press, 1970.

DAVIS, J. C. "Backing into Modernity: The Dilemma of Richard Hooker." <u>The Certainty of Doubt, Tributes to Peter Munz</u>, 157-179. Miles Fairburn and W. H. Oliver, eds. Victoria, B. C.: Victoria University Press, 1997.

DAWLEY, POWELL MILLS. John Whitgift and the Reformation. London: Adam and Charles Black, 1955.

DEAKEN, Q. E. "John Hooker's 'Description of Excester': A Comparison of the manuscripts." Devon and Cornwall Notes and Queries. 104. 229-238; 121; 264-71. [no publisher or date.]

DEAN, JOSEPH. Middle Temple Hall: Four Centuries of History. London: Middle Temple, 1970.

DENT, C. M. Protestant Reformers in Elizabethan Oxford. Oxford: Oxford University Press, 1983.

DEVON RECORDS OFFICE. Roger Hooker's Interest in Tin Works and His Debts. H.H.3.55, fol. 39; 57 fol. 148.

-------- Richard Hooker's Grants from the City of Exeter. Act Book 4, 1581-1588.

D'EWES, SIMONDS. The Journals of All the Parliaments During the Reign of Queen Elizabeth. London, 1682.

DICKENS, A. G. The English Reformation. rev. ed. Glasgow: Fontana Press, 1967.

DODD, A. H. Life in Elizabethan England. London: B. T. Batsford, Ltd., 1961.

DODWELL, C. R. Lambeth Palace. London: Country Life Limited, 1958.

DORAN, SUSAN AND DURSTON, CHRISTOPHER. Princes, Pastors and People. London and New York: Routledge, 1991.

DOUGLAS, C. E. AND FRERE, W. W., eds.. Puritan Manifestoes, 1907. London, 1954.

DOWLING, THADY, ed. Annals of Ireland. Dublin: R. Butler, 1849.

DUNCAN, C. D. "Public Lectures and Professorial Chairs," The History of the University of Oxford, III, 335-362. James McConica, ed.. Oxford: Clarendon Press, 1986.

DURSTON, CHRISTOPHER AND DORAN, SUSAN. Princes, Pastors and People. London and New York: Routledge, 1991.

ECCLESHALL, ROBERT. "Richard Hooker and the Peculiarities of the English: The Reception of the 'Ecclesiastical Polity' in the Seventeenth and Eighteenth Centuries." History of Political Thought, 2.1: 63-117. January, 1981.

EDELEN, GEORGES. "A Chronology of Richard Hooker's Life." The Folger Library Edition of the Works of Richard Hooker, VI: xvii-xxx. W. Speed Hill, ed. Cambridge and London: The Belknap Press of Harvard University, 1990.

-------- "Hooker's Style." Studies in Richard Hooker, 241-277. W. Speed Hill, ed. Cleveland: The Press of Case Western Reserve University, 1972.

-------- The Description of England (1587). William Harrison, ed. New York: Dover Publications, 1994.

ELTON, G. R. England Under the Tudors. London and New York: Routledge, 1974.

ERICKSON, CAROLLY. The First Elizabeth. New York: Summit Books, 1983.

FALLA, TREVOR. "Heavitree." Discovering Exeter. Exeter: Exeter Civic Society, 1983.

FARR, EDWARD, ed. Select Poetry Chiefly Devotional of the Reign of Queen Elizabeth. Cambridge: The Parker Society, 1845.

FINLAY, ROGER AND BEIR, A. L. The Making of the Metropolis: London 1500-1700. London and New York: Longman, 1986.

FLETCHER, ANTHONY AND ROBERTS, PETER, eds. Religion, Culture and Society in Early Modern Britain Essays in Honour of Patrick Collinson. Cambridge: Cambridge University Press, 1994.

FLETCHER, J. M. "The Faculty of Arts." The History of the University of Oxford, III, 157-200. James McConica, ed.. Oxford: Clarendon Press, 1986.

FORTE, E. P. "Richard Hooker as Preacher." Folger, V: 658-682.

FOWLER, JOSEPH. Medieval Sherborne. Dorchester: Longmans, 1951.

FOWLER, THOMAS. The History of Corpus Christi College. Oxford: Clarendon Press, 1893.

FREEMAN, EDWARD A. AND HUNT, WILLIAM, eds. Historic Towns. London: Longmans, Green & Co., 1906.

FULLER, THOMAS. The Church-History of Britain from the Birth of Jesus Christ until the Year MDCXLVII, III. London: John Williams, 1665.

-------- The History of the Worthies of England, I. London: J.G.W.L., 1662.

GAUDEN, JOHN. The Life & Death of Mr. Richard Hooker in The Works of Mr. Richard Hooker . . . London: J. Best, 1662.

GEE, ERIC A. Bishopsthorpe Palace An Architectural History. York: William Sessions Limited, 1983.

GIBBS, LEE W. "Introduction to Book VI." Folger. VI.I, 249-308.

-------- "Theology, Logic and Rhetoric in the Temple Controversy between Richard Hooker and Walter Travers." Anglican Theological Review, 65.2: 177-188. 1983.

-------- (with Philip Secor). TheWisdom of Richard Hooker. Bloomington. Ind.: Author Books, 2005.

GOSART, ALEXANDER B., ed. The Spending of the Money of Robert Nowell. Blackburn, Lancashire. Printed for private circulation. Townley MSS, 1877. British Library 2.326g.19.

GREENSLADE, S. L. "The Faculty of Theology," The History of the University of Oxford, III, 329-55. James Monica, ed. Oxford: Clarendon Press, 1986.

GRISLIS, EGIL. "Commentary." Folger, V, 619-55. W. Speed Hill ed. Binghamton, New York: Medieval & Renaissance Texts & Studies, 1993.

-------- "The Hermeneutical Problem in Richard Hooker." Studies in Richard Hooker: Essays Preliminary to An Edition of His Works. W. Speed Hill, ed. Cleveland and London: The Press of Case Western Reserve University, 1972.

HAIGH, CHRISTOPHER, ed. The Reformation Revised. Cambridge: Cambridge University Press, 1987.

HALLAM, HENRY. The Constitutional History of England, 5th ed., I. London: John Murray, 1846.

HAMMER, CARL I., JR. "Town of Oxford," The History of the University of Oxford. III, 69-116. ed. by James Monica. Oxford: Clarendon Press, 1986.

HARRISON, WILLIAM. The Description of England (1587). Georges Edelen, ed. New York: Dover Publications, 1994.

HARTE, WALTER J., ed. An Account of the Seiges of Exeter, Foundation of the Cathedral Church and Disputes Between the Cathedral and City Authorities by John Vowell alias Hoker. Exeter: Muniment Room. James G. Commin, 1911.

-------- ed. <u>Exeter City Monuments</u>, 52. Devon and Cornwall Record Society.

-------- <u>Gleanings from the Common Place book of John Hooker, relating to the City of Exeter (1485-1590)</u>. Exeter: Wheaton & Co. (no date).

-------- <u>John Hooker's Description of the citie of Excester</u>. Exeter: Devon and Cornwall Record Society, 1919.

--------with J. W. Schopp and H. Tapley Soper, eds. <u>Office of Arms Chart 1597.</u> Showing "Joan" as wife of Roger Hooker. Exeter City Muniments, 52.

HARTLEY, T. E., ed. <u>Proceedings in the Parliaments of Elizabeth I 1584-1589</u>, I. London: Leicester University Press, 1995.

HASTINGS, ROBINSON, ed. <u>The Zurich Letters 1558-1579</u>. Cambridge: The Parker Society, 1845.

HAUGAARD, WILLIAM P. <u>Elizabeth and the English Reformation</u>. Cambridge: Cambridge University Press, 1968.

-------- "The Hooker-Travers Controversy." <u>Folger</u>, V, 264-9.

-------- "The Preface." <u>Folger</u>, VI.1, 1-80.

-------- "Books II, III, IV." <u>Folger</u>, VI.I, 125-181.

HEADLAM, CECIL. <u>Oxford and its History</u>. London: J. M. Dent & Sons, 1926.

HERBERT, H. AND BRAYLEY, W. <u>A Concise Account Historical and Descriptive of Lambeth Palace</u>. London: S. Gosnell, 1806.

HIBBERT, CHRISTOPHER. <u>The English A Social History 1066-1945</u>. New York: W. W. Norton, 1987.

-------- AND WEINREB, BEN, eds. <u>The London Encyclopedia</u>. London: Macmillan, 1983.

HILL, W. SPEED. <u>The Doctrinal Background of Hooker's Laws of Ecclesiastical Polity</u>. Doctoral Dissertation. Harvard University, 1964.

--------, gen. ed. <u>The Folger Library Edition of the Works of Richard Hooker</u>. 7 vols. Cambridge, London, Binghampton, N.Y., Tempe, Arizona: The Belknap Press of Harvard University; Medieval and Renaissance Texts and Studies, 1977-1998 [cited in this bibliography as <u>Folger</u>.]

-------- Richard Hooker A Descriptive Biography of the Early Editions: 1593-1724. Cleveland and London: The Press of Case Western Reserve University, 1970.

--------ed. Richard Hooker Works: Index of Names and Works. Tempe, Arizona: Medieval and Renaissance Texts & Studies, 1998. [Published as vol. VII in Folger Library Edition of the Works of Richard Hooker.]

--------, ed. Studies in Richard Hooker: Essays Preliminary to an Edition of His Works. Cleveland & London: The Press of Case Western Reserve University, 1972.

-------- "The Evolution of Hooker's Laws of Ecclesiastical Polity." In Studies: 117-158.

HINTON, EDWARD M. Ireland Through Tudor Eyes. Philadelphia: University of Pennsylvania Press, 1935.

HOBHOUSE, CHRISTOPHER. Oxford As it Was and As it is Today. London: B. T. Batsford, Ltd, 1939.

HOOKER, JOHN. A Catalog of the Bishops of Excester, with the description of the Antiquitie, and first foundation of the Cathedrall Church of the same. London: Henry Denham, 1584. Also, 1584: Bk.2. Exeter: Devon Records Office

-------- Common Place Book. In Walter Harte, ed. Gleanings from the Common Place Book of John Hooker. Exeter: Wheaton & Co., 1919?.

-------- The Description of the Cittie of Excester, Colected and Gathered by John Vowell alias Hooker gentleman and Chamberlain of the same Cittie. London?: Blackletter, 1559; 1571; 1580 (in British Museum General Catalogue of Printed Books. London, 1964, CCL, 2430; 1587 (in Holinshed's *Chronicles)*, 1600. Devon Record Office. Exeter City Archives. Book 52. Also in Harte, ed. John Hooker's Description of the citie of Exeter. Devon and Cornwall Record Society, 1919. Pt. II, 8-25.)

-------- The Discourse and Discovery of the Life of Sir Peter Carew. In John Maclean, ed. John Hooker's The Life and Times of Sir Peter Carew (1584), 119ff. London: Bill & Daldy, 1857.

-------- Order and Usage of the keeping of a parlement in England. London: John Allde,1572. In Vernon F. Snow. Parliament in

Elizabethan England, John Hooker's Order and Usage. Hartford: Yale University Press, 1977.

------- A Pamphlet of the Offices, and Duties of everie particular sworne Officer, of the Citie of Exeter. London: Henry Denham, 1584.

HOOKER, RICHARD. The Answere of Mr. Richard Hooker to a Supplication Preferred by Mr. Walter Travers to the HH. Lords of the Privy Counsell. 1586. Folger, V, 225-57.

--------Autograph Notes on A Christian Letter, 1599-1600. Folger, IV, 1-79.

--------Dublin Fragments on Grace and Free Will, the Sacraments, and Predestination. After 1595. Folger, IV, 99-167.

--------The First Sermon Upon Part of St. Jude, 1582/83. Folger, V, 13-35.

-------- Of the Laws of Ecclesiastical Polity: Books I-IV. 1593; Book V, 1595; Books VI, VIII, 1648; Book VII, 1662. Folger, I-IV, 1977-82.

-------- A Learned and Comfortable Sermon of the Certaintie and Perpetuitie of Faith in the Elect, 1585. Folger, V, 69-82.

-------- A Learned Discourse of Justification, Workes, and How the Foundation of Faith is Overthrowne, 1585/86. Folger, V, 105-69.

-------- A Learned Sermon of the Nature of Pride. Folger, V, 309-61.

-------- Notes Toward a Fragment on Predestination. Folger, !V, 83-97

-------- A Remedie Against Sorrow and Feare delivered in a funerall Sermon, 1595-1600. Folger, V, 367-77.

-------- The Second Sermon Upon Part of St. Jude, 1582/83. Folger, V, 36-57.

-------- A Sermon Fragment on Hebrews 2.14-15. Folger, V, 402-13.

-------- A Sermon Fragment on Matth. 27-46. Folger, V, 1990, 309-401.

-------- A Sermon on Matthew 7.7, 1679. Folger, V, 385-94.

-------- A Sermon Fragment on Prov. 3. 1595-1600. Folger, V, 414-17.

-------- "A Pension to Richard Hooker," 21 September 1582. Act Book 4 1581-1588: 399. Devon Records Office.

-------- Richard Hooker's Will. Archdeacons Court, Canterbury Cathedral. PRC: 32/38, fol. 291.

HOOKER, ROBERT. Robert Hooker's Will, 1534. Devon Records Office: H.H.3-55, fol. 93.

HOOKER, ROGER. <u>Witness to Challoner's Will</u>. PRO, London: PCC47, Bakon: 375.

-------- <u>Interest in Father's Tin Works</u>. Devon Records Office: H.H.3.55: fol. 39.

-------- <u>Debts Recorded</u>. Devon Records Office: H.H.3.57: 148.

-------- <u>Letter from Ireland</u>. In John Maclean, ed., <u>John Hooker's The Life and Times of Sir Peter Carew</u>. London: Bill & Daldy, 1857.

-------- <u>Listed on Devon Muster Role</u>. Howard, A. J. and Stoate, T. L., eds. <u>The Devon Muster Roll for 1569</u>. Almondsbury, Bristol, 1977.

HOOKER, ZACHARIE (ZACHARY). <u>Will of Z. Hooker</u>. 1643. In Charles Worthy, Esq. <u>Devonshire Wills: A Collection of Annotated Testamentary Abstracts</u>. 124. London: Bembrose & Sons, LTD., 1896.

HOPE, VYVYAN AND JOHN LLOYD. <u>Exeter Cathedral</u>. Audrey Erskine, ed. Exeter: Dean and Chapter of the Cathedral, 1988.

HOPWOOD, CHARLES HENRY, ed. <u>A Calendar of the Middle Temple</u>. London: Butterworth & Co., 1903.

--------, ed. <u>Middle Temple Records</u>. London: Butterworth & Co., 1904.

HOSKINS, H. G. <u>History of Devon</u>. Tiverton, Devon: Devon Books, 1992.

-------- <u>Two Thousand Years in Exeter</u>. Chichester: Phillimore & Co., Ltd, 1960.

HOULBROOKE, RALPH A. <u>The English Family 1450-1700</u>. New York: Longmans, Inc., 1984.

HOWARD, A. J. AND STOATE, T. L., eds. <u>The Devon Muster Roll for 1569</u>. Almondsbury, Bristol, 1977.

HUNT, WILLIAM AND FREEMAN, EDWARD A., eds. <u>Historic Towns</u>. London: Longmans, Green & Co., 1906.

HUTCHINSON, JOHN. <u>A Catalog of Notable Middle Templars</u>. London: Society of the Middle Temple, 1902.

INDERWICK, R. A., ed. <u>A Calendar of the Inner Temple Records</u>. London, 1896.

INGRAM, MARTIN. <u>Church Courts, Sex and Marriage in England 1570-1640</u>. Cambridge: Cambridge University Press, 1987.

KEBLE, JOHN, ed. The Works of Mr. Richard Hooker. 3rd.ed.,3 vols. Oxford: Oxford University Press, 7th ed., 1887.

KEEN, ROSEMARY, ed. "Inventory of Richard Hooker, 1601." Archaelogia, Cantiana. Ashford, Kent: Headley Brothers, Ltd, 1957.

KENDALL, R. T. Calvin and English Calvinism to 1649. Oxford: Oxford University Press, 1979.

KER, N. R. "The Provision of Books," James McConica, ed., The History of the University of Oxford, III, 439-77. Oxford: Clarendon Press, 1986.

KNAPPEN, M. M. Tudor Puritanism. Chicago: Chicago University Press, 1939.

KNOX, S. J. Walter Travers: Paragon of Elizabethan Puritanism. London: Methuen & Co., Ltd, 1962.

LAKE, PETER. Anglicans and Puritans? Presbyterianism and English Conformist Thought from Whitgift to Hooker. London: Unwin Hyman, 1988.

LAMB, CHRISTOPHER. The Parish Church of St. Andrew Enfield. Gloucester: The British Publishing Company Limited, 1968.

LAURANCE, ANNE. Women in England 1500-1760. London: Weidenfeld and Nicolson, 1994.

LE BAS, CHARLES WEBB. The Life of Bishop Jewel. London: J. G. & F. Rivington, 1835.

LEE, SIDNEY, ed. Dictionary of National Biography, V, XXVII. New York: Macmillan, 1891.

LE NEVE, JOHN. Fasti Ecclesiae Anglicanae 1541-1857. Compiled by Joyce M. Horn. London: University of London Institute of Historical Research, 1986.

LEWIS, C. S. English Literature in the 16th Century Excluding Drama. Oxford: The Clarendon Press, 1954.

LITTLE, BRYAN. Portrait of Exeter. London: Robert Hale, 1983.

LLOYD, JOHN AND HOPE, VYVYAN. Exeter Cathedral. Audrey Erskine, ed. Exeter: Dean and Chapter of the Cathedral Publishers, 1988.

LOACH, JENNIFER. "Reformation Controversies," James McConica, ed., The History of the University of Oxford, III, 363-96. Oxford: Clarendon Press, 1986.

McADOO, HENRY R. The Spirit of Anglicanism. New York: Charles Scribner's Sons, 1965.

McCAFFREY, WALLACE T. Exeter 1540-1640. 2nd edition. Cambridge: Harvard University Press, 1975.

MACLEAN, JOHN, ed. John Hooker's The Life and Times of Sir Peter Carew. London: Bill & Daldy, 1857.

MACLURE, MILLAR. The Pauls Cross Sermons. Toronto: University of Toronto Press, 1958.

McCONICA, JAMES, ed. The History of the University of Oxford, III. Oxford: Clarendon Press, 1986.

MacCULLOCH, DIARMAID. The Later Reformation in England 1547-1603. New York: St. Martins Press, 1990.

-------- Thomas Cranmer A Life. New Haven and London: Yale University Press, 1996.

McGINN, DONALD J. John Penry and the Marprelate Controversy. New Brunswick: Rutgers University Press, 1966.

McGRADE, A. S. "Introduction to the Last Three Books and Autograph Notes." Folger. VI.I, 233-47, 309-83..

--------, ed. Richard Hooker and the Construction of Christian Community. Tempe, Arizona: Medieval & Renaissance Texts & Studies, 1997.

--------, ed. Richard Hooker of The Laws of Ecclesiastical Polity. Cambridge: Cambridge University Press, 1989.

--------, AND VICKERS, BRIAN, eds. Richard Hooker Of The Laws of Ecclesiastical Polity. New York: St. Martins Press, 1975.

MARSHALL, PETER. The Catholic Priesthood and the English Reformation. Oxford: The Clarendon Press, 1994.

MELLOR, HUGH. Exeter Architecture. Chichester: Phillimore & Co., Ltd, 1989.

MILNE, J. G. The Early History of Corpus Christi College. Oxford: Basil Blackwell, 1946.

MILTON, ANTHONY. Catholic and Reformed The Roman and Protestant Churches in English Protestant Thought 1600-1640. Cambridge: Cambridge University Press, 1995.

MOORMAN, JOHN R. H. A History of the Church in England, 3rd ed. Harrisburg, Pennsylvania: Morehouse Publishing, 1980.

MORGAN, IRVONY, The Godly Preachers of the Elizabethan Church. London: The Epworth Press, 1965.

MORRIS, CHRISTOPHER. Political Thought in England, Tyndale to Hooker. London and New York: Oxford University Press, 1953.

-------- Richard Hooker Of the Laws of Ecclesiastical Polity. Everyman's Edition. London: J. M. Dent & Sons, Ltd., 1907.

MORYSON, FYNES. The Itinerary of Fynes Moryson, II. Glasgow: James MacLehose and Sons, 1907.

MUNZ, PETER. The Place of Richard Hooker in the History of Thought. London: Routledge & Kegan Paul, 1952.

MURRAY, MICHAEL G. Middle Temple Hall, An Architectural Appreciation. London: The Middle Temple, 1991.

MYERS, JAMES P., ed. Elizabethan Ireland, A Selection of Writings by Elizabethan Writers in Ireland. Hamden, Connecticut: Anchor Books, 1983.

NEALE, J. E. Elizabeth I and Her Parliaments 1584-1601. London: Jonathan Cape, 1957.

NIJENHUIS, WILLEM. Adrianus Saravia (1523-1631). Leiden: E. J. Brill, 1980.

NOVARR, DAVID. The Making of Walton's "Lives". Ithaca: Cornell University Press, 1958.

O'BRIEN, MARIE AND CRUISE, CONOR. The Story of Ireland. Englewood Cliffs: The Viking Press, 1968.

O'DAY, ROSEMARY.The Debate on the English Reformation. London: Methuen & Co., Ltd., 1986.

ORGAN, TOM AND AUSTIN, PETER. Report on the Conservation of the 14th Century Wall Paintings. Unpublished research paper from St. Mary's Church, Bishopsbourne, Kent, 1995.

ORME, NICHOLAS. Education in the West of England 1066-1548. Exeter: University of Exeter Press, 1976.

-------- Exeter Cathedral as It Was 1050-1550. Exeter, Devon County Council: Devon Books, 1986.

OSSORY, JOHN. "The Father of Richard Hooker." The Irish Church Quarterly, V. 6. Dublin, 1913.

OXFORD UNIVERSITY. A Concise Guide to Colleges of Oxford University. Oxford, 1992.

-------- New Illustrated History of Oxford. Oxford, 1993.

PAGET, FRANCIS. An Introduction to the Fifth Book of the Laws of Ecclesiastical Polity. Oxford: Clarendon Press, 1899.

PAM, DAVID O. The Rude Multitude, Enfield and The Civil War. Edmonton: G. G. Laurence & Co., 1977.

-------- The Story of Enfield Chase. Enfield Preservation Society, 1984.

PARKER, MATTHEW. Correspondence. Cambridge: The Parker Society, 1853.

PARRY, H. LLOYD. The Founding of Exeter School. Exeter: James G. Commin, 1913.

PEARSON. A. F. Thomas Cartwright and Elizabethan Protestantism 1535-1603. Cambridge, 1925.

PITMAN, H. D. GERALD. Sherborne Observed. Sherborne: The Abbey Press, 1983.

-------- The Church of St. Mary Magdelen at Castleton, revised edition. Published by the Church, 1975.

PORTER, H. C. Puritanism in Tudor England. Columbia: University of South Carolina Press, 1971.

-------- "Hooker, the Tudor Constitution, and the Via Media." Studies in Richard Hooker. Essays Preliminary To An Edition Of His Works, 77-116. W. Speed Hill, ed. Cleveland and London: The Press of Case Western Reserve University, 1972.

PORTER, ROY. London, A Social History. Cambridge: Harvard University Press, 1995.

POWICKE, F. J. Robert Browne Pioneer of Modern Congregationalism. 1910.

-------- Henry Barrow and the Exiled Church in Amsterdam. 1910.

PRIDHAM, T. L. Devonshire Celebrities. London: Bell & Daldy, 1869.

PRINCE, JOHN. The Worthies of England. London: Longman, Hurst, Rees, 1810.

PROCKTER, ADRIAN AND TAYLOR, ROBERT. The A to Z of Elizabethan London. No. 122. London Topographical Society, 1979.

QUENNELL, MARJORIE AND C. H. B. A History of Everyday Things in England, 1500-1799, 7th ed., V. II. London: B. T. Batsford, Ltd., 1945.

QUINN, DAVID BEERS. The Elizabethans and the Irish. Ithaca: Cornell University Press, 1966.

RABB, THEODORE K. Jacobean Gentleman Sir Edwin Sandys, 1561-1629. Princeton: Princeton University Press, 1998.

RAINOLDS, JOHN. Oratio in Laudem Artis Poeticae [circa 1572]. Intro. by William Ringler. Princeton: Princeton University Press, 1940.

RAPPAPORT, STEVE. Worlds Within Worlds: Structures of Life in Sixteenth Century London. New York: Cambridge University Press, 1989.

REECE, SUSAN. Research Notes, card 3539. Exeter: The Devon and Exeter Institution.

RIDLEY, JASPER. The Tudor Age. London: Constable and Company, Ltd., 1988.

RINGLER, WILLIAM. Stephen Gosson. Princeton: Princeton University Press, 1942.

ROBERTS, PETER AND FLETCHER, ANTHONY, eds. Religion, Culture and Society in Early Modern Britain Essays in Honour of Patrick Collinson. Cambridge: Cambridge University Press, 1994.

ROBISON, HASTINGS, ed. The Zurich Letters, 1. Cambridge: The Parker Society, 1845.

ROSE-TROUP, FRANCES. The Western Rebellion 1549. London: Smith, Elder & Co., 1913.

ROSENBERG, ELEANOR. Leicester Patron of Letters. New York: Columbia University Press, 1955.

ROTHSTEIN, NATALIE, ed. Four Hundred Years of Fashion. London: Victoria and Albert Museum, 1985.

ROUTH, C. R. N. Who's Who in Tudor England. London: Shepherd-Walwyn, 1990.

ROWSE, A. L. Court and Country: Studies in Tudor History. Athens, Georgia: The University of Georgia Press, 1987.

-------- Oxford in the History of the Nation. London: Book Club Associates, 1975.

-------- The Elizabethan Renaissance The Cultural Achievement. New York: Charles Scribner's Sons, 1972.

-------- The England of Elizabeth. London: Macmillan and Co., Ltd., 1950.

SAINT, ANDREW AND DARLEY, GILLIAN. The Chronicles of London. London: Weidenfeld and Nicolson, Ltd, 1994.

ST AUGUSTINES WATLING STREET. General Parish Register 1559-1653. Guild Hall Mss. Rm., Ms. 9535, 2.

SALGADO, GAMINI. The Elizabethan Underworld. Stroud: Alan Sutton Publishing, Ltd., 1992.

SALISBURY CATHEDRAL. "Penruddocke." Chapter Act Book, 16.15r.

-------- Sub-deans Act Book, 1589-1596. D4/3/2,fol.6r, Dec.1,1591. Wiltshire Public Records Office, Trowbridge.

-------- Box 34, Dec.30,1591. "Letters patent of John Coldwell. . ."

-------- Press IV. "Procuratoria," Dec.2,1591. "Letters of John Brydges. . ."

-------- Sub-deans Act Book 1589-1596. D/4/3/2,fol.6. Trowbridge: Wiltshire Public Records Office.

-------- Dean of Chapter Records, Presses 1,2: p.10; Press 4. Trowbridge: Wiltshire Public Records Office.

SANDYS, SIR EDWIN. Notes of Mr. Hooker's Sixth Book. Corpus Christi College, Oxford Archives. MS 295, fol. 3.1.

-------- A Relation to the State of Religion; and what Hopes and Policies it hath been framed and is maintained in the several western parts of the World. London, 1605. (Also published as Europae Speculum .. .). British Library, C. 110e12.

SARAVIA, ADRIAN. Of the Diverse Orders of the Ministers of the Gospel . . .London: John Wolfe, 1591. Lambeth Library 1591.29.

SAVOY, CAROLYN AND WINTER, JANET. Elizabethan Costuming For The Years 1550-1580, 2nd.ed. Oakland, Cal.: Other Times Publications, 1979.

SCHOFIELD, JOHN. The Building of London from the Conquest to the Great Fire. London: British Museum Press, 1984.

SCOTT, ANDREW AND DARLEY, GILLIAN. The Chronicles of London. London: Weidenfeld and Nicolson, Ltd., 1994.

SEAVER, PAUL S. The Puritan Lectureships, The Politics of Religious Dissent, 1560-1662. Stanford: Stanford University Press, 1970.

SECOR, PHILIP B. Richard Hooker and the Christian Commonwealth. Unpublished doctoral dissertation. Duke University, 1959.

------------ "In Search of Richard Hooker: Constructing a New Biography." McGrade, Arthur Stephen, ed., <u>Richard Hooker and the Construction of Christian Community</u>, 21-37. Tempe, Arizona: Medieval & Renaissance Texts & Studies, 1997.

------------ <u>Richard Hooker Prophet of Anglicanism</u>. Tunbridge Wells: Burns & Oates and Toronto: Anglican Book Centre, 1999.

------------ <u>The Sermons of Richard Hooker: A Modern Edition</u>. London: SPCK, 2001.

------------ <u>Richard Hooker on Anglican Faith and Worship: A Modern Edition of Book V of The Laws of Ecclesiastical Polity</u>. London: SPCK, 2003.

------------ (with Lee Gibbs). <u>The Wisdom of Richard Hooker</u>. Bloomington, Indiana: Author Books, 2005.

SISSON, C. J. <u>The Judicious Marriage of Mr. Hooker and the Birth of "The Laws of Ecclesiastical Polity, "</u>Cambridge: Cambridge University Press, 1940.

SMITH, ELSIE. "Hooker at Salisbury." <u>Times Literary Supplement</u>: 233. March 30, 1962.

SNOW, VERNON F. <u>Parliament in Elizabethan England, John Hooker's Order and Usage</u>. Hartford: Yale University Press, 1977.

----------- "John Hooker's Circle: Evidence from his New Year's Gift List of 1584." <u>Devon and Cornwall Notes and Queries</u>. 140. 273-77; 161. 317-24.

STOATE, T. L. AND HOWARD, A. J., eds. <u>The Devon Muster Roll for 1569</u>. Almondsbury, Bristol, 1977.

STONE, LAWRENCE. <u>The Family, Sex and Marriage in England 1500-1800</u>. New York: Harper and Row, 1977.

STOW, JOHN. <u>A Survey of London</u>. Stroud, Gloucester: Publishing Ltd, 1994. (Reprint from 1603 ed.)

STRONG, ROY. <u>The English Renaissance Miniature</u>. London: Thames and Hudson, 1984.

STRYPE, JOHN. <u>Historical Collections of the Life and Acts of John Aylmer, Lord Bishop of London in the Reign of Queen Elizabeth</u> (1700). Oxford: Oxford University Press, 1821.

------------ <u>The Life and Acts of John Whitgift, D.D. The Third and Last Lord Archbishop of Canterbury In The Reign of Queen Elizabeth</u>, V.II. Oxford: Clarendon Press, 1822.

STURGESS, H. A. C., ed. Register of Admissions to the Honourable Society of the Middle Temple, I. London: Butterworth & Co., Ltd, 1949.

TAYLOR, ROBERT AND PROCKTER, ADRIAN. The A to Z of Elizabethan London, No.122. London Topographical Society, 1979.

THOMPSON, W. D. J. CARGILL. "The Philosopher of the 'Politic Society': Richard Hooker as a Political Thinker." In W. Speed Hill, ed., Studies in Richard Hooker: Essays Preliminary To An Edition Of His Works, 3-76. Cleveland & London: The Press of Case Western Reserve University, 1972.

TRAVERS, WALTER. Disciplina Ecclesiae Dei Verbo . . . et Anglicnae Ecclesiae . . . Explicato (Book of Discipline). 1587. In Francis Paget, An Introduction to the Fifth Book of Hooker's Treatise of the Laws of Ecclesiastical Polity, 238-51. Oxford: Clarendon Press, 1899.

------------A Supplication Made to the Privy Counsel by Mr Walter Travers. 1586. Lambeth Library, Fairhurst Papers 3470, fols.8287; Folger, V, 187-210.

TREVOR-ROPER, HUGH. Catholics, Anglicans and Puritans. Chicago: University of Chicago Press, 1987.

------------ Renaissance Essays. Chicago: University of Chicago Press, 1961.

TYACKE, NICHOLAS. Anti-Calvinists and The Rise of Arminianism 1590-1640. Oxford: Clarendon Press, 1987.

VICKERS, BRIAN AND McGRADE, A. S., eds. Richard Hooker Of The Laws of Ecclesiastical Polity. New York: St. Martins Press, 1975.

WALTON, IZAAC. The Life of Mr. Rich. Hooker, The Author of those Learned Books of the Laws of Ecclesiastical Polity. London: Richard Marriottt, 1665.

------------ "Preface to the First Edition of the Life of Hooker." John Keble, ed. The Works of . . . Mr. Richard Hooker: With An Account of His Life and Death by Isaac Walton, 3rd ed. Oxford: Oxford University Press, 1845.

WEINREB, BEN AND HIBBERT, CHRISTOPHER, eds. The London Encyclopedia. London: Macmillan, 1983.

WEINSTEIN, ROSEMARY. <u>Tudor London</u>. Museum of London, 1994.

WHITGIFT, JOHN. <u>A Defense of the Ecclesiastical Regiment in Englande defaced by T. C. In his Replie against D. Whitgift</u>. London: Henry Bynneman, 1574. (Original in Lambeth Library.)

------------ <u>Letters</u>. Assorted Correspondence: 1587-94. Lambeth Palace Library: Fairhurst Papers, MSS 3470, fols. 89, 99-103, 109-113, 115.

------------ <u>Notes on the Hooker-Travers Controversy</u>. 1586. Lambeth Palace Library: Fairhurst Papers, 2006, fols. 6-15; *Folger* V..

WILLIAMSON, J. BRUCE. <u>The History of The Middle Temple</u>. New York: E. P. Dutton and Company, 1924.

-------- <u>The Middle Temple Bench Book</u>, 2nd ed. London: Chancery, 1937.

WILSON, H. B. <u>The History of the Merchant Taylors Schools</u>. London, 1812.

WINSTANLEY, WILLIAM. <u>The Honour of Merchant-Taylors</u>. London, 1668. (The British Library.)

WINTER, JANET AND SAVOY, CAROLYN. <u>Elizabethan Costuming For The Years 1550-1580</u>, 2nd ed. Oakland, Cal.: Other Times Publications, 1979.

WOOD, ANTHONY. <u>Athenae Oxonienses, An Exact History of all the Writers and Bishops Who Have Had Their Education in the University of Oxford</u>, 1691-92. V.I. Philip Bliss, ed. London, 1813.

WOOD, REGINALD. <u>Sir Walter Ralegh, Gold Was His Star</u>. Lewes, Sussex: The Book Guild, Ltd., 1991.

WOOLTON, JOHN. <u>The Christian Manual</u>, 1576. (Parker Society Edition). Cambridge: Cambridge University Press, 1851.

YOUINGS, JOYCE. <u>Sixteenth Century England</u>. Harmondsworth, Middlesex: Penguin Books, Ltd., 1984.

------------ <u>Tuckers Hall Exeter</u>. Exeter: The University of Exeter Press, 1968.

About the Author

PHILIP SECOR has been a "follower" of Richard Hooker ever since he wrote his doctoral thesis on Hooker's political thought in 1959. In recent years he has written a number of books on Hooker including, *Richard Hooker Prophet of Anglicanism* (1999); *The Sermons of Richard Hooker* (2001); *Richard Hooker on Anglican Faith and Worship* (2003); *The Wisdom of Richard Hooker* (with Lee Gibbs), 2005. He holds MA and PhD degrees from Duke University and has taught at Duke, Davidson and Dickinson. He has been Dean of Muhlenberg College and President of Cornell College. Secor lives with his wife, Anne, in eastern Pennsylvania.